From the Spool
to the City

First published in 2023
as part of the Design Principles and Practices Book Imprint
https://doi.org/10.18848/978-1-957792-55-2/CGP (Full Book)

BISAC Codes: DES011000, POL002000, SOC026030

Common Ground Research Networks
2001 South First St, Suite 201 L
University of Illinois Research Park
Champaign, IL
61820

Library of Congress Cataloging-in-Publication Data

Names: D'Elia, Luca, author.
Title: From the Spool to the City / Luca D'Elia.
Description: Champaign, IL : Common Ground, 2023. | Series: Design
  principles and practices | "Based on the research activities carried out
  at Sapienza University of Rome, over the three-year period of a
  doctorate in Planning, Design, Technologies of Architecture (35th cycle,
  PDTA Department)"--Acknowledgements. | Includes bibliographical
  references and index. | Summary: "This book is the result of a three
  years of iterative Research which explores the ways in which technology,
  community, and urban design can work together to create more sustainable
  and productive cities. Through an in-depth analysis of the city of Rome,
  the Research focus on community building and new urban models toward
  more sustainable, resilient, and productive cities. The outcome of the
  Research is a hyper-local tool that enables bottom-up initiatives to
  respond to specific needs and help develop new economies. This approach,
  combined with top-down initiatives from Administrations, would be useful
  for policymakers, urban planners, makers, designers, and citizens who
  want to design and advocate for sustainable urban development models and
  thriving neighborhoods. With its practical insights and real-world
  examples, this book offers a roadmap for building more resilient and
  sustainable cities in the 21st century"-- Provided by publisher.
Identifiers: LCCN 2023014129 (print) | LCCN 2023014130 (ebook) | ISBN
  9781957792545 (hardback) | ISBN 9781957792538 (paperback) | ISBN
  9781957792552 (pdf)
Subjects: LCSH: City planning. | Urban ecology (Sociology) | User-centered
  system design. | Public spaces--Italy--Rome--Design. | Sustainable
  development.
Classification: LCC NA9035 .D47 2023 (print) | LCC NA9035 (ebook) | DDC
  711/.40945632--dc23/eng/20230810
LC record available at https://lccn.loc.gov/2023014129
LC ebook record available at https://lccn.loc.gov/2023014130

From the Spool
to the City

Luca D'Elia

COMMON
GROUND

DESIGN PRINCIPLES
AND PRACTICES

Acknowledgements

This book is based on the research activities carried out at Sapienza University of Rome, over the three-year period of a doctorate in Planning, Design, Technology of Architecture (35th cycle, PDTA Department).

This work has been made possible thanks to those very individuals who have made my personal journey in the world of Research and Design possible, enjoyable and enriching. Each person I've encountered has contributed to my professional growth, enriched my life so far (as well as most of them still keep up). I will never fully express my gratitude for every person I've met along the way, but I sincerely hope that each of them knows how deeply grateful, esteemed, and respectful I am for each contributions, for every feedback, for the commitment and endeavors shown along the path that is shaping myself as designer, researcher and as a person.

In particular, I need to express my heartfelt appreciation to those who played significant roles along this path: to Lorenzo Imbesi, who has been more than a professor or a supervisor, but a mentor who guided me through the challenging, marvelous, and ever-evolving realm of the Research. To Loredana Di Lucchio, which advice and wisdom are an invaluable source from which I continually draw. I am grateful to Viktor Malakuczi for his competence and patience, which have taught me so much, and I hope to reciprocate his kindness in the near future. To all the collaborators and individuals at Centro Sapienza Design Research, precious colleagues and friends, who welcomed me and made me feel like an integral part of a community from the outset. I am grateful to Lina Monaco, whose dedication has been a guiding beacon in times of uncertainty. To Massimo Menichinelli, a dear friend and esteemed role model, whom I have been lucky enough to met along the path, and to which I would like to resemble one day for competence and humanity. I am glad to have met Safouan Azouzi, whose sincerity and kindness have left a profound impact on me, and whom I hope to cross paths with again. To Thomas Fabio Borrelli, not only a business partner but a trusted friend, and someone I know I could always rely on. Last, but certainly not least, my work could not be possible without the support of my family and relatives, who always support me: to my parents, without whom I wouldn't have had the opportunity to experience this wonderful journey called life; to Mara, for being to my side everyday and for being the driving force behind my aspirations.

To all of you: your unwavering support and love are gifts I will cherish forever, and for which I could never be grateful enough.

When we refer to the architect of a foreign policy program or the designer of a scientific experiment, we acknowledge that programs and experiments are as designed as are buildings, posters, and traffic circles.

Design itself is often what survives. And design is in large measure what civilizations and their governments are remembered by.

Chermayeff et al., 1973

CONTENTS

INTRODUCTION

Technology, Community, and City

Faced with the series of recent global crises, from the lowering of the planet's resources to the most recent global emergency of COVID-19, the current model of consumption and production leads to questioning many practices implemented so far. While numerous critics and scholars of the current economic system have theorized and proposed 'lateral' alternatives to development, the research presented in this book proposes that the quantitative approach, according to these studies, must move towards a systemic and qualitative approach.

The Research analyzed the post-industrial panorama established in the urban context, through activities aimed at identifying types of products and users close to the Maker culture, a culture of 'know how' which still suffers from a condition of identity and economic ambiguity which risks diminishing the technological potential of distributed production. To do so, the research took into consideration three fundamental aspects:

- Technology, as an enabler, especially when accessible and always usable, where the increasing social role of information and interconnection (ICT) along with the growing accessibility of operational machinery (OT) has allowed the birth of alternative and distributed economic models (DIY, Makers) connoting them to forms of open and collaborative culture (Menichinelli and Cangiano, 2021);

- The community, as the hybrid set of manufacturers, designers, artisans, and enthusiasts who, thanks to enabling technologies, with different forms of aggregation on site as well as dislocation, have been able to demonstrate a growing will aimed at greater inclusiveness as well as new forms of self-organization (Castells, 2009);

- The city, which through the union of the two aforementioned factors has known how to make it increasingly smart, supporting a fertile ground for innovation, a habitat capable of optimizing infrastructural, economic, and ecological resources in a distributed and interconnected ecosystem (Micelli, 2016).

The present book is a continuation of a project that studied the changes and the consequences that recent events in the world had on Maker culture as part of an outcome of the Design discipline towards these dimensions. Hopefully, insights can offer a useful solution for mapping the knowledge and skills that are being formed and organized within urban contexts, giving substance to those characteristics of quality and flexibility of the digital age.

Above macro-systemic studies which lead the theoretical frame, the Research intends to contribute to this dialogue with a local case study which investigates the Lazio Region and focuses specifically on the metropolitan city of Rome. The general objective of the Research activity described has been motivated by the will to understand the ability of local Makers and communities to pursue projects which could possibly see the involvement of Public Administrations, where the latter would possibly be seen active in promoting specific actions for and with local communities.

The production activities examined and mapped in this way will be able to interact directly through the design activity, expanding the catchment area of their services, and the business network of any suppliers or collaborators. This Research therefore takes this close-knit network into consideration as a new production chain which, starting from participatory and open planning, can pass through a distributed and limited production, up to a distribution that can be evaluated based on the type of product, the insertion context, the reference market, and the end user. The Research intended to compile a study that can give a clear picture of both the technologies and the skills currently present to stimulate the development of new urban practices of distributed production node. Aimed to better understand, in punctual manner, the assets and the development of Maker culture at local scale, the Research investigated major stakeholders present at regional levels and lastly profiled the potential factors which has been considered valid to enable worthy Maker and Design-led practices. This last objective foresees the proposal and experimentation of a tool which could possibly enable community-based projects.

In 1952, Ernesto Nathan Rogers coined the slogan "from the spoon to the city" with the intent to explain an architectural approach in which the project must start from the microscopical aspect of the project such as a lamp, a chair (the spoon) intended as mirror of behaviors and dynamics of people, up to those containers that are made of streets, building, skyscrapers. This book starts from this consideration and re-contextualizes it in the contemporary world: a world in which it's no longer just the architect or the designer who takes on the burden of designing for the citizens (the others), but is actually those empowered citizens who, through technologies and knowledge, redesign the city and reconfigure it based on their own needs. And everything can start just from a spool[1] to build up a city.

[1] In the Maker context, a very low entry level technology is the filament 3D printer (commonly known as FDM): a very practical and "ready to use" machine which printing material is sold in "spools" of plastic filament that are then processed and deposited by the machine to replicate the digital model.

Read it layer by layer

This book is divided into four parts and eight chapters (two chapters each). Each level of investigation (Technology, Community, City) consists of a preliminary part of Desk Research (DR) followed by the corresponding Field Research (FR). Therefore:

Part I) Chapters 1 and 2 are respectively dedicated to DR and FR on *Tech* (i.e. Technologies);

Part II) Chapters 3 and 4 are respectively dedicated to DR and FR on *Cmty* (i.e. Communities);

Part III) Chapters 5 and 6 are respectively dedicated to DR and FR on the *City*;

Part IV) Chapter 7 is a preliminary reflection made with Professor Massimo Menichinelli, from which crucial consideration has been made to establish the activity of the last chapter, dedicated to the final FR results of the MakIN'Rome project. The Research journey concluded with chapter 8 with the formulation of a toolkit introduced along with specific guidelines, which has been used for the design of community-based projects, followed by some fine examples provided as a report of the test carried on within the city of Rome. The Conclusion chapter collects final considerations on the overall experience.

Look... don't just look

"This book does not follow the academic conception of 'theory and practice.' It reverses this order and positions practice before theory, which, after all, is the conclusion of practice." (Albers & Weber, 2013, p. 1)

Before getting into the matter, it is necessary to delve deeper into the study of the Action Research methodology through a comparison with the most current practices in Design Research such as Co-Design (Norman, 2014), Emotional Design (Norman, 2005), Interaction Design (Norman, 1998) and a series of facets that the discipline has taken on during its evolution. Among all the research methodologies previously described, Action Research seems to occupy a position of relevance in design research for its participatory, generative, and destructive aspects, but even more so, for the experiential value it attributes to practice. Action Research originated in the field of social sciences, but its application in the field of design research has had a fundamental impact, starting with its disciplinary implications. In fact, it was through the recognition of a research methodology such as Action Research that the research process was no longer divided into a dichotomy of those who discover, invent - scientists, inventors, researchers - and those who apply, construct - craftsmen, workers, industries. For these reasons, Action Research has assumed and perhaps still does, a founding dimension for the discipline of Design as it recognizes through its research process a knowledge dimension to "doing".

Design action thus becomes not just practical knowledge but also theoretical knowledge, or we could say "design knowledge," meaning a form of knowledge that alternates between practical knowledge and theoretical knowledge by borrowing knowledge from each. Action Research originated around the 1960s in sociological research, but its application in design research has had a fundamental impact, tracing its philosophical foundations back to the theories of learning by doing (Dewey, 2010).[1] Indeed, "doing" is now seen as something capable of generating knowledge, and what was once considered purely practical, manual knowledge gains a theoretical base carrying innovation. In the Design context, the first teachings promoted by the Bauhaus can be traced back to their basic courses which were accompanied by numerous laboratory and experimental activities that relied heavily on prototyping or experimenting with materials, finishes, and colors to acquire and produce new knowledge. It became imperative for the Design discipline to reflect on the importance of Research in practice-based (or practice-led) design, highlighting how this approach can be related to the research categories described by Frayling (1993), such as: Research on Design, Research for Design and Research through Design (which will be discussed in the next paragraph). Although the different shades of Design converge in different types of research, the correspondences between them have two main common (while peculiar) characteristics of Action Research:

1. The first aspect is related to the context dependency of the activity. Unlike any other forms of Design Research, in Action Research, the context changes along with the research process itself. All information or data retrieved feeds the investigation process and opens up new possibilities towards the use of different tools, techniques, and methodologies to examine the design problem in question. Therefore, it is possible to argue that it is a non-linear approach which proceeds through continuous observations of the context which it operates in. The ability of Action Research to operate in different fields, feeding the latter through data and planned actions, makes the Action Research methodology capable of responding much more precisely to needs and of identifying problematic matters.[2]

2. The second aspect, which would justify the prominent position that Action Research occupies within Design Research, is characterized by its strong inclination towards experimental participatory methods. The participatory nature of this approach is characterized by a constant dialogue between the stakeholders involved and is particularly strong when the participants can see themselves as a research-led community, in which the designer assumes the role of mediator.

[1] The theory of the philosopher and pedagogue had a fundamental impact within the educational field as it overturned the idea of indoctrination as a necessary point for the development of knowledge, reformulating instead the idea of learning from experiential data, from 'learning by doing'
[2] In the study of social sciences, the 'positivist paradigm' empirical, objectivist, and explanatory is followed by the interpretive paradigm - humanistic, subjective - and it is aimed at understanding rather than gaining certain knowledge.

These aspects make an Action Research approach particularly effective as a methodology both for the opening of the democratic nature of its method of investigation (finding correlation with the thematic that will be explored in the next chapters), and for the necessarily self-reflexive and relational aspect of the Design process itself.

It is possible to notice that, although practice constitutes the fundamental seed for modern Research in Design, it is the cognitive dimension (therefore that codifies the 'doing') that the Design actions move from the pure crafting knowledge or the "thinking with your hands" (Porcari, 2016, p. 83) to disciplinary knowledge capable of combining practice and theory (Laureti, 2020). Action Research's approach has been identified for its paradigm that is well suited to Design due to its cognitive value and the many aspects that characterize it. This has led to the hypothesis that Action Research could be considered the genuine research paradigm of Design and serve as the basis for constructing a disciplinary gnoseological foundation. Furthermore, the approach as it has been introduced, shows an inner attitude of Design towards interdisciplinarity or more probably towards "anti-disciplinarity" (Ito, 2016), intended as the peculiar attitude of Research to get out of a particular discipline seeking relationships between different disciplines looking for new forms of languages and systems. Factors such as tacit knowledge, creativity, and intuition can significantly impact the development of research and design. These factors can make a difference in the success of any research approach, and the ability to leverage them in combination with an appropriate research method can lead to better problem solving and innovation in the field of Design.

Research Through Design in the Action Research approach assumed a founding dimension as much for the Design discipline as for the present Research itself. Through its iterative process of action and research, it does not limit itself to highlighting the importance of practical knowledge as a starting point for the construction of the theoretical knowledge but goes much further, recognizing a cognitive dimension to the action of the project itself, to the 'design practice'.

The practices carried on in the last thirty years are a set of tools, procedures, and toolkits aimed to guide the designers in the participatory management of users, researchers, and designers thanks to the adoption of cognitive tools sensitive to the reference system, therefore not unrelated to the transversality of the Design Thinking approach (Brown, 2009).

A Research (Journey) Through Design

"Design thinking is not a linear path. It's a big mass of looping back to different places in the process." (Kelley, 2020)[1]

When referring to Research through Design (RtD), we are discussing design activities that contribute to the generation of knowledge: the activities developed around this approach typically involve actions that can be recognized as design practices by one of the design professions, and depend on the professional skills of designers that take part to the flow by gaining actionable understanding of a complex situation, framing and reframing it, and iteratively developing prototypes that address it. Therefore, RtD is capable of providing specific concepts aimed at developing a different paradigm of research in design, which, although epistemological, "is also a condition for methodological development" (Jonas, 2007, p. 187), consistent with the thought of Findeli (2010), who reports two important aspects of RtD: the shift of research from artefacts that investigates processes and experiences; the essential role for the development of a research project-grounded paradigm in Design (Glaser and Strauss, 1967)[2]. One example of an RtD case study is the Design for Sharing project, which explored how design can help to create a sharing economy. The project involved a team of designers and researchers who worked with local communities in the UK to develop and test new models of sharing. The team used a range of design methods, including participatory design and co-design, to engage with local communities and to develop new ideas. The Design for Sharing project is an excellent example of the power of the RtD approach to generate new knowledge and insights. By using design methods to engage with local communities and to develop and test new ideas, the project produced outcomes that went beyond traditional academic research.

The project demonstrated how Design can be used as a means of inquiry, and how this approach can generate new insights and ideas that are relevant to real-world problems. The designer's contribution can be as simple as creating stimulus material for use in someone else's Research, but it often involves developing a prototype or artefact that can be mistaken for a product and plays a central role in the knowledge generating process. For instance, the prototype may present a previously non-existent combination of factors to provoke discussion, or it may create the possibility for people and products to engage in interactions that were not possible before, and these can be brought into existence and observed through the design process.

[1] Quotation retrieved on December 15th, 2023 from IDEO blog https://www.ideou.com/blogs/inspiration/david-kelley-on-design-thinking
[2] Project-grounded research refers to a methodology formulated in the sociological field by Glaser & Strauss (1967). According to Grounded Theory, observation and theoretical elaboration proceed simultaneously in a circular and bottom-up approach: the theory is derived from the analysis of local and contextual data.

In the process of ideation, concept development, and making that led to the pro-totype's creation, the designer(s) will have encountered and navigated around re-al-world obstacles to build the best bridge between the product and its users. This process generates specific insights, some of which can be made explicit and shared, bringing facts to light, and contributing to future endeavors.

Given the context in which Design, as a project, is called to respond, a research methodology such as RtD would allow us to better respond to the ever-increasing need to produce process innovation rather than artefact innovation. Design seems to have two main characteristics which in some way differentiate it from the other disciplines: the ability to create connections (Buchanan, 2009) and to have pre-cisely subjective methods, which are intended as those Research strategies that could be vary based on researchers' personal influence. Design, in this sense, en-ables connection with different fields and topics related to different disciplines to-wards a transdisciplinary understanding of complex problems towards new forms of knowledge and further creativity. In this regard, it is important to point out that creativity is considered as an act of perception or a way of grasping wholeness to explain how designers and creators make or discover things, such as products, artefacts, ideas and more.

Thus, grasping the completeness of a system could be a way of learning to see, which is linked to the ability to intuit. Intuition is not something irrational, it is something profoundly rational but not so formulated a priori. It must also be dif-ferentiated from a form of "tacit knowledge" (Friedman, 2008). Tacit (or implicit) knowledge is not codified through structured communication flows, which exist in the heads of individuals, and which often arises from work experience. As such, it is connected to the ability to understand the contexts of action, intuitions, sen-sations that can hardly be understood by those who do not share this experience. Intuition guides us towards the new, it allows us to move from what is known to what is unknown, it is something we trust but often it can also fail (Laureti, 2020).

The perception of this connection is what we often identify with the term inno-vation or creativity. Creativity is nothing more than a perception of what is not familiar, of what we do not know, of what we do not have in front of us. In this sense, creativity can go far beyond the imagination, it can be a way of perceiving and seeing variations; perception thus becomes the key.

"I see intuition as a very significant matter in creativity. In reading Spinoza, for instance, in his Ethics, he says that the sequence is imagination and reason, but beyond imagination and reason it is intuition that gives us the greatest knowl-edge. Now what could he possibly mean by that, except the ability to perceive some deeper connection, some deeper system that goes beyond our arguments and our rational structures? To grasp a wholeness. And I think this is what designers do. I think they grasp the wholeness of a product." (Henriksen & Mishra, 2018, p. 217)

TECH / MAKING TECH

PART I
TECH
CHAPTER 1
MAKING TECH

This chapter introduces a series of reflections built around the technological dimension of the Maker Movement and its evolution. It offers insights into the technological advancements achieved and accessed by this culture, thereby aiding in better comprehension of the technological state of art available in Maker production and enabling the prediction of possible future developments.

Technology as consequent approaches to design, producing, distributing, and consuming, has transformed the industrial paradigm of designer/producer/distributor/buyer, shifting the focus from products capable of suggesting changes and controlling the manufacturing process themselves to manufacturers and individuals. The various forms of technology that have become integrated into our daily lives are explored as products, tools, and systems of economy, highlighting the need to view technology not as an exogenous force that will determine our future or a mere tool but as an integral part of our behaviors, thinking, and design processes.

Before talking about the technological matter, a semantic premise is necessary. Historically speaking, 'technique' and 'technology' are quite recent concepts. In the Middle Ages and the Renaissance, we spoke rather of practical or useful arts; later, starting from the 17th century, 'mechanics' and 'machine' became the new dominant concepts. More recently 'technique' and 'technology' have also entered the common language, and do not give rise to any misunderstanding. However, although their meaning appears clear, a precise delimitation of the semantic scope of the two terms is extremely difficult. It would undoubtedly be legitimate - similarly to other pairs of concepts such as, for example, psyche/psychology - to designate a real phenomenon with 'technique' and with 'technology' the knowledge or science relating to physical reality, but in fact a distinction of this type is not systematically implemented in any language. In English, 'technology' is mostly used in both cases, while in German it is preferred to speak of *technik*. In English, on the other hand, 'technique' has a much narrower meaning, and designates specific practical skills, or *"a way of carrying out a particular task, especially the execution or performance of an artistic work or a scientific procedure"*[1].

In Italian, the two terms are often used interchangeably, implying concept that embraces a wide variety of domains, encompasses practically all forms of goal-oriented agency that adopts some tool or specialized knowledge, and lends itself little to demarcating a particular field of study. It would be therefore appropriate to use a narrower concept of 'technique' for analytical purposes, which presupposes the existence of artefacts created by humans and used in the context of goal-oriented action. This narrow concept refers not only to material artefacts, but also includes methods and processes; for example, the production technique of the chemical industry includes both technical devices (artefacts) and special procedures. Therefore, the term 'technology' refers both to artefacts and to processes and materials. This first chapter reflects a priori on the role of technology, investigating in first place what technology therefore means in society and what cultural, socio-economic correlation it has.

1.1 It is always a matter of time

Introduced as such, the concept of 'technology' could be seen in a holistic view compared to the 'technique', which is the specific object of study of a multiplicity of disciplines; therefore, 'technology' could refer to broader fields of technically relevant knowledge and skills (or 'techniques') based on scientific knowledge, from which practical applications can be developed. Apart from the engineering sciences, which concern the construction of technical artefacts and the development of new procedures, there is a philosophy (Feenberg, 2009; Ihde, 2004), a history (McNeil, 1996), and a sociology (Pinch and Bijker, 1984) of technology.

---

[1] Definition retrieved from the Oxford Dictionary

Economics and political science are also concerned with this issue, the former regarding innovation and economic growth, the latter in connection with technology policy problems. The study of technology from the perspective of the humanistic sciences embraces a variety of approaches. A decisive boost to the development of the sociology of technology, as it has been necessary especially in the last thirty years, was given by the critique towards the so-called 'technological determinism' (Drew, 2016). Both the development of technology and its consequences follow an inherent logic or its own dynamics and are therefore subtracted from conscious control by humans. The development of a new technology, therefore, would essentially depend on the stock of knowledge and capacities present and be available at a specific historical moment (Mayntz, 1998). Regarding this latter aspect, the research has been strongly influenced by a concept that will be referred to several times in the next paragraphs on all three levels of inquiry: time. De Kerkove (2011) stated that technological development is an unstoppable movement that reveals in social dynamics a new objective related to the temporal dimension.

> "[…] I am currently interested in what I call 'the conquest of time,' which is a technological and social innovation that will allow us to expand our lives both quantitatively and, more importantly, qualitatively. Since we conquered the moon and wired the planet into a global network through electrical and electronic communication technologies, we have completed the conquest of space. We did this by using its own simulation, bringing it into a virtual reality. Now the new frontier of technological and social development is time. Today people buy space and still say that time is money. But tomorrow the same people will buy time as a possibility of choice, or, economically speaking, as a market of choice. I am also very interested in the idea of time as a market. A wide and global market."[1]

Once a new technique is introduced, it will necessarily cause certain social changes (Mayntz, 1998). A series of ethical issues have become evident in the last forty years, concerning (among other things) the influence of technological development on the quantity and quality of jobs, the occupational structure, corporate organization, and their relevance in the economic growth - which is also a consequence of the technological improvement that has impact on at local and global scale. So, technologies, as techniques, have become relevant themes for the social sciences when they began to be perceived as a problem. The sociological study of technique, a conscious technological policy, and the systematic attempt to develop and institutionalize an assessment of technology consequences represent three parallel and mutually related answers to the same matter (MacKenzie and Wajcman, 1999).

[1] Transcript retrieved from the intervention of Derrick De Kerokhove in the article on Intervention at the International Conference "Journalist Profession: New Media, New Information," retrieved from www.e-journal.it/special_event/relatori/articoli/de_kerckhove.htm

For the design practice, these elements becomes extremely relevant when the formal dimension can directly communicate and shape itself through and with the technological dimension. This approach recognizes that technology is not neutral and that decisions about its development and application can have far-reaching consequences. Designers can contribute and as will be discussed further are called to action by advocating for technologies that are aligned with social and environmental values and by working with policymakers to shape technological policy.

On *Techne* and *Poiesis*

"[...] saw that all other living beings harmoniously possess everything, and that instead man is naked, barefoot, without a bed or weapons: the fateful day was now imminent, the day when man too must leave the earth and come to light. Prometheus, findlng himself in great distress for the salvation of man, then stole from Hephaestus and Athena the technical knowledge along with fire [...] and thus he gave it to man."[1]

With these words, Plato defined the technical action as a force inherent in the human evolution, who achieve the capacity to develop the ability to produce tools, developing their technical knowledge even before being able to think about it. This works introduces the concept of Homo faber (who thinks with his hands) that can modify surrounding reality. During a lesson held on November 18th, 2022, by the globally famous designer Denis Santachiara for the Master Course in Product and Service Design at Sapienza, an important concept was introduced through the presentation of his products: the relationship between *Techne*[2] (i.e. technical knowledge) and *Poiesis*[3].

"You know that creation is something multiple. In fact, every cause for which everything passes from non-being to being is always a creation; so, productions that depend on all the arts are creations, and all the craftsmen of these things are creators. However, you know that not all of them are called creators, but they have other names, and a distinct part of the whole creation, namely that which concerns music and poetry, is designated by the name of the whole. Only this is called creation, and those who possess this art of creation are called creators."[4]

The historical concept of *Techne* can more easily be associated with the artistic context as the ability to seek the useful and good in what concerns it (art, therefore, as ability, capacity, responsibility, not in and of itself but in relation to the fixed purpose).

[1] The present quotation comes from Platone, Protagora, (V century a. C.
[2] From the Greek téchne which stands for "art" and is intended as "expertise" or "know-how"..
[3] The noun "poiesis" (from ancient Greek) stands for " make from nothing" (Plato, Symposium, 205b), first appeared in Herodotus with the sense of "poetic creation" (ii, 82).
[4] Text extracted from Marco Vignolo Gargini's elaboration of Platone, Symposium, edited by France Ferrari, RCS Rizzoli Libri, Milan, 2003, 173-203.

Poiesis, on the other hand, is decidedly more complex to define because it is not linked to the common concept of 'poetics' but implies the ability of the homo faber to access a higher level, as in the creative and generative process of nature for those 'new' forms that become things, works, artefacts. It follows that the creative process does not have its seat in Plato's being (that is, in the psyche, sensations, nature, sociology) but descends, through intuition, from a higher, antecedent level. In this sense, Santachiara has fundamentally expressed how the Design project moves from this *Techne* to *Poiesis*, and its success is based on the balance between these in which the function (expressed by technology such as IoT and smart actuators) has a restricted and limited echo in time, but it is beauty, wonder, creation, precisely, that gives longevity to the project in its user. The time of the project is determined by the juxtaposition - not perfect as it is a median between the two, but adequate to the context and the purposes of the same - of the project between these two elements.

> *"The magician strategy increases the distance between cause and effect."* *(Santachiara, 2022)*

A concept not dissimilar to Clarke's third law (1984): *"Any sufficiently advanced technology is indistinguishable from magic"*. In the sense of Design, Santachiara makes it clear how the designer must move between these two concepts to produce, from a technological effect, an immediate and fundamentally "brief" impact in the mind of the observer, a wonder, a surprise, that can remain impressed in the mind of those who have experienced it.

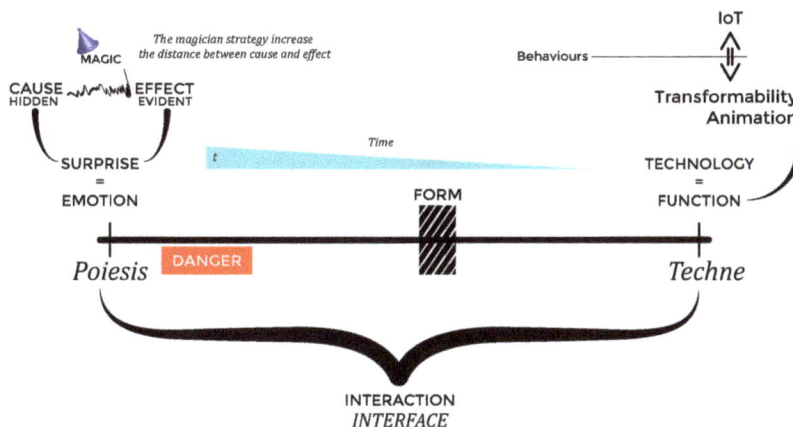

A graphical representation of the concepts expressed by Denis Santachiara during his lecture in Sapienza at the Interaction Design class on November 18th, 2022.

Santachiara thus defines his "magician's strategy," the designer's ability to surprise the user by "hiding" the technology inside the design's form. In this sense, it becomes crucial to know technology to integrate it not only to make use of it, but because through this combined action, Design and technology can generate more enduring impacts over time, surviving technological advancements and formal changes in product culture. As a final warning, it is important to emphasize that if the transition from function to emotion is not fully satisfied, the highest risk will be to have a 'disillusioned' user.

1.2 It is not "rapid prototyping" anymore

"Industrial development is one of those mysterious cumulative phenomena that grow on themselves, like epidemics." (Ruffolo, 2009, p. 160)

The industrial production development spread, fueled at the same time by technological, social, and economic advancement, could be traced with exponential more difficulties which generates serious barrier to the reconstruction of the chain of events that led to certain results "due to the dense interplay of interdependencies" (Ruffolo, 2009, 160). Within the scenario of the Fourth Industrial Revolution, a series of phenomena that define the transformations taking place have formed and are continuing to form. Technologies and new digital approaches have changed the configuration of classic industrial production, building a totally new production reality known as "Industry 4.0"[1] (Henning et al., 2011). Regarding this evolution, it is possible to highlight in the first place the main actors that made possible the birth of the "4.0" concept. Indeed, it is possible to point out that previous production facilities have been essential in preparation for the fourth industrial revolution. It is therefore necessary to make a little retrospective of it:

- First Industrial Revolution (1760 – 1830) involved the introduction of mechanical production systems, characterized by the advent of machinery in the production compounds and energy generation facilities;

- Second Industrial Revolution (1856 – 1878) saw technological development in the energetical sector led to the advent of the electricity which enable the mass production of consumer goods opening to production movements and reconceptualization of the industry dynamics such as Fordism and Taylorism;

- Third Industrial Revolution (1950) has increased this last trend towards the automation of production processes by resorting to electronics and information technologies, thanks to the implementation of the last great innovation reality: the Internet.

---

[1] This term, which has now entered the daily lexicon of modern industry, was used for the first time at the Hannover Messe 2011 by Henning, Wolf-Dieter e Wolfgang (2011): in their report "Industrie 4.0: Mit dem Internet der Dinge auf dem Weg zur 4. industriellen Revolution" [Industry 4.0: the Internet of Things towards the Fourth Industrial Revolution], exposed what changes the Fourth Industrial Revolution would bring on a global level.

The improvement of production assets led the industrial systems to end up with everyday products through the introduction of products with integrated memories, communication capabilities, wireless sensors, integrated actuators, and intelligent software. These aspects enable direct connections and interactions between the virtual world (cyberspace) and tangible reality, allowing a fine synchronization between the digital models of the devices and the physical reality, introducing concepts such as the "digital twins" (He & Bai, 2021) up to those phygital systems (Mikheev et al., 2021) that strategically merge the digital information with physical actions of users (commonly referred to a marketing strategy).

According to Henning et al. (2011), the upcoming business models of the next decades will be feasible only with the involvement of cyber-physical systems (CPS), for which development has already provided the starting point for numerous research projects based on the concept of product memory. Understanding this concept is crucial to grasp how technology can drive innovative solutions. This shift marks a complete change in the industrial paradigm, empowering products to play an active role for the first time. Rather than being controlled, products now become semi-finished goods capable of suggesting changes during different phases of the process. With prototypes and products monitoring environmental parameters through integrated sensors, they can even "control" the manufacturing process themselves and behave in an active way. This concept represents the essence of new industrial production, made possible by the technologies enabled by the Fourth Industrial Revolution. These technologies, considered strategically relevant for business activities, can define new business models (Schwab, 2017). When discussing this transformation, it is possible to notice how prototyping tools became more integrated in production processes over time, enabling changes as much in the flows as in the inner identity of the product itself. Prototyping process is required, in as much as a possible easy and economical way, to understand the functions of an object which define its shapes as the future user behavior. It is therefore an iterative virtuous process, made also of trials and errors in which we can distinguish three main phases of analysis: the process to make the product, the content, in terms of user behavior and features of the product and the esthetical quality of the result. Designing successful products requires careful consideration of a multitude of factors, including the user experience, technical feasibility, economic viability, and social and environmental responsibility (Brown, 2009) in which prototyping, is the physical comprehension of a product.

Graphical readaptation of Brown (2009) scheme (p.19) on innovation process.

Desirability focuses on the user experience and emotional response to a product, therefore related to its quality; its feasibility, related to process, considers the technical and economic aspects of design; the viability is instead related to its content, while addressing the social, environmental, and ethical implications of a product. By considering these three aspects together, designers can create products that are not only attractive and functional but also socially and environmentally responsible, economically feasible, and technically feasible. Through this framework, designers can create products (in the core and still unknown until the very end) that are both successful in the marketplace and sustainable in the world.

To understand the industrial and digital revolution, it is necessary to understand the technology of hardware, software, and digital networks, synthesized respectively as exponential, digital, and combinatorial (Brynjolfsson and McAfee, 2015):

- The exponential adjective is a term that has arisen due to the growth in technological advancements and is viewed through the lens of Moore's law[1]. According to it, the pace of digital progress today appears faster than in the past as the exponential growth predicted by Moore's law is accumulating. This has led to a new regime in the use of computers, and they are now highly widespread. Digitization is not just a simple shift from physical to digital but rather a process that encompasses a range of changes.

- The digitalization evolution of research systems and knowledge production models has resulted in a transformation of physical information into 'binary data', which is both accessible and inherent. This transformation has given rise to a new market and industry, which has allowed for the efficient production, collection, and storage of information in existing systems.

1.3 Enabling technology through Design

"[...] it is supposed that in the near future we can contribute to changing the productive sphere, making it no longer centered only on the industrial production-consumption dichotomy, but also on the autonomous development of products by those who need them." (Cecchini, 2012, p. 107).

The technological aspect and the applications of the aforementioned enabling technologies determine more extensive and open innovative approaches, which can characterize the production and design environment of this new phenomenon (Hirshberg et al., 2016; Lipson, 2012; Pearce, 2012). Nevertheless, it should be noticed that this revolution can also be seen as a resource that must be exploited at its best, which is not only linked to a change dictated by technology.

---

[1] The Moore's Law states that the power of computers doubles every 18-24 months, while the cost remains the same. This has led to a rapid evolution of technology and an exponential growth in computing performance.

"[...] it is necessary to review the approach with which we observe and examine the important technological innovations that are transforming our society. In fact, we cannot think of technology as an exogenous force that will inexorably determine our future, nor, on the contrary, we can imagine new technologies as a mere tool that man can choose to use whenever he wishes."
(Schwab, 2022, p. 14)

In fact, we should pay attention to outlining specific approaches within a system that is not based only on practical aspects related to the production sphere; both Design, at the center of the process, and the technologies themselves should be able to make the best use of each other using data retrieved (Schwab, 2017). The result is an increase in productivity, which, however, is increasingly faster and devoted to improving products based on customer requests or needs. This also leads to an increase in the efficiency of the resources used, as well as the possibility of creating new forms of collaboration that lead to the transformation of production models. Some approaches are already starting to appear, even if not yet completely developed, while others are starting to be applied, and it is possible to summarize them by looking at the factors that describe an industrial production in which it is possible to outline a trend of developments defined by the following innovative approaches described by the literature so far produced.

On Open Innovation

From the second revolution onwards, the founding principle of Fordism production has been seen as linked to the technical division of work-based duties sectorization and the assignment of different tasks related to individual skills (Dinetti, 2012). By this consideration, each worker is therefore required to produce only a part of the product itself which then, assembled to that built by others, constitutes the entire final product. This process constituted a sort of collaboration process between the layers of the factory which, however, was not aimed at obtaining any sort of product innovation through it. Nowadays, those Open Innovation participatory tools offered by the web and the digital environment, where the information era, as well as the "democratization" of the production processes, question traditional organizational models, producing a decentralization and participation of the reference assets (Frate, 2018). Actors involved intervene and collaborate with each other both within the design process and in the production (Elmquist et al., 2009), the process aiming to advance both the product and the process. These factors go beyond the technical impact and productivity implication and can be understood as a socially empowering set of tools. Open Innovation is a business strategy that involves seeking and incorporating external ideas, knowledge, and resources into a company's innovation process, as opposed to relying solely on internal resources.

The concept was introduced by Henry Chesbrough, who argued that the most successful companies are those that collaborate with external partners to innovate and create value (Chesbrough 2007, 2010). The growing amount of innovation that is emerging thanks to radical and widespread movements such as Open Source, which from early experiments such as the human genome project (HGP) has evolved to the present day, distinguishing itself as a real means of innovation on a global scale (making the term 'Open Innovation' coined in just ten years), favoring the advent of new thought tools such as the Thinkering, a portmanteau of 'thinking' and 'tinkering' (Antonelli, 2011). Speaking of this, Andrea Branzi, in an interview for the magazine Abitare states that the widespread and distributed nature of modern design (referring to design as much as to architecture) makes it difficult to identify a single will, defining it a militant and fluid bond.

> *"[...] Just think that during the Salone del Mobile there are more than 400 exhibitions at the same time, all projects not intended for the market, but an expression of an idea of reform of the environment, the city, the habitat, to realize that it is a widespread avantgarde form. Less evident, perhaps, but with an anarchist, reformist base and with a certainly greater number of employees than us." (Lanza, 2017)*

1.4 From BITs to Atoms

Digital manufacturing makes it easier for people or collaborative teams to design or produce end products and reduce the barriers to innovation. The manufacturer of products, which can be hindered in a traditional bureaucratic context with difficult requisitioning processes and long logistical waiting times, now would have options to make products faster. For intercompany collaboration, design teams can literally 'fax' their parts around the world to work with tangible products. When the necessary design or engineering resources are not collocated or even virtually connected, companies have turned to crowdsourcing. There is a global movement towards sustainability for the home and for companies of all sizes. Rapid manufacturing reduces transport costs when the 3D printer is placed near the production line. There are also efficiencies in terms of operating costs when airplanes are built with lighter materials.

Having said this, when the first user adopts the use of 3D printing technologies, there are often factors that are lacking in cost-benefit analysis; for example, power and heat are fundamental for 3D printing processes. Moreover, the advantage of a simple iteration of projects can increase the amount of non-recyclable waste. As result, digital manufacturing environmental benefits do not come without care and planning but are achievable. There is a wide range of materials that can be used, including plastic, wood composite, natural fibers such as hemp or carbon, ceramic, steel, graphene, titanium, and other metals.

On the market it is possible to see many different variations of materials and alloys, and it is interesting to notice how most of these applied for 3D printing technologies comes from SMEs and small research labs. Mulgan (2019) clarifies how the artefact, the physical object, in each of its declinations, facilitates large-scale coordination (referring to the interaction created in large connective intelligence systems and collaborative societies). We are used to thinking about things and we struggle to do it in their absence. Large-scale cooperation and coordination generate schematization and vice versa. The design process evolved with technological improvement and vice versa; technologies have been influenced by the Design discipline. Originally, rapid manufacturing was limited to prototyping. Now, printing methods such as direct laser sintering of metals, selective metal sintering and electron beam fusion have advanced digital fabrication up to the industrial applications level and final assemblies. When considering the applications, the question that companies should consider is which supply chain resource network and which mix of old and new processes will be optimal (Vargas and Yamnitsky, 2014). Some processes may take advantage of the input of a part made on demand with 3D printing, but others may not be suitable for it. It is therefore essential to consider alignment of existing processes with new ones providing data and awareness suitable to match them, in which, as D'Aveni states:

> *"Those that control the digital ecosystem will sit in the middle of a tremendous volume of industrial transactions, collecting and selling valuable information."*
> *(D'Aveni, 2015, p. 46)*

Technology as a shared service

Technology has revolutionized the way we live and work, and it has become an integral part of our lives. Traditionally, technology has been seen as a tool that assists humans in carrying out their tasks. However, with the rise of the internet and the emergence of the digital age, the way we conceptualize technology has evolved. In recent years, there has been a shift towards viewing technology not as a tool, but as a service that provides a range of benefits to users. This shift has been driven by the growth of the technology industry and the increasing demand for technology-based solutions in various industries. Today, businesses and consumers alike are looking for ways to leverage technology to improve their operations and enhance their experiences. In response, many technology companies have begun to offer their products and services as a service rather than as a one-time tool purchase. One example of this shift towards technology as a service is the rise of cloud computing by which, rather than buying software and hardware outright, businesses can access resources through cloud-based services based on a subscription system. Another example can be found in the growth of the Sharing Economy model, which is based on the idea of using technology to share resources and services (Sundararajan, 2016).

Platforms like Airbnb and Uber have disrupted traditional industries by allowing individuals to share their homes and cars with others for a fee. These platforms provide a service that enables people to access resources they may not have been able to otherwise, and it also provides an opportunity for individuals to monetize their assets.

The intervention of digital technologies is fundamental for the realization of a dialogue that, beyond the simplistic technological advancement for production they represent, it is required to rethink the design discipline approach that should operate in favor of the innovation of the product as well as of the process. This dialogue is based on the horizontal communication[1] between the product and the processes that (as we stated in previous paragraphs) has been made possible by the fact that enabling technologies. Thanks to this approach, each component of the system is capable of sharing, exchanging and producing parts of the whole process by generating constant innovation (Anderson, 2014). In this sense, concepts such as the Sharing Economy becomes an approach since it is not an end but aims to be a continuous, democratic, and potentially endless advancement and exchange. It can therefore be asserted that it is the digital and diffusive approach that makes products innovative since sharing makes it possible to have a horizontal and widespread intervention on a global scale. After introducing and outlining the meaning and impact of horizontal dialogue within the system, the sharing approach requires that the weight of vertical dialogue[2] within the system itself be defined. The shift towards viewing technology as a service has important implications for the way we approach technology. Rather than simply using technology as a tool to achieve a specific task, we can now view technology as a partner that can help us achieve our goals in a more efficient and effective way. This approach allows us to leverage the full potential of technology and to take advantage of the many benefits that it can provide.

The concept of technology as a service becomes an important evolution in the way we perceive and use the technology. As technology continues to advance and become more ubiquitous in our lives, the shift towards technology as a service will likely become even more pronounced. By embracing this approach, we can unlock the full potential of technology and use it to improve our lives and our businesses. The development of digital technologies, based on interconnection between different production components and on an approach oriented towards process and product innovation, makes the Fourth Industrial Revolution different from previous ones.

[1] With horizontal communication, also known as Horizontal Integration, we refer to the interaction established between different systems, such as companies operating in the same supply chain, even if they are seemingly competitors (Martin 2019, p.9).
[2] Vertical integration refers to the exchange of information between customer and supplier within the value chain (Martin 2019, p.9).

This aspect requires a change also from the point of view of organizational structure, where Design can be seen as a tool capable of developing a new approach supported by strategies such as the decentralization and recomposition of the value chain, personalized offering, elimination of barriers between industry and services, and mixing of production and consumption (Tullini, 2016). The effort needed to achieve this model cannot ignore the need to reach these objectives without a significant upheaval from both a process and product perspective where:

> "[…] a manufacturing solution that provides such flexible and adaptive production processes that will solve problems arising on a production facility with dynamic and rapidly changing boundary conditions in a world of increasing complexity." (Radziwon et al., 2014, p. 1187).

Obviously, the project of such a reorganization requires significant investments of time and money, generally manageable only by large enterprises, which could lead to discrimination against small and medium-sized enterprises (SMEs) that mostly maintain a craft production and do not have the necessary tools to implement such applications (Micelli, 2016). This critical issue has been accentuated, due to factors beyond control, by the pandemic crisis of 2020 which in Italy:

> "[…] did not stop the growth of Industry 4.0, confirming that it was not a passing trend but a planning approach that is persistently renewing the Italian industrial sector. [...] To launch pervasive, multi-technological, and cloud-based digitalization projects on innovative networks, a long-term vision, the courage to experiment with new applications for the new challenges that have arisen, and a strong investment in 4.0 skills will be necessary." (Osservatorio Industria 4.0, 2021)

In countries such as Italy, where small and medium-sized enterprises represent the heart of the productive fabric of the so-called 'industrial districts' (which will be discussed in detail later), much of their economy is based on production, and therefore, on the survival of these entities. The term "survival" is used purposely: according to the Italian Ministry of Economic Development (2018), it is still difficult to identify real leading figures capable of guiding the transformation of this type of manufacturing within the Italian panorama. According to Micelli (2016), SMEs lack the resources and managerial discipline to manage an organizational project and make large investments in research and development. The lack of knowledge means that SMEs and startups involved in updated small and medium-scale production systems (including historical craft activities) always remain a poorly competitive reality in constant crisis (Angolino et al., 2019). According to a more recent analysis (Angolino et al., 2022) Italian SMEs reacted promptly to the shock of the pandemic, showing remarkable resilience in limiting the damage caused by the crisis and a strong dynamism in recovering losses.

However, the prospects for recovery were abruptly limited at the beginning of 2022 with the outbreak of the Russo-Ukrainian conflict and the intensification of the energy shock. These two events have triggered a series of changes at the geopolitical and macroeconomic levels, determining a rapid change of scenario. Moreover, they demonstrate that, despite the responsiveness of the national entrepreneurship, the system of SMEs cannot be considered stable, proving instead to be fragile in the face of rapid changes. Specifically, it is possible to frame the development of these technologies between 2019 and 2020 by looking at the three areas of application in the entire production process, which are 1) Smart Lifecycle, including the development process of a new product, the management of its life cycle, and the management of the suppliers involved in these phases; 2) Smart Supply Chain, which includes the planning of physical and financial flows in the extended production logistics system; 3) and Smart Factory, which includes the processes that represent the heart of manufacturing, namely production, internal and external logistics, maintenance, quality, safety, and compliance with regulations. These aspects are linked to the establishment of new processes of both economic and ecological sustainability, which, following the pandemic crisis, focus on an increasingly local and precise dimension to identify and systematize processes, production, and distribution on a shorter range, extending the network of knowledge and cross-contamination of competence. This last aspect is of particular interest to parallel research lines on communities as ecosystems of competencies capable of generating economies, and the study of the city that contains such systems.

1.5 Distributed and shared responsibilities

The different trends and applications outlined so far have direct implications at different levels on culture and subculture evolution and in different aspects of the production systems. It could be possible to consider three categorized trends which have seen digital manufacturing as a critical factor of change outlined by the renowned international organization and digital business observatory Ernst and Young (Thewihsen et al., 2016): the technological improvements, described in present chapter, the market development, which will be discussed in the fourth chapter of this manuscript as result of the exchange dynamics within a specific environment (which in this case is related to urban context), and the business model evolution, which will be discussed in the sixth chapter as part of the evolution of strategies derived from a series of updated and empowered interactions. For this reason, it becomes imperative to endorse critical thinking towards a system that develops responsible and empowering policies. In this way of thinking, Responsible Design, which has a relationship with the market, defines itself as 'commercially available,' and whose primary intent is not a profit maximization but rather advocacy for a 'right cause' (e.g., a public tap that closes itself after a certain period).

Otherwise, we could talk about an *Empowering Design*, which has little to do with the market but is closer to a critical intervention towards an attitude to be rectified (e.g., a tap that shows how much water is used, providing environmental impact awareness). In the world of 3D printing, it is not difficult to associate the role of plastics, and it has been, fortunately, equally easy to find alternative and ecological solutions to the question. Today, various materials are developed directly deriving from industrial plastics that would otherwise risk ending up at the expense of governments or the environment itself. Instead, what is most difficult to see is what has been carried out in productive consumption and waste management. For instance, the waste generated around the food sector and how digital manufacturing has offered an answer. We have pseudo meats and edible compounds are produced deriving from food waste, used for the feeding of domestic or farm animals, and there is nothing that excludes that one day it

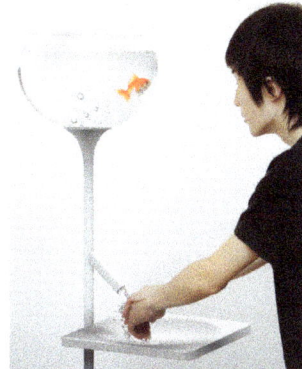

Poor Little Fish Basin, designed by Yan Lu, is a traditional shaped fish bowl and a basin. While using the water, you will notice the water level in the bowl gradually falls, it will go back to the same level once the water stops.
Image retrived from https://www.tuvie.com/poor-little-fish-basin-your-fish-will-die-if-you-waste-water/

will reach our meal consumption. In 2018 Giuseppe Scionti patented, with its company Novameat[1], a solution for the first plant-based substitute of meat[2] and its consequent application via FDM 3D printer: a revolution in the food-technology sector: from a design perspective is still proclaimed and printed as a steak. These factors led the reflection put in place on the role that past habits has on innovation processes: Artigiani (1988) stated that even in front of radical changes, some elements of the previous system must be maintained, in order to achieve a minimum perceptual and existential stability. We have increasingly sustainable materials (in economic and ecological terms), derived from the recycling of the same bioplastics, technologically performing and aesthetically appealing, but which are produced in a less ecological way (given the limited accessibility of industrial complexes to renewable energies), in an increasingly aggressive and competitive market context and distributed in ABS cases, sealed in common plastics, delivered by fuel based vehicles. These aspects recall a bit of a famous provocative question made by the architect Cedric Price in 1966 during his lecture while debating trust put into new technologies by the (at that time) British prime minister Harold Wilson:

"Technology is the answer, but what was the question?" (Price, 1966)

[1] www.novameat.com
[2] EU patent WO2020030628A1. https://patents.google.com/patent/WO2020030628A1/en

TECH / TECH IN PRACTICES

PART I
TECH
CHAPTER 2
TECH IN PRACTICE

Following a first phase of analysis of the technological landscape, the market, and the potential opportunities dictated by the possible accessibility of technological tools, a series of open and distinct labs were established with two different types of users in order to measure the actual accessibility of technology and its relationship with the discipline of Design. The experiment worked with design practitioners, whose projects has been placed in an unpredictable technological context to validate the coherence of the discipline in the face of technological potential.

The results of the experiments have shown that Design, although able to operate independently of technology, is not completely detached from the production phase, but rather attracted to it in a form of curiosity and willingness to experiment, with the aim of understanding its limits and approaching it as much as possible to stimulate possible developments.

Design tools and approaches are put into play and often challenged, contributing to the implementation of an objective moderated by an advanced technological tool, which, although it has enhanced the expectations of the project, has also imposed limitations for its realization.

2.1 Living Tech lab

European policies already announced guidelines for 2020 based on smart, inclusive and sustainable growth by promoting and developing an economy based on knowledge and innovation, more aware and rigorous in terms of resources, in order to support their own development if they don't want to see their production system reduced to what Bauman (2000) call an economy of transit only and the exchange of goods and people. An attitude which, at the same time, favors social and territorial cohesion through new indicators of well-being which, according to the "Report by the Commission on the Measurement of Economic Performance and Social Progress" (Stiglitz et al., 2009), they try to outline aspects that go beyond merely economic/monetary values, trying to conceive well-being as the union and balance of social, environmental and economic capital.

Issues related to the relationship with technological resources and the sustenance of activities linked to the territory are the basis of projects, studies, and actions in various sectors of industrial design and in particular in the field of design applied to corporate territorial systems. The economic crisis due to the global emergency of COVID-19 broke into a crisis process already underway and dramatically accelerated its times. As Daclon (2020) stated, the problem of the future will not be that many people in industrialized societies will have difficulty finding a job or will temporarily lose it due to a crisis such as the pandemic: *"The problem will be that work itself will no longer exist and a large part of the work positions, as we understand them today, will simply no longer exist"*.

The evolution of technology is driving changes in paradigms and dynamics that are impacting both the economy and society. This research explores new production and management models for cities that empower citizens to redesign the networks of information, services, and products that surround them.

These models involve hybridizations, connections, and distributed productions that go beyond just exchanging data to include goods and services, and they are changing the relationship between suppliers and users as well as the dynamics of urban life. Popular and participatory applications of technology are subverting traditional urban models and empowering citizens to take an active role in data collection. Over the years, several scholars of machines and electricity have theorized the role of the consumer as a producer (McLuhan, 1972) up to identifying the distinctive features in the dynamics of production and consumption which, going to invalidate the logic of the market, have allowed the birth of the definition of *prosumer* (Toffler, 1980).

The birth of the figure of the *prosumer* was made possible by technological discoveries and the growth of user participation, which blurred the boundary between production and consumption activities.

The wide panorama of changes and improvements outlined so far radically changes the asset of a production system, questioning how the concept of product is evolving by including those that are being created nowadays.

To answer this question, perhaps the issue can be circumvented with a change of perspective, taking into consideration the future ConsumAuthors (Morace, 2016). Although access and understanding of digital systems have become increasingly widespread, the physical interaction and contact with tangible materials remains essential for establishing relationships and tactile experiences. This "generational gap" arises from a society with a material culture that values physical touch.

This part of the research aimed to explore the urban productive assets of specific urban areas in the city of Rome, which is constantly rediscovering itself, from artisan shops to independent production laboratories with undefined catchment areas. In line with some European programs for social innovation and the improvement of the citizen's quality of life, such as "European innovation partnership on smart cities and communities" (EIP-SCC)[1], this part of activities carried on during this phase aimed to capitalize on the experiences of self-production techniques for their disruptive and proactive potential in the area through a critical analysis of the Smart Cities models that have favored the use of technology superimposed on the city.

2.2 A as STEAM

The concept of citizen empowerment has gained significant attention as a means of fostering community engagement and participation in decision-making processes. At the same time, STEAM practices, which integrate science, technology, engineering, arts, and mathematics, have also emerged as a powerful tool for enhancing innovation and creativity. In this context, it is important to examine the connection between citizen empowerment and STEAM practices, as these two concepts are closely intertwined. STEAM education can promote sustainable development and societal transformation (Taylor and Taylor, 2019). By integrating science, technology, engineering, arts, and mathematics, STEAM education offers a more comprehensive understanding of the world and fosters creativity, innovation, and problem-solving. A transformative approach is therefore necessary to challenge future people's assumptions and values to inspire them to become agents of change.

> *"[…] digital has the ability to change content and form, a digital content does not remain identical but can be declined into very different versions from each other" (Magone & Mazali, 2016, p. 110)*

The aforementioned statement requires a deeper reflection on the different skills and abilities designers must have to manage and control the processes involved in modern processes.

[1] https://smart-cities-marketplace.ec.europa.eu/

The focus, indeed, is shifting from 'design for Industry 4.0' to 'education for Industry 4.0' (Paoletti et al., 2018) providing necessary knowledge and skills from the early stages of education with a particular attention on "learning by doing" in Design education. Different criticisms emerge in the critical shift from high school education when facing real world challenges and the new world paradigms and approaches which, if properly handled, shorten the dichotomy between designer (as homo faber) and industrial designer, thanks to those technological and social dynamics enabled by the cloud and the internet (Anderson, 2006). Educators increasingly promoted the idea that to succeed in the future society, the next generation must be equipped with 21st century skills such as creativity, innovation, and entrepreneurship (Caprile et al., 2015)1. Instead, there is a growing debate among educators that "Arts" should be integrated into STEM curriculum to spur creativity and innovation (Guyotte et al., 2014), leading to the transformation of STEM into STEAM (Liao, 2016).

Despite that premise, British Educational Research Association reports some concerns about STEAM education due some inconsistencies and lack of conceptual clarity in STEAM terminology, pedagogy, and research (Colucci-Gray et al., 2017) as well as confirmed by other studies carried by the Ministry of Science, Innovation and Universities in Spain (Aguilera & Ortiz-Revilla, 2021). A primary point of confusion is the matter of defining the arts within the STEAM acronym (Perignat and Katz-Buonincontro, 2019). STEM education has been often described as ambiguous, with differing conceptualizations arising from the context in which it is used (Breiner et al., 2012), geography (Ritz & Fan, 2015), and lack of theoretical foundations (Bybee, 2013). As a result, STEM education has undergone a complex transformation, resulting in various educational experiences, despite its commitment to a similar educational approach, but, nonetheless, with differences in practice (Martín-Páez et al., 2019). Perignat and Katz-Buonincontro (2019) pointed out that in order for STEAM education to be an effective pedagogy, research must understand its implications in practice. While STEAM is thought to enhance creativity, critical thinking, and other skills, there is limited evidence to support this notion (Henriksen and Mishra, 2018; Khine and Areepattamannil, 2019; Stroud and Baines, 2019). Despite evidence of cognitive and academic benefits from arts education, there is limited research demonstrating transferable benefits to STEAM education. This gap is compounded by a lack of research linking STEAM learning outcomes to arts standards or education objectives. Future research should focus on outcomes such as creativity, critical thinking, problem-solving, perseverance, and self-efficacy, which are commonly associated with arts education. Such research has the potential to significantly impact the development of effective STEAM models. This case study offers various STEAM education approaches using design methodologies to teach students hard skills in implementing and managing new technology machinery.

2.3 Like the egg and the chicken

Assuming therefore that the technology is present and available to support not only production but development, the focus of the question on "how comes first" also has a shift; how much therefore design is capable of handling technology, rather than questioning its level of accessibility, delegating the production problem to a lexical question that divides the designer from the engineer. The advent of digital manufacturing has shortened the distance between the designer and production environments.

The designer today gets their hands dirty and becomes a Maker, creating an ever-closer link between the conceptual and the real thanks to increasingly accessible and efficient tools. The rapidity of the proliferation of communities, places of social prototyping, such as fab labs and co-hubs, and of widespread production also ethically redefines the role of design. Consumers increasingly buy experiences rather than products or services (Jaworski, 2018; Klaus and Nguyen, 2013). They enjoy physical experiences, such as attending concerts, or buying in concept stores, but also digital experiences, such as playing video games, browsing the internet, or experimenting with virtual reality applications. Today, a new set of hybrid consumption experiences, 'phygital' (physical + digital), combining the characteristics of both worlds, have emerged (Batat, 2019, 2021; Wided, 2022).

The design thinking process itself enables the opportunities offered by digital manufacturing, but above all the way of conceiving production and consumption changes. The question raised is mainly related to the role does design plays in digital manufacturing practices, to understand if and how it can operate ethically and effectively towards the ongoing social, economic, and ecological changes.

To reply to this question, the research project decided to simulate what happens to the design, when there is no certainty of the technology support. The initiative Design for a Phygital World[1] investigates how it is possible to reconcile digital manufacturing with the urgent challenges of the contemporary world generated by the ever more dramatic climatic, health, and political upheavals and which require us to review the very meaning of the things that surround the everyday. A space where physical and digital are no longer alternatives to each other but a new dimension of necessarily sustainable action.

The 'experimentation' was carried in two days between May 12th and13th 2022 and was organized on the occasion of the tenth anniversary of the Sapienza Design Factory, which created the event, hosted in the SAPeri&Co. laboratory, which offered the space, and technologically powered by the Selltek[2] company, which provided the technologies.

[1] www.facebook.com/events/747582076428996
[2] www.selltek.it/ a brand of DEDEM S.p.A.

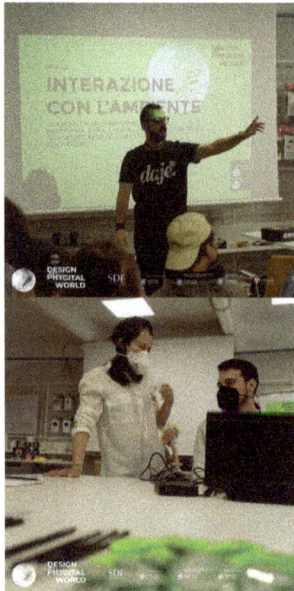

All the partners will be discussed in detail in the next chapter. The challenge of Design for a Phygital World called designers and makers under thirty to present product ideas that have already faced the potential of digital manufacturing to reply to the expressed urgencies by contemporary society and well represented in the Sustainable Development Goals (SDGs). In particular, the challenge looked for projects that could actively face the following challenge themes:

- DESIGN WITH NATURE. The challenge has always been to deterritorialize (Deleuze and Guattari, 1972) the magnificence and strength of nature to integrate innovative solutions into its products, create self-supporting structures for its projects, and adopt ever more performing generative tools. It's time for design to give back its space to nature. The ideas that respond to this challenge propose solutions for inserting the natural elements we desperately need in places where they no longer exist or have never been.

- DESIGN FOR PEOPLE. The recent pandemic crisis has shown all the fragility of people and their habits who must primarily deal with the issue of well-being and health. Therefore, the challenge is not only that of medicine called to cure but there is also an open challenge to prevent to which it is possible to respond effectively through new habits and new spaces and objects for living. The ideas that respond to this challenge propose solutions that manage to involve humans in an increasingly physically active, healthy, and independent life.

- DESIGN IN CITY. Cities, increasingly multicultural and multigenerational, are the place to imagine changes and innovations that are not just something that falls from above but include bottom-up actions. Thus emerges the challenge of revising the forms of appropriation and re-appropriation of public spaces and common goods in a more shared sense. The ideas that respond to this challenge propose solutions that stimulate the life of urban spaces and improve quality.

This experimentation has been carried on in the form of an hackathon[1] therefore designed to compare the design, and the production dimension of one's project, with an additive manufacturing technology that was unknown until the start of the activities.

[1] An *Hackathon* is a competitive event in which people work in groups on software or hardware projects, with the goal of creating a functioning product by the end of the event. Definition retrieved from https://www.dictionary.com/browse/hackathon

The hackathon took place for a total of sixteen hours, during which the students were first introduced to the technological potential of the machines adopted for the challenge, which included a Stratasys SLS machine for depositing Nylon PA12 with a volume of 400x400x400 [mm], a Carbon L1 DLS printer for resin printing, and the FFF D3-XP printer from Selltek for processing high-performance filaments. The entire production system and material investment was kindly supported and sponsored by the Selltek company.

The works resulting from the hackathon were delivered and evaluated by its representative and main mentor, Francesco Puzello, an Additive Manufacturing specialist and professor of the same subject at the National Institute of Nuclear Physics (INFN) of Gran Sasso. The event gathered thirty project proposals from fifty-four students from four Italian universities - specifically, the Sapienza University of Rome, the Rome University of Fine Arts (RUFA), the University of Camerino and the University of Pescara. Following an internal preselection, thirty-three students for sixteen projects were then accepted to participate in the hackathon. To understand the actual accessibility of technology and design tools beyond professionalization in undergraduate educational context, our research investigated the relationship of those tools most available, and the role covered by design methodologies in approaching those nonexpert users. Design led the practice not only as a disciplinary approach which could develop a reiterative process (Brink, 2015) but also as cognitive dimension. The project, although is still on working on further exercises which will be carried out in other points and with other students to test the efficiency of the structure and confront the results, already gave back a clearer idea of the dynamics and the lexicon needed to develop a true empowerment through more sensible citizens. If the citizens have been therefore confirmed to be open to empowerment through "*Design-led Technologies*", on the hand it has been considered relevant to understand if Design as discipline handled by experts, is capable of endorse a "*Technology-led Design*". Therefore, discussing the solid base that Design-led practice has compared to digital manufacturing transformation, to understand if and how those approaches can still operate effectively towards the ongoing social, economic, and ecological changes.

Results have highlighted that designers (referring to the participants) are not only capable of adapting themselves to and merging with other disciplines, but they have also been able to rapidly mitigate the necessity they have of the technology with the principles of the project. This has been highlighted especially by the original brief attendees presents and the outcome they had at the end of the Hackathon which, despite the challenges and the opportunity, has been able to persist and be improved. These experiences, which do not claim to be totally exhaustive in terms of research terminology, but represent the beginning of a journey that has brought to light various fundamental aspects useful for the constitution of the following results:

1. Young practitioners got closer to the concept of STEAM, with a process of gamification in which skills and competence necessary for the realization of both physical and digital artefacts has been put in question and under pressure to validate their consistency. It was understood therefore how preliminary STEAM skills in university education are necessary in the field of design for a smoother integration of new designer education into the new technological and social context of Industry 4.0 (and it is also hoped that the experiences undertaken may have contributed in this sense towards its participants);

2. The possibility of developing virtuous practices based on both Design Thinking and highly performative digital production was identified in the network of regional technology producers with characteristics like large industries (but outside the pure discipline of Design). Similarly, the collaboration between university and industry constituted for the designers the creation of a portfolio of projects usable both within the academic context and within industrial production.

"Design and technology point toward the transformation of something into something else while keeping the original substance" (Duarte & Álvarez, 2021, p. 15)

PART II
CMTY
CHAPTER 3
MAKING COMMUNITIES

Since the previously introduced influence of industrial transformations, processes, and technologies, in this chapter, the shift in the role of the designer in society is introduced and explored. In the past, production of artefacts was an artisanal process where the master craftsman knew and managed every single production phase. Technology accessibility and closer production systems shifted the role that creative communities' transformations whether technologies have shaped within society.

The contemporary understanding of design practices has been influenced by the advent of enabling technologies and the idea that anything can hold cultural or symbolic value. The capitalist system has led to the creation of artificial needs to maintain consumption, resulting in the transformation of the society from production-driven to consumption-driven. This has led to a detachment from consumerism and the need for a general change to meet evolving subjective needs. Consumption influences production, and individuals create paths of acceptance or rejection through competition that displays its offerings through media and the web. The growth of neo-tribal aggregation mechanisms and social networks has facilitated the creation of communicative matrices that give rise to solidify and dissolve groups with different configurations and goals, reminiscent of the archaic structures of tribes.

3.1 Designers of cultures

"Design that works outside of utilities is valid and a huge part of culture, just like art and music are, in a way. Design doesn't need to justify itself by saying users are at the centre of that process to be a welcome part of our society. Design is about culture invention" (Schulze, 2021)

This sentence has been retrieved from video interview with Jack Schulze, "Cultural Invention" for the Design NonFiction Archive by Tellart[1]. This statement led to reflect on the specializations Design has had to undergo during the course of its history which led to a shift of the role of the designer, highlighting the necessity of understanding how industrial transformations, in terms of processes and technologies, have influenced and shaped the role of the designer within the society.

Before the advent of industry, the production of artefacts was an artisanal process in which the master craftsman alone knew and managed every single production phase. Know-how passed through a continuous synthesis between thought and action, abstract knowledge and real experience (Buono, 2018). The understanding of contemporary design is instead largely influenced by the advent of IoT and *"the internet of things that are not things as such"* (Hill, 2014, p. 34) which implies the idea that anything can hold cultural or symbolic value. This was true even before the internet era, as Potter (1969) argues, designers could be seen as "culture generators" among others. What changes along with industrial revolutions is the sustainability of the economic system which becomes more and more dependent by its increasing production.

This results in an ongoing introduction of goods and services, rapid obsolescence, and creation of artificial needs to maintain consumption. Society transforms from being production-driven to consumption-driven (Angelisi, 2016). Behind the image of a wealthy society, made of sustainable products and communities, lies the issue of human freedom and detachment from consumerism[2]. The capitalist system, marked by recurring economic, environmental, and energy crises, also brings widespread discomfort due to the reification of human relationships and practices as external objects. The economic crisis dragged on from 2009[3] up to the present, results from societal transformation and the exceeding of societal limits, necessitating a general change to meet evolving subjective needs.

---

[1] Retrieved on October 8th, 2022, from https://www.tellart.com/projects/designnonfiction/#jack_schulze.
[2] Marx identified in capitalism a trend towards consumption, defining it as the fetishism of commodities. In his theory of value, goods, once pure and simple products of human labor, become a social relationship and, symmetrically, social relationships take on the appearance of relationships between things in exchange.
[3] To contextualize it better, the Italian manufacturing sector, which grew according to a development model based on exports, suffered a heavy setback due to the decrease in demand for goods from abroad. The collapse of exports determined a negative growth of GDP in 2008 (-1.2%) and one of the worst performances in 2009 (-5.5%).

Angelisi (2016) pointed out that the crisis stems essentially from two main factors: 1) from the development of society, which inevitably leads to a radical transformation of human life; therefore, the manifestation of a development that society has not yet been able to positively metabolize; 2) from reaching a limit and a subsequent collapse by society that goes beyond its rules, causing disorder, and this then necessarily presupposes a general change suitable for subjective changes (a break in balance). This factor has direct consequences on the development and transformation of human relationships, which can lead to new lifestyles starting from the sphere of consumption. In theory, through consumption, individuals influence production, shape industrial choices and strategies, and create paths of acceptance or rejection.

Thus, according to Bersano (2019), a context has formed where subjective identities form to give order and meaning to one's existence through existential projects entrusted to a specific lifestyle as a *"result of adopting a specific way of selecting and merging what the market provides"* (Codeluppi, 2015, p. 15). This results in the growth of neo-tribal aggregation mechanisms, supporting sociality by networking minority communities with temporary structures and a widespread hedonism, where desire strategies are aimed at satisfying the present day. Recently facilitated by digital technologies and social networks, this creates a communicative matrix that gives rise to, solidifies, and dissolves groups with different configurations and goals, reminiscent of the archaic structures of tribes (Maffesoli, 1998).

> *"The only notable difference of the electronic galaxy is certainly the temporality characteristic of these tribes. In fact, differently from what this notion usually suggests, the tribalism in question can be completely ephemeral and is organized according to the opportunities that arise." (Maffesoli, 1998, pp. 193–194)*

Within those 'tribes' of design this dialogue has determined a specification and a specialization of fields of action in which it intervenes, making Design adaptable upon several levels (Bassi, 2013). Maldonado (1977) defined Industrial Design as a process which:

> *"[…] must carry out its task within this process[1] and whose ultimate aim is the "concretization of a technical individual".[2] According to this definition, designing the form means coordinating, integrating and articulating all those factors which, in one way or another, participate in the constitutive process of the shape of the product. And precisely we allude to factors relating to the individual or social use, enjoyment and consumption of the product (functional, symbolic or cultural factors) as for those relating to its production (technical-economic, technical-construction, technical-systemic, technical-production and technical-distribution factors)" (Maldonado, 1977)*

[1] Referring to the productive process
[2] See Simondon, 1958

Design no longer concerns only the shape of machine-made objects but is a complex and overall profession, meaning overall that quality of Design capable of incorporating and communicating with all those scientific, technical, and social disciplines that influence the production of an artefact.

However, Design must constantly confront the reality of the contemporary and evolve coherently with it. Digital technologies have indeed outlined Design paradigms which seem to be more adherent to artisanal practices rather than industrial ones. Therefore, if DIY practices have been able to renew themselves and exploit the possibilities that the Fourth Industrial Revolution has to offer, Design is mandatorily required to developed methods and approaches that adhere to the new way of 'doing'. In this context, it is necessary to ask how Design and the designer can exploit these possibilities.

> *"[...] We are witnessing profound changes within the various production sectors, characterized by the birth of new business models and by the questioning or rethinking of the current production and consumption, transport and shipping systems" (Schwab, 2017, p. 14)*

3.2 Community-based productions

In response to these needs, there is a fervent return to the local, a new economy from below, sustainable, and respectful of the diversity of the territories that could truly outline a strategic vision of the productive future. Just think of the role of the makers and the rapid social responsiveness of rapid manufacturing which has led to the proliferation of communities and places such as fab labs and co-hubs, where the interdisciplinary exchange of skills is in favor of the development of innovative start-ups and cultural growth of the cities in which they operate. The technological update of Industry 4.0 and the adoption of certain production technologies (such as FDM or SLA/DLP) run in aid of an increasingly demanding market attentive to the central role of the final consumer.

This rapid expansion has moved the planned obsolescence market above all, which has obviously felt called into question in the face of an instrument that can reset its competitiveness. An interesting program launched by Groupe SEB (which includes industry giants such as Moulinex, Tefal, Rowenta), is the "10-year reparability commitment," a mapping of 'repairers' that offers the possibility of finding 3D printed parts to replace the components that can break over time in the products Jan Middendorp of LettError describes as the importance of tools for a designer, referring however to artisans as their ancestors. The latter, according to Middendorp, were like disgruntled customers in the 'tools' market and for this reason they have always tried to make their own, to personalize their work environment.

"They always had the tendency to personalize their tools, to appropriate them by honing them, converting them or expanding them. The more specialized the work, the greater the demand for customized or individually made instruments." (Middendorp, 2000)

The opportunity offered by some experimental and consolidated technologies, gained thanks also from the Open-Source communities and the digital manufacturing machinery industry, to be able to apply these tools and innovations to any production sector. In addition, design has become more evident participated and a fundamental part of the most disparate disciplines, so the role of the designer is redefined under an ethical key for which the design process itself is the fulcrum of the activity and acts as a coordinating element capable of managing the various skills at stake and work and production flows. Indeed, according to Paul Brody, US Advisory Technology Sector Strategy Leader at the Ernst & Young[1] global network: *"It is not just about 3D printing technology adoption. Inserting a 3D printing subprocess into traditional stamping will likely require process redesign"* (Thewihsen, 2016, p. 10). Another example of that could be found in the Danish designer Olivier van Herpt, who launched in 2014 the project, Adaptive Manufacturing, a collaborative project with the help of Sander Wassink. The project starts from the assumption that technological production has replaced the craftsman and therefore removed all traces of human and local influence and how this 'ambiguous' digital manufacturing process can mediate the language between the two realities. As it states on his website:

"At the foundation of every product there is the production process. When we replaced the craftsmen by machines, we lost the translation of local influences into our products. What if our machines could become more sensory? What if the machine could sense the local environment and incorporate it into the production process?" (Van Herpt, 2014)

The research of the two designers examines the ways in which it becomes possible to regain that lost connection between the production of objects and the objects themselves. To do this, they decided to design scripts that distil shapes and textures from external phenomena.

[1] https://www.ey.com/en_gl

External information, measured by sensors, is then translated into specific printer behaviors via software. A sensory and sensitive machine perceives the environment and therefore binds to a specific territorial context, translating the input into a specific movement, position, or raw material. Here the designer still plays a fundamental role by defining the degree of sensitivity of the machine and the elements to be considered. These approaches and experiments allow one to think about the role of the digital manufacturer. In addition to demonstrating a willingness to declare themselves through their products, making them unequivocally attributable to their work, they show an exquisitely melancholy taste in their past, artisanal, traditional, and local realities. Through the readjustment of past products or the use of traditional materials, the need to combine digital manufacturing with a world in decline seems to emerge until questioning if it is out of a real nostalgia or a secret will to confront the massive industry.

Maker culture distribution

The economic and social crisis, mentioned above, focuses on the need to identify new development models that consider the deep interdependence now active between the different economies and the potential expressed by the development of communication and data exchange systems. According to the study by Claire Warnier (2014) the development of new small-scale production techniques will allow the transfer of power from the hands of industries and those who regulate the infrastructure to those of the designer and consumer, who today more than ever is identifying himself as the only figure. Indeed, Morace (2016) redefines the role of the consumer, referring mainly to the Italian context, that is becoming more aware of the production and creative processes and is increasingly interested in them so much that he wants to be an integral part of them. From *prosumer* (Toffler, 1980) they (we) have evolve up to *ConsumAuthor*, the hybrid figure who directly participates in defining and selecting the prototyping lines of products and services, assuming their identity and involvement. A concept that is closer to the world of luxury and an almost elitist market, but which in an increasingly social and open context is spreading like wildfire on almost all market levels. Since the days of Apple, the concept of branding has been introduced, or no more than just brands. A fluid, inclusive system, in constant transformation and improvement where the consumer, the community, and feedback play a fundamental role in the development of the activities themselves. Therefore, our research investigates the responsibilities that design has developed around everyday products, particularly referring to those products which new generations refer to. With this regard, the analysis of this layer of investigation related to the Maker Movement and the birth of the subcultural community refers to those cultural and social values of a developing context of belonging should be handed down, who today more than ever are able to define, recreate, hack, reprogram, redesign the context in which it operates.

During the industrialization period, the removal of the craftsman's direct involvement in the manufacturing process led to a decrease in the product's quality, as the focus shifted towards mass production. To address this issue, some intellectuals promoted artistic-industrial initiatives that aimed to incorporate fine arts into the industrial system. They believed that the inclusion of art could restore the artisanal quality that had been lost in the production process. In 1845, Sir Henry Cole, one of the leading figures of the emerging design culture of the Victorian era, coined the term "*art manufacturer*" to describe a new role that blended the artistic and the artisanal, responsible for designing industrial products that combined aesthetic and intellectual qualities. This term can be seen as the precursor to the modern concept of the designer (Fusco, 2009).

The industrial revolution made everyday objects more accessible to the masses, but it also brought about significant changes in society and lifestyle. As a result, a new figure was needed to address the needs and interests of the consumers and guide them towards new behavioral patterns (Buono, 2018), rather than just the artisanal technique. Thus, the role of the craftsman was gradually replaced by that of the designer, who could conceptualize projects based on the requirements of mass production. From the 1950s onwards, as the influence of Fordism declined and the digital age began to emerge, industrial design started to incorporate computer technology. This led to the development of scientific communities in major industrialized countries, resulting in a range of scientific and methodological approaches that had a significant impact both socially and geographically (Malakuzzi, 2015).

In the late 2000s, the Massachusetts Institute of Technology (MIT) introduced the Fab Lab concept (N. Gershenfeld, 2005), which brought together digital fabrication technologies, such as computer controlled cutting machines and 3D printers, in a central location for people to use. This allowed makers to quickly prototype and fabricate their ideas on a larger scale, leading to the growth of the Maker culture movement and its increasing popularity and recognition. Over the years, Maker culture has continued to evolve, incorporating new technologies, such as artificial intelligence and the Internet of Things, and attracting a wider and more diverse group of participants. The term "Maker culture" has been finally expressed for the first time by Dale Dougherty in 2005, with the advent of Maker Media and Make magazine which has since been widely embraced and discussed in both academic and popular contexts. Born from the evolution of hackerspaces, as places for the dissemination of an active technological culture, makerspaces understood as places of doing in their heterogeneity (repair cafés, makerspaces and Fab Labs to name a few formats) have established themselves as potential places of widespread production throughout the territory, elevating these traditionally informal spaces to experimental laboratories of the next industrial revolution (Anderson, 2006; N. Gershenfeld, 2005).

This movement of hackers and creatives had such a significant impact on the public sphere that it has drawn the attention of governments, generating new models of governance and inspiring a new generation of urban entrepreneurs who are actively working *for* and *with* the local community to collaboratively achieve common objectives that are beneficial to society (Smith et al., 2016). As an example, we can refer to the Fab Lab network which, thanks to the support of Public Administrations in the United States, started spreading in 2011. By 2018, the global number of labs had doubled every year and a half, transforming an informal network of self-managed spaces that started from the bottom-up, into a new cultural infrastructure that is now top-down (Capdevila, 2015).

The peculiarity of each context makes the comparison and the analysis of the real effects of this institutionalization process on the wider phenomenon of makerspaces quite challenging, since more recent data record the reduction in the absolute number of laboratories: in October, 2020 it has been registered a total number of 1027 active Fab Labs[1] and 991 Hackerspaces[2], highlighting a decrease from 1120 Fab Labs (Fasoli and Tassinari, 2017) and of 1331 Hackerspaces registered in 2017 (Niaros et al., 2017). Along with the numerical reduction, important signs of qualitative consolidation can be observed, guided by the need (and will) to establish economically sustainable models, particularly in cities with a more extensive maker community, such as Barcelona, where the Smart City plan already in 2014 placed the goal of a new model of productive city based on digital manufacturing (N. A. Gershenfeld et al., 2017) - even if ten years later it is the same network of public makerspaces distributed throughout the urban territory it has still become an educational infrastructure for technological capability.

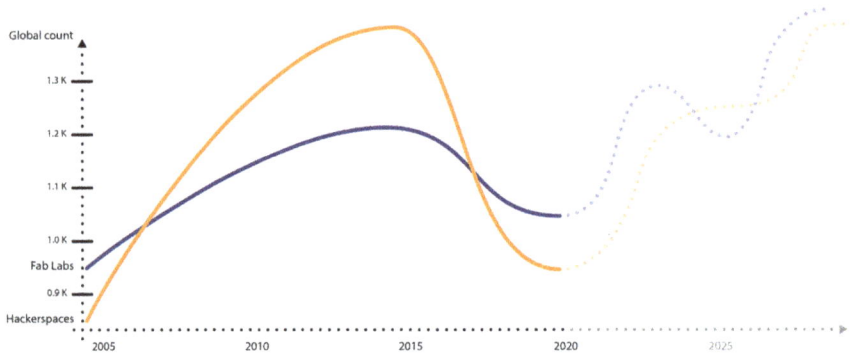

[1] www.fablabs.io
[2] wiki.hackerspaces.org

Taking note of the transition phase in makerspaces, this article questions which policies can be put in place to safeguard their function as open laboratories at the service of the public and encourage the development of their potential, illustrating a method elaborated and applied to within a European project.

> "The territorial and production context is defined by the set of skills and experiences settled over time, productive knowledge consolidated at individual, family and group level and, moreover, by the bonds, which are also consolidated between companies and people." (Tosi & Rinaldi, 2010, p. 14)

It could be possible to argue that modern production systems find their foundation in the artisan realities and in the culture of know-how typical of a tradition that is slowly disappearing. A production that, in addition to being a pride in the world, is a central sector of an economy that reflects the mechanisms of the society itself (Follesa, 2017). The building blocks of the development process of the global society, the liberalization of markets, have intervened as devastating factors SMEs facing with a crisis in the planet's resources.

Current consumption and production model leads us to redefine and question many practices that have been implemented so far. There are numerous critics and scholars of the current economic system who propose 'lateral' alternatives to development, through the application of concepts such as the necessary degrowth (Latouche, 2006). The quantitative approach, according to these studies, shifts towards a qualitative approach.

3.3 Catastrophic innovations

Taking note of the transitional phase in which makerspaces find themselves, questions arise as to what practices can be put in place to safeguard their function as open laboratories while promoting their potential development. Tools such as Open Source and digital manufacturing technologies have popularized DIY design practices, pushing millions of people to engage in projects, even if they are not yet intended for public consumption but rather directed towards personal needs. It is in this context that the figures of the Maker and the 'digital artisan' of Dougherty emerge and thrive within the Makers Movement.

> "First, they're using digital tools, designing on screen and increasingly outputting to desktop fabrication machines. Second, they're the Web generation, so they instinctively share their creations online. By simply bringing the Web's culture and collaboration to the process of making, they're combining to build something on a scale we've never seen from DIY before." (Anderson, 2014, pp. 20–21).

This definition could also be applied to the concept of the digital artisan, but with a substantial difference. Giovanni Longo, who was the curator of the "Open Manufacturing" section for the business-oriented information portal TechEconomy2030[1] until 2018, clarifies this difference precisely: if Makers choose an Open-Source economic development model, which can be represented by the definition of Sharing Economy, digital artisans, with a propensity to collaborate among themselves, are more likely to choose a Shared Source model.

Uncontrolled and distributed productions values

The most recent social and economic transformations have shown, both in the context of global development and in the national economy, a crisis of production balances and questioned the development models that have defined and guided local production in the last forty years, reducing progressively the degree of competitiveness of craft businesses. This loss is exacerbated by the constant contamination of culture carried out by globalization and by the massive industry which tends to amalgamate cultures to expand its catchment area. Lyotard (1979) defines the end of the great narratives as a loss of identity dictated by a single cultural strand composed of the sharing of certain values. The homologation of these paradigms, which aim at a more economic than ethical model, determines the end of this meta-narration of which the philosopher speaks and marks the departure from traditions and cultural values generating radical movements and disruptive works. Regarding this, Mari (2002) speaks of an almost criminal role of design in its being an instrument of proliferation of new goods in a world already submerged by them. In fact, Mari condemns the creative process and the search for innovation by attaching an almost criminal role to the current landscape which is dominated by unnecessary overproduction and a senseless frenzy. According to this and the Open Innovation revolution described by Branzi (which has been anticipated in the first chapter) it is possible to recognize the traits described by Gagliardi (2017) of a revolution that is not guided by a thought or a will capable of evaluating the social impacts that such innovations can have, which fills our time of 'tools', but with ambiguous ends.

According to Mari, the designer must consider human needs outside the market conditions when developing a project. With a severe denunciation of the progressive deterioration of today's design work, the main culprit for this situation is the global market that requires an object to be producible and saleable in every part of the world. The role of the designer is thus diminished to a simple 'signature' to be affixed to series of objects in which any construction philosophy is lacking. The designer should be able to respond to this 'ambiguity' by providing a complete and reproducible analysis tool that is able to put a more willing and interested market at the service of technological innovation, aware of its development and potential.

[1] www.techeconomy2030.it

A working method that would be able to create products from a synergistic process between technological research and the morphological and social spheres is necessitated. Frateili (1969) defines Design as the result of the combination of three factors: language, function and meaning as indeed they refer respectively to three specific morphological, technological, and social fields of study. In this sense, the role of the designer acts as director of these categories to favor their synergistic development of these fields, aiming to offer a result greater than the sum of the parts. However, the designer is not at the core of the action, but he becomes a multifaceted and dynamic figure that insinuates himself into the individual disciplines and regulates their input and output. The result is a series of small, unpredictable innovations (Gagliardi, 2017), which collides with a practical market that tends to favor 'planned change'. Innovations that fit into a planned pattern or that are easily recognizable in an economy that, while dynamic, must remain predictable. Problems related to the relationship with local resources and territorial identity are the basis of projects, studies and actions in various sectors of industrial design and in particular in the field of design applied to corporate territorial systems.

Object and place's identity

Thanks to these tools, it has also been possible to build new research and development places that go beyond the cultural and immutable *Genius loci*[1]. In this sense, the project is not limited to the internal dynamics of the company or the individual designer but uses a distributed model that opens up to a whole network of entities that act on it, generating a new intrinsic value. The productive and industrial scenario that has emerged in the previous paragraphs has highlighted the numerous descriptive aspects and approaches of this new way of thinking and has also highlighted how this new scenario requires an equally new and adherent design and production model (Schwab, 2022). The new industrial systems will necessarily have to update their organizational assets that should (but can already be said to 'must') be characterized by qualities that look to these enhancement systems that are both technological, economic, and social (Celaschi et al., 2017).

- Interoperable, promoting communication between objects, machines, and people in order to establish a homogeneous workflow in which decision-making is also supported and facilitated by information exchange;

- Virtualized, not to be misunderstood as 'dematerialized', but as openness to the possibility of simulation in order to evaluate the effect beforehand to limit its impact and therefore increase productive, economic, environmental, and social sustainability;

[1] The Genius Loci is a natural and supernatural entity linked to a place and an object of worship in Roman religion.

- Modular, opening up to the understanding of open products, services, and processes intended as independent and interchangeable modules, in order to adapt to changes in physical, economic, productive, and social contexts. A form of adaptability that allows for the collection, storage, and analysis of data useful for overcoming emergencies;

- Decentralized, as an organizational form of processes, in which every node of the network becomes a place of production, validation, and consumption. (OECD Multilevel Governance Studies, 2019; World Bank and Decentralization Thematic Team, 2013).

Regarding this last concept, Magone and Mazali (2016) argue that the decentralized production model enables interconnections with society that occur through the digitalization of relationships among market operators, which could be seen vertical - between the company and the supply chain or between the producer and the consumer - as well as horizontal - between entrepreneurs, consumers, and even the objects themselves.

> *"In the new scenario, the relationships of communities currently available in the realm of relationships between individuals can be replicated within the market, with the creation of communities that involve entrepreneurs, consumers, machines, objects, and workers. Within these communities, digital communications will determine circular flows of information and involve everyone."* *(Magone and Mazali, 2016, p. 155)*

The issues related to the dynamics of business (and its sustainability) are essential elements to understand how the design product could change in order to face a critical evolution (not always easy to tackle and leaving behind various "victims") as a driving force for innovation in companies and entrepreneurial objectives that in the short and long term allow activities to demonstrate resilience (or even antifragility) in the face of an emergency crisis such as the pandemic, up to the acquisition of tools capable of integrating "antifragile" solutions and development models (Taleb, 2013), able to exploit these unexpected events to their advantage. Unlike the traditional concept of "resilience," which refers to the ability of a system to resist and recover from shocks, antifragility is the property of a system that benefits from volatility, uncertainty, and disorder. Antifragile systems not only withstand stressors but thrive and become stronger as a result of them. A system like that one just introduced finds correlations with the description provided by Gandolfi (2008) of a complex system, which combines the advent of digital, electronic computing, at the moment of true understanding of what really is a complex system and the realization of how this complexity is inherent in everything that surrounds us, from the physical and biological nature of things to the texture of the social fabric, from production systems to political systems.

These systems are in fact represented as hierarchical constructs where each level of this scale is regulated by a network of interdependence and continuous circulation of data (input and output) which, thanks to the complexity of the system and of the individual parts that compose it, are to generate outputs of greater importance than the sum of the inputs. In this socio-economic evolution, design plays a primary role: on the one hand because of its being an important discipline in the development of production systems, and therefore central in defining new possible alternative economic scenarios, and its ability over time to have become so multifaceted and interdisciplinary as to play a role in every production system; on the other hand, for the responsibility that is unanimously attributed to it in the development of those consumer dynamics that have accompanied the progress of globalization. Having outlined the context, and the futureable directions that this Research will take, it becomes necessary to filter from the pool of potential results and sectors to which this Research can be applied.

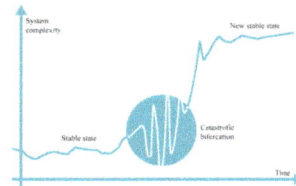

Gandolfi (2008) graphically reconstruction of the evolutionary path of a complex system. The system experiences relative stability, but eventually reaches a point of instability known as catastrophic bifurcation. During this phase, even small fluctuations are amplified by positive feedback, making the future unpredictable. Finally, one fluctuation prevails, leading to a new stable state.
(Adapted from Laszlo, 1986, p.53)

If we consider ourself in the middle of what Gandolfi (2008) calls a 'catastrophic bifurcation', we could catch a glimpse micro-oscillations of confusing revolutions (entropy) about to transport us into a future in which everyone will have full responsibility (enthalpy) for their own work and creation: it can no longer be said that we are at the gates of a revolution. The risk becomes that of letting it get out of hand or worse of using these tools unconsciously. We usually think of production systems with two distinct figures: designer and developer, architect and worker, mind and arm. This gap is about to disappear. If we have now witnessed a series of movements that have generated individual verticalized figures on single themes (art, engineering, craftsmanship, gadgets, small and medium productions and so on) now we see hybrid figures capable of operating (not just knowing how to operate) in a more active way on the production scene. Such a change is not only the result of technique or sensitivity, but a way of acting that has been able to generate a result greater than the sum of its parts. Awareness of the tools and design by virtue of these.

The following steps aim to analyze the post-industrial panorama and the role of its actors. With a particular attention to the relationship established between the digital manufacturer and his role as producer, the 'Maker' figure places himself in a context that no longer sees him only as customer of instruments trading, but an active part of a market that has spread their production potential to all.

An open, distributed, (still) free scenario, which however carries with it the burden of moral, ecological, civil responsibility, of a power that has long since declared its potential. In 2020 Menichinelli and Bianchini (2020) argued that discussions on the Open and Distributed Design (and Production) phenomenon should focus on long-term strategies, rather than solely exploring common features and how to scale it. This should include addressing critical issues that have an impact on Strategic Design, and how Strategic Design can impact on design and production. Design practices have evolved over the last two centuries and new technologies, processes, and approaches have influenced them. The Maker movement is an example of such evolution (Menichinelli, Bianchini, 2020). While trying to still find an evaluation for the Maker movement and explore potential strategies, including increasing democratization through the participation of *non-Expert* users and assessing the impact of these practices, the design discipline has evolved in line with the technologies that have allowed this material to express itself in new forms and, precisely because it is driven by this impetuosity, it has evolved and become more complex itself over time taking on so many facets to become an extremely difficult subject to understand. Without a convincing, truly taxonomic way of organizing the design activity, the latter risks leading to misunderstood results; the risk, for the designer, becomes that of being scattered and vague.

Different thinkers argue that errors are an inherent part of any complex system, and that attempting to eliminate all errors is neither possible nor desirable. In fact, they argue that trying to eliminate errors can make the system more fragile and prone to catastrophic failure. Giorello (2019) suggests that embracing errors and using them to refine scientific theories and models can make the scientific enterprise more robust and less prone to error. Similarly, Taleb (2013) argues that systems that are antifragile - which are those systems that benefit from stressors and shocks - are more adaptable and resilient than systems that are merely robust. In both cases, the idea is that errors and stressors can make the system stronger and more able to adapt to changing circumstances. Rather than trying to eliminate all errors or risks, it is better to embrace them and use them to build a more robust and adaptable system. The system has to be able to foresee the occasion, the chance to grow and thrive. As Mao Zedong (probably) said: *"Great is the chaos under heaven [...] the situation is excellent"*[1].

If, by its definition, Design is a process, it does not have a single interpretation and result but provides tools to understand a whole series of social, productive, and fruitful processes: an interdisciplinary discipline that has now imposed itself in almost all sectors of research and development, as well as production.

---

[1] According to MacFarquhar and Schoenhals (2008), Mao Zedong expressed his determination to create "great disorder under heaven" for the purpose of ultimately achieving,"great order under heaven." in a letter wrote to his wife on July 8, 1966.

"We are not experts in a specific subject ... we are experts in the process that leads a specific subject in bringing innovation" (Kelley, 1999)

Having to represent these mechanisms, it becomes possible to notice graphic affinities of representation and it is equally easy to identify assonances with more recurring and impactful themes such as blockchain, open source, and community exchange systems. We are no longer regulated and centralized, but distributed and widespread, free to make choices and therefore responsible for them. At the basis of the reflections outlined so far, this Research dealt with the relationship between design and production and the different ways in which the design discipline must be placed towards a post-industrial production, paying particular attention to the identity, defined by as much by the tools themselves as by geopolitical and cultural characters. It must investigate the identity of objects and the different ways in which these are built in relation to the social context and from there with both material and immaterial resources. This reflection led us to consider the correspondence between objects and places and how such correspondence has been interrupted (or at least weakened) with the advent of the machine society (Frateili, 1969), the expansion of an economic system always more open and inclusive, and with the substitution of codified knowledge for practical knowledge.

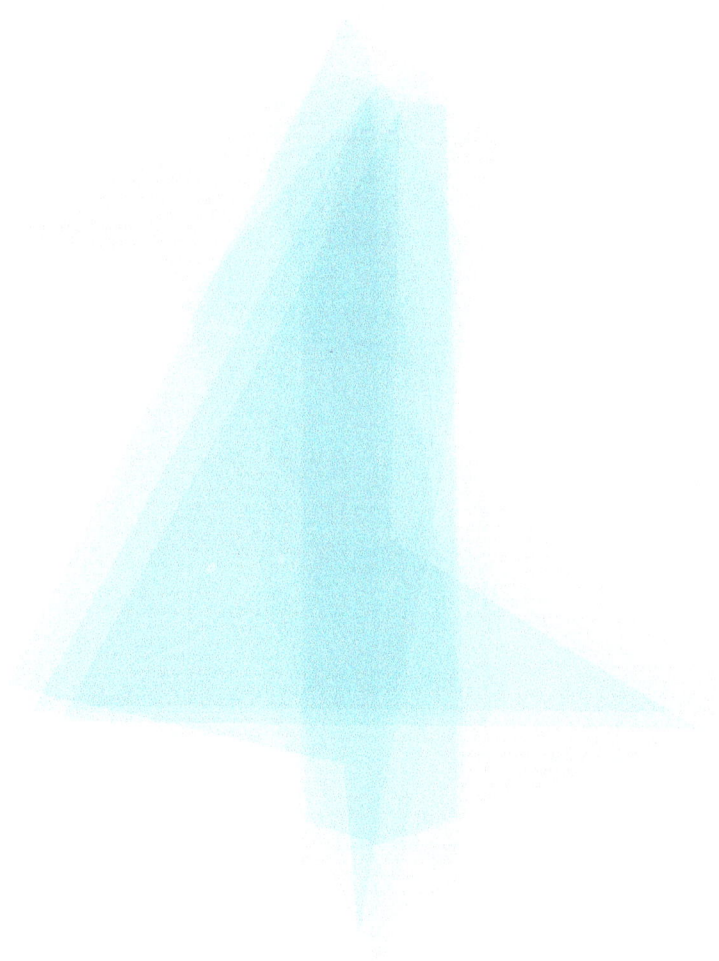

CMTY/ COMMUNITIES IN PRACTICE

PART II
CMTY
CHAPTER 4
COMMUNITIES IN PRACTICE

The various types of creative communities and spaces distributed in the regional and urban context can be recognized as an organism capable of optimizing resources, producing ideas and artefacts in a participatory culture that is also a tool for citizen engagement and self-organization.

This chapter reports a series of surveys aimed at identifying and evaluating the network of manufacturers, spaces, and users, across the Maker community in the Italian Lazio region (therefore amplifying the lens of the physical territory but focusing on specific users) in which actors are involved in a framework of public and private initiatives and cover solid social role within the urban fabric.

Based on the information available online, the Research identified 'somatic traits' have been clustered as such: services provided, technological equipment, openness of the projects initiated at the lab, customer care, original projects developed, inclusion or relationship with a specific business network (including outsourcing). The screening and the interviews have been carried out based on simple binary questions on those traits (yes/no) which have been collected for each reality identified in Record Cards to have a solid base for coordinating digital manufacturing resources. This study focuses on exploring the current condition of digital manufacturing small and medium-sized enterprises (SMEs), makerspaces, and Fab Labs within the Lazio Region of Italy as a resilient social response capable of stimulating social innovation actions, shared economies, and good daily practices.

4.1 Temporary cultural productions

As per the technology, time plays a fundamental role: temporary communities and autonomous spaces are not oppositional types of spaces, but instead there is a synergy between them, and we can learn more from autonomous geographies if we consider their temporal aspects. Learning from these spaces as forms of temporary urbanism that have not been co-opted can also help us to think differently about what temporary uses of the city are. Overall squats and autonomous social centers help us create new imaginaries within cities, to think about cities based on the people experiencing them. This allows us to imagine a different type of city and to think about what an alternative city could look like. With the advent of digital technologies and social networks, the concept of temporary communities arises.

Temporary communities refer to groups of individuals who come together in temporary, often makeshift, spaces within urban areas. These communities form for a variety of reasons, including, but not limited to, political activism, artistic expression, and social engagement offering individuals an opportunity to come together outside of traditional institutional frameworks and to experiment with alternative forms of social organization. One of the key features of temporary urban communities is their temporality - they are designed to be short-lived, often lasting only a few days or weeks. This temporality is seen as a strength by some, as it allows individuals to experiment with new forms of community and organization without the pressure of sustained commitment. At the same time, however, this temporality also makes it difficult for these communities to establish a lasting impact or to create more sustained forms of resistance against dominant power structures.

> *"Only the autonomous can plan autonomy, organize for it, create it" (Bey, 1991, p. 100)*

The concept of Temporary Autonomous Zones (TAZ) as put forward by Bey, (1991) has had a significant impact on the discussion raised about urban communities, particularly those that exist in a temporary or ephemeral manner. In his writing, Bey argues that the TAZ is a space that exists outside the reach of state control and regulation, characterized by a lack of hierarchical structures, and the presence of creative freedom and experimentation. This concept has been taken up by various groups and movements, who view it as a way to reclaim control over their lives and environments in the face of increasing homogenization and globalization, as well as increasing surveillance and control exercised by the state. For instance, temporary urban communities such as pop-up stores, street art festivals, and unpermitted squats often embody the values and principles of the TAZ, including a rejection of state control, the embrace of experimentation and creativity, and a desire for community and connection (Luckman, 2011). However, the influence of this concept has been the subject of ongoing debate among scholars and researchers.

On the one hand, some argue that the TAZ represents a powerful tool for subverting state power and asserting individual and collective autonomy. Bey argues that the TAZ is a space where individuals can challenge dominant power structures and experiment with alternative forms of social organization and expression. On the other hand, others scholars argues that the TAZ is often seen as a 'playground' for privileged individuals, who are able to engage in acts of experimentation and subversion, but who are largely removed from the experiences of marginalized and oppressed communities (Beveridge, Koch, 2016). While the TAZ concept, as it has been outlined, continues to have a relevance on the discussion around temporary urban communities, it is still a subject of ongoing debate on their role in modern urban community planning and effectiveness (Newman, 2011; Schuhmann, 2014; Sellars, 2010) up to more recent adaptation of it as the López (2022) re-adaptation and proposal of Temporary Autonomous Home (TAH)[1]. Urban temporary communities are a vibrant and important aspect of contemporary urban life, as they offer to individual opportunities to experiment with alternative forms social organization while providing space for resilient practices and self-sufficiency (a concept that will be discussed in the *City* chapters).

The current political and economic condition is progressively transforming the social models as known so far. Capitalism thus becomes both the cause of the capitalistic model fall and the original point of the collaborative production growth that spontaneously came through network technology (Rifkin, 2015). In fact, technology has facilitated the formation of this model since it has given the possibility to the educated and connected human being to act as "*a new agent of change in history*" (Mason, 2016, p. 17), tracing the footsteps of Cosmopolitan Localism (Manzini, 2014) and the interregional and planetary networking of place-based communities that share knowledge, technology and resources.

This is contributing to making Design an autonomous discipline capable of "*building the common as a design space*" (Escobar, 2018, p. 186), thus overturning its capitalist and modernist heritage. However, according to Fry et al. (2015), lots of leaders and decision makers do not understand this quality of Design, making the communication work of academics and professionals more complex than it could be. The reflection on the methods and approaches that Design can adopt towards the different living communities starts from the hypothesis of Manzini (2018) that a virtuous circle can be triggered between social planning and 'Politics' (Manzini, 2018)[2], in a set of various experiences that produce a change in the system where they operate (Transit, 2017).

[1] The TAH concept proposed by López moved from Bey's notion to explores the night and how these are felt and articulated for a group of migrants from southern European countries in the city of Bristol (UK)
[2] Ezio Manzini in the working paper of the conference "Social and Political Planning", organized by cheFare at the Milan Triennale on October 19th, 2018, defines Politics (with a capital P) as "the set of contents, organizations and methods that allow a company diversified and complex to exist and, if possible, progress towards higher forms of civilization".

Consequently, designers would have to transform themselves into politicized agents of change (Fry, 2010) to overturn many deeply rooted political, economic, ideological and technological foundations. Self-generated movements provide practices and models that, with a view to preserving their social identity, must be able to be protected and cultivated by generating public services or even public policy (Selloni, 2018). In this sense, Design and Research are involved in the construction of co-design processes aimed to produce different outputs, depending on the reference context, in a form of social activism that develops a counter-narrative for social innovation (Fuad-Luke, 2009).

Community-based productions

Over the past decade, the term "design culture" has become increasingly prevalent. Conceptually, it refers to the interconnectivity of the realms of design, production, and consumption, which are central to considerations of value, circulation, and practice. Within the context of neoliberalism, the deliberate promotion of design cultures and the engagement of individuals and objects with this movement are seen as particularly significant. As networks, the density, scale, and speed of interactions within design cultures are worthy of examination (Julier, 2013).

In response to the recent crises of neoliberalism, design activism has emerged as a movement, which shares some common themes with mainstream design culture, such as intensification, co-articulation, temporality, and territorialization. Nonetheless, design activism does not necessarily operate independently from mainstream design culture. Thus, a sort of Design activism develops that, according to Thorpe (2012), can become a tool in the public domain and a cultural, spatial and governmental tool only if the role of Designer is properly understood in a context of distributed and collaborative making, to design, modify, and adapt products (like in the case of hacking design) and make them available to everyone. The Research investigated in the past the collaborative capacity of Design and its tools in a social context where the citizen is the core, but they have not been able to aggregate in a consistent form.

According to a World Bank (2013) report, social innovation and inclusion is a process of improving the conditions for the participation of individuals and groups in society, improving their skills, opportunities and dignity regardless of their identity. In other words, a given society becomes inclusive when all individuals are valued. It is in the face of situations of marginalization and exclusion that social innovation initiatives make sense in offering new alternatives. In recent years, this theme of social innovation has become an integral part of the vocabulary of urban regeneration, where space plays a radical role in the production of this innovation (Ostanel, 2017). Savoldi (2007) associates this inclination with a common distrust of institutions due to a reduction in forms of public investment.

4.2 Lazio Making Network

"Design is necessary because it serves human needs. As human needs have become more complicated, and human beings more numerous, the design necessarily has become more intense." (Chermayeff et al., 1973, p. 5)

The Maker Community social response to the insufficient mass production and distribution of personal protective equipment during the COVID-19 sanitary emergency, characterized by globally diffused bottom-up initiatives of volunteers' DIY production of sanitary supplies, has finally proved the role of maker practices in determination of local community resilience, already theorized in response to the 2009 economic crisis. Most of the scientific literature recognizes in maker practices, intended as the combination of digital fabrication technology and open design, a revolutionary potential to define more resilient development models, identifying the Maker community's social response phenomenon extended the awareness to the Public Administration (PA) that in some cases was participating to managing the distribution and mediating the acceptance of products. Indeed, the present contribution stems from a previous collaboration with the Lazio Region Administration on the Maker network's potential in defining a new model of citizenship, based on renewed proximities.

A pre-pandemic overview on the maker economy was showing an extraordinary proliferation of the Maker network. Referring to the Fab Lab Network subset, diffused in the US thanks to the pioneering Public Administrations support received since 2011, the global number of Fab Labs, as discussed in previous chapter, was doubled in everyone and a half year until 2017 (Gershenfeld et al., 2017). The European declination of the Maker network model has been strongly characterized by Governments support, which act as a top-down enabler for makerspace foundation and from a shift of perspective over the maker movement that, between 2016 and 2018, moved from the civic role of social technological empowerment and educational commitment to a local economic booster role (Monaco et al., 2021). This institutionalization process has been followed by a global contraction of the Maker Network, visible in the decreasing number of Maker entities registered in the most representative platform (such as the fablab.io website and wiki.hackerspaces.org), measured in Europe since 2015 according to the JRC report on EU makerspaces (Rosa et al., 2018). Subsequently the role developed by the Maker community in rebuilding proximities during the sanitary emergency has highlighted again the intrinsic social vocation of maker practices beyond the governments orientation, and how necessary they are to increasing the resilient response of a territory. This renewed scenario covers new meaning to the investigation of the causes of the global crisis of the Maker Network, from resource improvement to which raises a question: How are Maker realities evolving and which future awaits them?

To understand the ecosystem and the inner dynamics, it has been considered particularly relevant to the consideration of the proximity concept, where the term 'proximity' has been intended both in the 'horizontal' definition of geographical vicinity, necessary for resilient response, and in a 'vertical' definition between multi stakeholder interaction, equally necessary to the resilience improvement (Zheng and Chan, 2013). As result of this, the emerging new kind of functional and relational proximity also generates communities along with new opportunities that will require to be sustained by proper service distribution (Manzini, 2021).

4.3 Innovation space *for* and *with* communities

Local interaction (in terms of economies) systems encourage the substitution of external economic energies and territorial coercion, leading to the constitution of community-based economies. This concept refers to the dream of a supportive and egalitarian community, which has always crossed the history of humanity (Anitori, 2012). Community-based economies and social innovation enable the birth of innovative community initiatives which therefore could be seen as ethical practice of locality (Gibson-Graham, 2003), where local needs are viewed both from individual and social perspective. Thus, local social innovation aims for dignified livelihoods and political voice as integrated with community development strategies (Moulaert et al., 2005). Projects of Integrated Area Development, for instance, start and support community enterprises development improving individual living conditions while strengthen the local economy and its social, cultural and physical infrastructure (MacCallum, 2009; Moulaert, 2000; Phillips & Marothia, 1981). From a community economies perspective, cooperative enterprises indeed do not simply reply to unmatched needs of the locals but they provide specific places in which such needs are denaturalized, deterritorialized (Deleuze and Guattari, 1972), and opened for discussion. Similarly, while in the very different context of the labor movement, it is possible to glimpse a negotiated status of necessity; as the movement has struggled to increase workers' wages and improve working conditions, workers have redefined what is necessary for a fair and decent life (Gibson-Graham, 2006, p. 89). Those needs are negotiated and redefined in the process of establishing differential taxation, through which wealth is collected from some individuals and redistributed to others based on a malleable and changing vision of what is necessary to support human existence. Indeed, ethical decisions around needs are made in all sorts of contexts, signaling the presence of community-based economies (or part of them) in unexpected places and at a variety of scales (Gibson-Graham & Roelvink, 2009). The impact that those empowered citizens had on public affairs has attracted the attention of the governments, pushing towards the establishment of new governance models and new generations of urban entrepreneurs, which are active 'for' and 'with' the local community to collaboratively achieve common goals useful to the society itself (Smith et al., 2016).

Indeed, the European policies, that hoped for a growth of local realities in more inclusive and sustainable contexts for 2020, conceived those factors of well-being as a union of social, environmental, and economic capital, opening up to collective scenarios such as those implemented by Commons policies (Rifkin, 2011), where makerspaces play a crucial role as social driven tool in supporting thematic exploration, accessing to technology, and citizen empowerment (Taylor et al., 2016). However, there is a critical need for stable policies and practical solutions to the challenges posed by the organization of work, which, according to the Science for Policy JRC, have been treated in an increasingly marginal way both at a media and political level (Rosa et al., 2018). This process should seek inclusive methodologies that would allow the society to envision a participatory future, where studies, experiments and dialogues can promote the co-creation of the necessary knowledge addressing more important social problems.

In a broader perspective, design supports communities by proposing solutions to problems that, according to Manzini (2014), neither the market nor the state have solved. In a highly self-organized context, design becomes a useful tool for understanding and developing social innovation by mediating public and private needs. Regional context such as the one found in Lazio, with its satellite distributed "self-productions" realities, constitutes interesting research contexts to develop reflections on development processes and forms of self-organization seen as a structural fact of contemporary cities. Technologies have assumed a social role through time in supporting the births of hybrid communities in physical spaces, that therefore requires a deeper thought on replacing those technologies *"that recreate or reinforce the connections between people and physical places thanks to digital spaces"* versus displacing ones *"that moves people and their relationships out of physical places towards only digital spaces"* (Manzini and Menichinelli, 2021). Approaching then the case study of the Lazio Region territory, the Research includes in its investigations several different productive realities, questioning their proximity with the Institutions and local community in order to address the role played by the enabling technologies as social mediator in which it is possible to recognize new ways of networking, transfer knowledge, and developing competence even within a global crisis.

4.4 Trace regional Makers

Research identifies forty-nine entities which have been catalogued and profiled depending on equipment, sharing and access policies, and activities. Starting from the analysis of the information available online, direct interviews have been conducted with each entity, by mail and phone calls (prioritizing direct interviews instead of surveys sent online with anonymous and tautological replies).

Research distinguishes in the vast panorama of laboratories, private businesses, production companies and aggregation centers, which have made the accessibility of technologies and the openness of the Maker movement the basis of their business, two main categories of spaces: Private (Priv) and Public (Pub). Regarding the latter, it was considered important to make a further distinction between laboratories open to the public (that will be indicated as *PubO*) and those open to a referenced public (that will be indicated as *PubR*) such as University laboratories which basically allow access only to students. Only those laboratories and private entities that adopt digital manufacturing for the research and development of internal products not directly connected to digital manufacturing systems were excluded from the screening. It is important to point out that the latter represent an important part of the innovation market that feeds this important transformation, but that does not directly benefit the constitution of a community except thanks to the influence it can have on subjects already enhanced by the present technological system. The impact that these technologies have on production remains within the company's supply chain, which is exempt from or indifferent to the local context. Therefore, those private businesses were taken into consideration which offer their services under the various forms that we will see later of education, training, distribution of products and rental of machinery open to the public (that will be indicated as *PrivO*).

The first compiling has been conducted starting with the inner knowledge of the territory considering the personal involvement both as Researcher and as member of the Maker Movement for many years, Research adopted an integrative review approach (Snyder, 2019) in order to organize contributions, models and concepts that have been already encountered in both Research and practice, also thanks to renowned events such as Maker Faire[1] which, by chance is particularly distinguished in Rome at the international level. Moreover, the active presence of this movement on the internet, facilitated the individuation of other realities through platforms as Digital Innovation Hub[2], Lazio Innova[3], Italian Coworking[4] and of course including mainstream social networks such as Facebook and Instagram. Based on the information available online, the Research identified 'somatic traits' that have been clustered as such: services provided, technological equipment, openness of the projects initiated at the lab, customer care, original projects developed, and inclusion or relationship with a specific business network (including outsourcing). The screening and the interviews have been carried on based on simple binary questions on those traits (yes/no) which has been structured in *Services, Technologies, Sharing, Access, Project* and *Network*.

[1] www.makerfairerome.eu/
[2] www.fablabroma.it/on/
[3] www.lazioinnova.it/
[4] www.italiancoworking.it/

Services

The range of services offered to the public by laboratories can be clustered into the following categories: *Design*, conceived as the design activities performed both for the development of internal projects and for third parties; *Post-production*, considering that not all laboratories carry out (or have the logistical possibility of carrying out) post-production works such as painting, sandblasting, lacquering or even the processing of materials that cannot be directly processed by numerical control machines (in other cases, these jobs exclude up to the simple removal of supports or cleaning of the prints); *Assessment,* some of the laboratories integrate the knowledge and certified machinery useful for the validation of materials, processes, and products; *Education, as* one of the most profitable and long-lived activities in the Maker world.

Technologies

The technological system of a laboratory represents the maximum expression of the working potential of an activity. We could say that machinery is also a representation of your investment and ability to orchestrate complex and dynamic workflows in a space. So, the map considers the presence of *Textile lab, Wet lab* - used for the treatment of chemical compounds (often liquid) such as resins and silicones, but also for the development of materials and biomaterials made with the local resources available - *Soldering station, 3D printer, Laser cutter, 3D scanner, CNC Milling* (divided in *large and mini*), *Vinyl cutter, plotter cutter,* and finally a classical and over comprehensive *workshop*. If every radical revolution brings with it a characteristic element of the previous system (Artigiani, 1988) it is important to establish the type of legacy carried forward by workshops that practice modern forms of craftsmanship, and the workshop for traditional manufacturing is its direct manifestation. Those machines are often DIY builds or kits assembled by the technicians themselves, which ultimately hack them and adopt them for other purposes.

Sharing

As one of the characterizing aspects of this Maker Movement, the presence and the connective potential of the Internet along with the autonomy of the projects to "navigate" through the network this part of the interview aims first of all to understand how much individual laboratories rely on or participate in Creative Commons practices, therefore, by investigating whether the publication or re-sharing of projects are *Mandatory, Partial* (i.e., if the lab is well-meaning to share it, but have to ask permission to third parties), *Only on open/public days* (e.g., during workshops), *Not declared or absent* (considering that most of third parties project do not comes from a common ground perspective, therefore, labs are forced to respect the intimacy of those realities which struggle to integrate Open-Source concepts and put NDAs in front of any agreement they have.

Access

This is intended as physical access to the makerspaces and technologies. The Research considers it extremely important to be aware of the type of interactions that these laboratories allow and how they manage relations with the public and their collaborators. They can be categorized as *Once a week, For events, By subscription, By selection, By booking* an appointment where it is then possible to divde each of them as *Free* or *By Fee.*

Projects

This part investigated the involvement of the laboratories in the development of third parties' projects representing the relation the labs' owner and manager have with the Maker urban culture or business collaboration intents. They have been divided in *Consultancy,* in which the laboratory not only undertakes to make modelling and conceptualization skills available to the customer, but also offers a specific package that embraces various aspects, including production and management, of a project induced by the customer; *Project's check,* as a natural continuation of the consulting together with the assessment service (this does not mean that it cannot be requested as a stand-alone service, as can happen in laboratories that conduct training courses); and *Incentives Research,* one of the most difficult parts is raising the funds needed to start an initiative or business, in which we could identify those who sustain tenders and funding or crowdfunding platforms (e.g., Kickstarter[1], Indiegogo[2], GoFundMe[3]) to support those projects they deem valid.

Network

The network is the main source of income for maker activities; therefore, it is a crucial factor in evaluating the extent of the impact of individual activities. An impact that is not measured only in the reachability of one's products, but also in extensions of a concatenation of workflows. These streams can be defined by the presence, collaboration or support from/for *Incubation or Acceleration* programs. This aspect is fundamental to understanding the relationship that individual entities have with other entities. Some labs could be clustered as *Public or Cultural Service.* Some of the businesses established or affiliated with larger industries are already part of a network capable of redistributing skills and knowledge which often is categorized as *Franchise.* Like many of the young and enterprising activities, the laboratories tend to meet and exceed customer expectations by offering processes not available in their machinery, therefore some of those networks are direct consequences of an *Outsourcing* process.

---

[1] www.kickstarter.com
[2] www.indiegogo.com
[3] www.gofundme.com

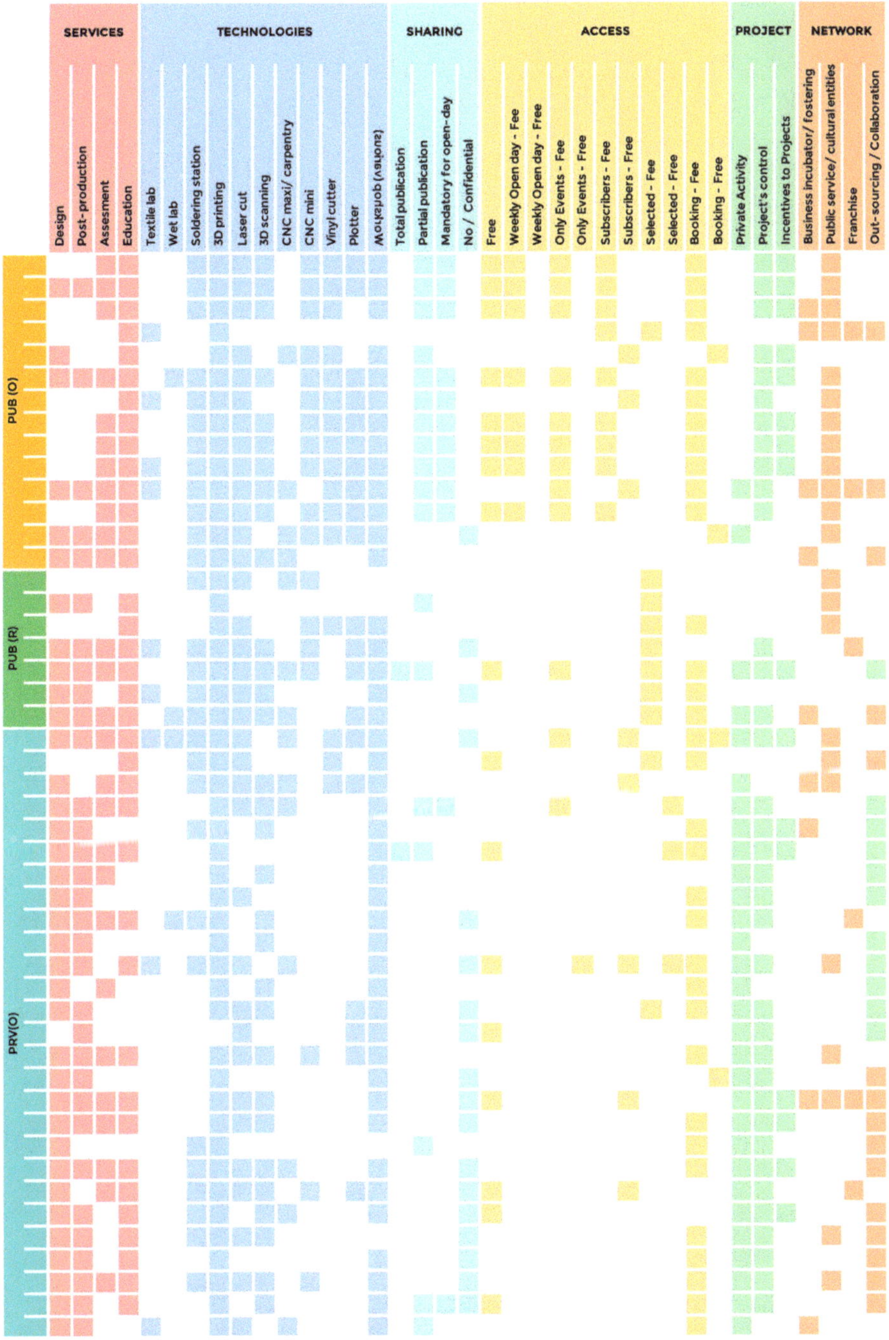

SERVICES
- Design
- Post-production
- Assesment
- Education

TECHNOLOGIES
- Textile lab
- Wet lab
- Soldering station
- 3D printing
- Laser cut
- 3D scanning
- CNC maxi/ carpentry
- CNC mini
- Vinyl cutter
- Plotter
- Mokujob (anyone)

SHARING
- Total publication
- Partial publication
- Mandatory for open- day
- No / Confidential

ACCESS
- Free
- Weekly Open day - Fee
- Weekly Open day - Free
- Only Events - Fee
- Only Events - Free
- Subscribers - Fee
- Subscribers - Free
- Selected - Fee
- Selected - Free
- Booking - Fee
- Booking - Free

PROJECT
- Private Activity
- Project's control
- Incentives to Projects

NETWORK
- Business incubator/ fostering
- Public service/ cultural entities
- Franchise
- Out- sourcing / Collaboration

Row groups: PUB (O), PUB (R), PRV (O)

The table above shows the preliminary information retrieved from the internet and the feedback given to the specific questions made via phone calls by the laboratories.

**Maker labs distribution
Lazio Region**

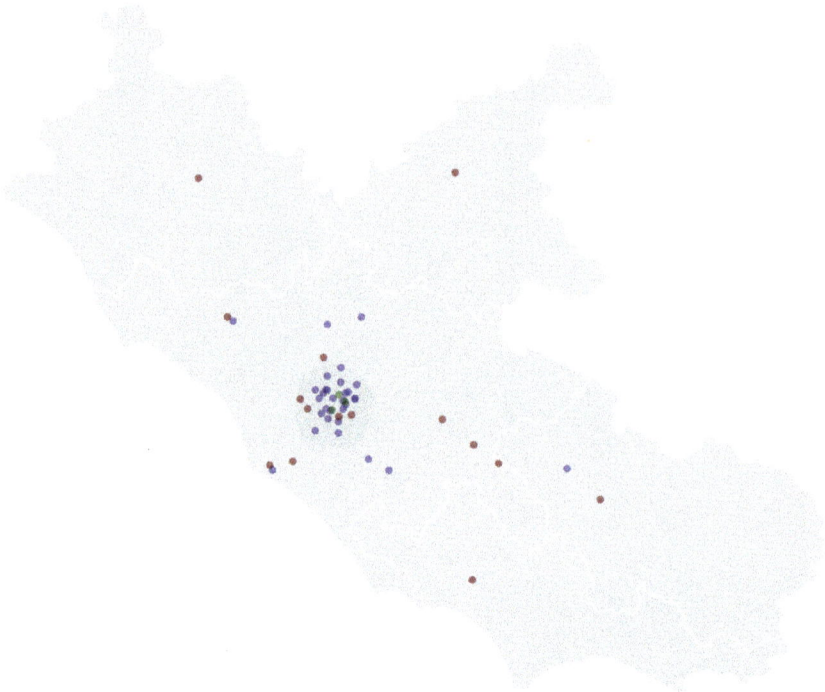

● Public spaces

● Public spaces (with selected audience)

● Private spaces

Regional geolocation of Maker different realities in Lazio

**Maker labs distribution
Rome Municipality**

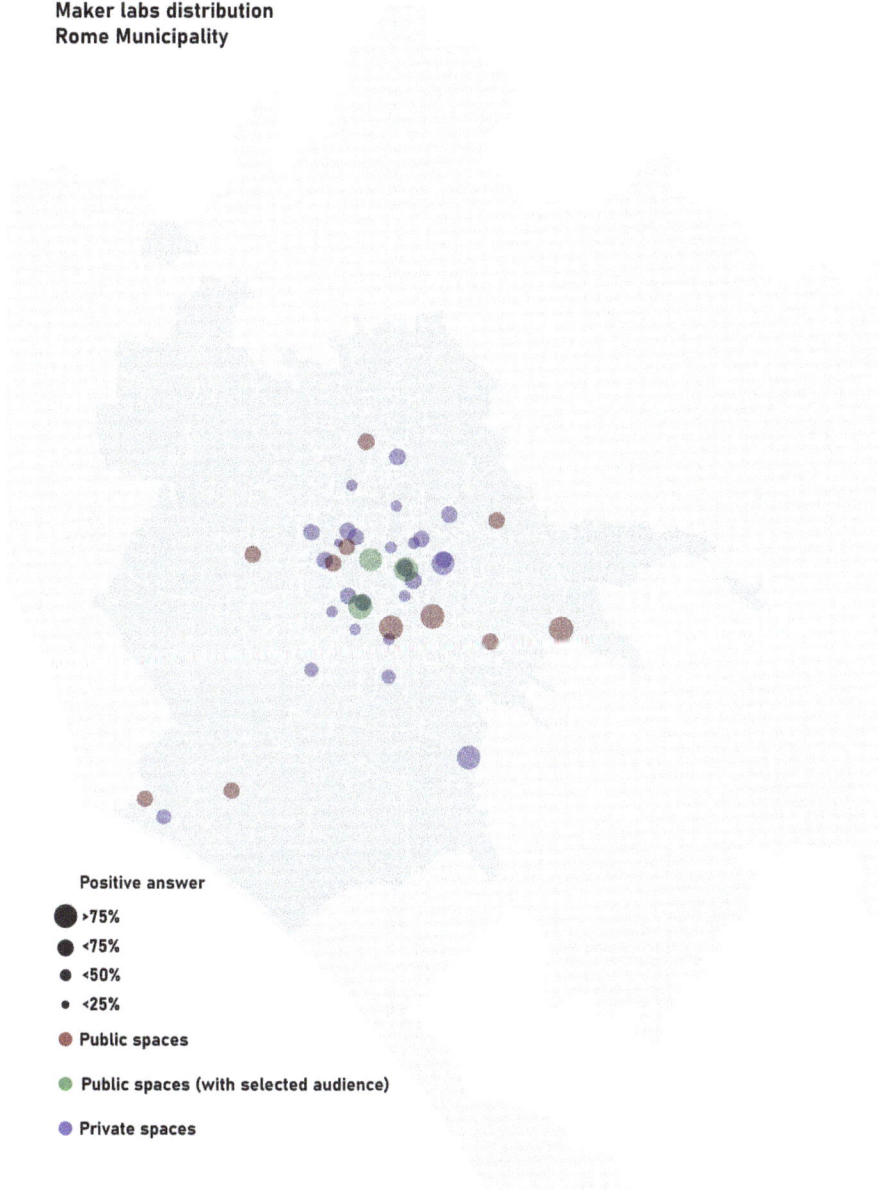

Positive answer
- ● >75%
- ● <75%
- ● <50%
- ● <25%
- ● Public spaces
- ● Public spaces (with selected audience)
- ● Private spaces

Urban geolocation of Maker realities identified for percentage of positive answers in the matrix

It is important to acknowledge that each of the labs has been reached with direct phone calls or physical visiting in order to know as much as possible, but due COVID-19 restrictions in which this part of the Research has started, some of these realities were not able to host anyone, and therefore some data has been forced to rely on the information available online. All this information and data has been collected in a temporary Excel files from which it has been possible to manage and retrieve a clear picture of each of them. Each trait (Tn) has been put in a matrix and divided in categories (Tx). Then, they have been put in relation one each other to always have that the total "score" of each trait would have been equal to the total "score" of another category (*Scale T*). Mathematically, it could be possible to represent this simple operation as such:

$$Scale\ T = (Tx1+Tx2+Tx3+\ldots+Txn)\ /\ Tn$$

Each sum has been put in relation in a radar graph where it could be possible to visualize the relation between each trait (as shown below). Therefore, based on the answer given to the survey and the data collected, it has been possible to see the relation of those traits: if a lab relies more on its network or on sharing activity to extend work impact; if its workflow comes from a community which is welcomed in the space or if its preferably 'directed' outward the lab; if the lab relies more on its machineries and technologies or on its skill and building oriented approach.

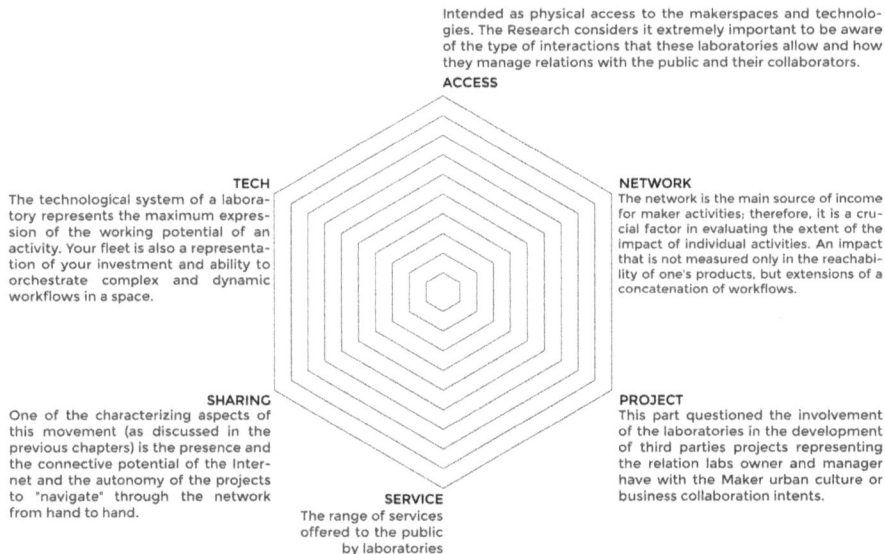

ACCESS
Intended as physical access to the makerspaces and technologies. The Research considers it extremely important to be aware of the type of interactions that these laboratories allow and how they manage relations with the public and their collaborators.

TECH
The technological system of a laboratory represents the maximum expression of the working potential of an activity. Your fleet is also a representation of your investment and ability to orchestrate complex and dynamic workflows in a space.

NETWORK
The network is the main source of income for maker activities; therefore, it is a crucial factor in evaluating the extent of the impact of individual activities. An impact that is not measured only in the reachability of one's products, but extensions of a concatenation of workflows.

SHARING
One of the characterizing aspects of this movement (as discussed in the previous chapters) is the presence and the connective potential of the Internet and the autonomy of the projects to "navigate" through the network from hand to hand.

PROJECT
This part questioned the involvement of the laboratories in the development of third parties projects representing the relation labs owner and manager have with the Maker urban culture or business collaboration intents.

SERVICE
The range of services offered to the public by laboratories

2BE3D

3D ITALY

3DZ

A3D LAB

Fab Lab ARCH. SAPIENZA

Fab Lab S.A. BRACCIANO

CANTIERE ANALOGICO DIGITALE

Fab Lab S.A. CASILINA

SPAZIO CHIRALE

Fab Lab S.A. COLLEFERRO

DESIGN MAKERS

DMAKE

Fab Lab I.C. ELISA SCALA

FABFACTORY

FAMOCOSE

Fab Lab FARADAY

Fab Lab S.A. FERENTINO

FIRAS

Fab Lab FREZZOTTI CORRADINI

Fab Lab FROSINONE

GULP 3D

IED LAB

KENTSTRAPPER

LAB3D PRO

FABLABARO

Fab Lab S.A. LATINA

M3D

MAKE A SHAPE

MASI 3D

NIDO 3D

Fab Lab OSTIENSE

OZ - OFFICINE ZERO

PHYRTUAL INNOVATION GYM

PRINT3D ROMA

PUNTOLUCE DI OSTIA

Fab Lab S.A. RIETI

RUFA LAB

SPAERI&CO.

SAPIENZA DESIGN FACTORY

SELLTEK

SETIT LAB

SHAREMIND

SMARTLAB

STUDIO ST

TRETIGRI

TRIDIMENSIONALE

TUMA STUDIO

Fab Lab S.A. VITERBO

Fab Lab S.A. ZAGAROLO

The regional PubO innovation network works as a unique diffuse workshop, with complementary equipment but similar services. Apart from the similarities within this network, there are no strong differentiating factors among private and public entities, suggesting that there is a migration from public to private models. Focusing on the services offered, education is transversely offered in public and private structures, while the private ones are more interested in offering design consulting.

Another observation is that there are several PrivO and PubR realities which are "isolated" from the maker community, not participating or proposing innovative projects on their own but only providing fabrication services. Many laboratories responded negatively to the question about sharing policies highlighting that they do not require or promote the sharing of design files (for us this suggests that there is a space for improvement of the open innovation culture in the examined context).

One of the aspects noted during the first phase of compiling the forms using the material available online was the type of "advertising" and the level of communication language that passes through both their sites and social pages. In fact, it was possible to notice how PubO laboratories tend to communicate through the product of their own work, showing formal and practical qualities as well as the performances of their own manual or design skills. On the other hand, PubO laboratories, which have to manage the discretion of the projects they host, hardly publish the result of their actions and services, communicating exclusively through the image of the workspace offered and suggesting the intrinsic potential of the own work areas.

Digital manufacturing has made a significant impact at both the digital and organizational levels, creating opportunities for technological and social innovation. Governments have recognized its potential as a strong competitive factor and have provided support for its development (Cooke and Schwartz, 2012). Despite the promise of a more sustainable production system, however, digital manufacturing in Lazio has not yet achieved the vision of a "zero marginal cost society"(Rifkin, 2015). Although it has access to a global market through a network of equivalent production tools and spaces, the ideal economic model for this system has yet to be identified (Holman, 2015).

Distributed production, in this sense, is still seen as not valid alternative to mass production systems, which requires direct connections to the clients along with a deep understanding of the end users and eventually in-person knowledge of the available resources (technologies, materials, processes). Distributed manufacturing, on the other hand, serves this connection, relying on comparable – and not always fully trustable – digital manufacturing. A physical product that is created and distributed purely as "digital" is therefore realized in an uncontrollable situation: this presents new challenges in terms of impact measurement (on different scales of retribution, success, infrastructures requirements).

Within Design's discipline various approaches through the years have been developed from the Open-Source approach inspired by software development to a collaborative (co-design) practice, since it has been facilitated by the easy access to distributed creative resources and facilities (Gasparotto, 2019). Uncountable designs have been developed and diffused through the internet via 3D model, projects, and design sharing platforms (e.g., Thingiverse, Instructables, Github, Opendesk, and Distributed Design Market Platform) open to feasible and useful product designs for Distributed Manufacturing, and some major online service bureaus offer their open marketplaces, which can provide revenues for designers.

The field of additive manufacturing across different channels has been also intensively discussed during the recent health crisis on how distributed production processes have contributed: the announcement of the state of emergency has immediately revealed in the health facilities, as in the distribution of public activities, a serious shortage of technical devices. During this lack of medical supplies for private sectors, DIY techniques are applied to help personal fabrication solutions.

Several items have been designed and produced in response to this crisis, and the scientific community has collected and medically evaluated dozens of open-source medical device designs opening to many ethical discussions about it since such contributions were coming from non-certified experts (makers) able to generate non-certified, but nonetheless useful, tools (Baudisch and Mueller, 2016).

It appears, then, that Lazio Maker ecosystem needs to not only re-visit the literature but also continuously update its alternative conceptualizations of the economy and its role in structuring its relationship to the real world. For more resilient communities, the distributed system concept has emphasized good environmental performance, local people's preferences, and quality of life and well-being (van den Dool et al., 2009), while particularly examining privileged regions in northern Europe. Distributed systems stand as a useful framework for understanding how local economies could be shaped, even within a rapidly transforming, global environment with many industrial and post-industrial trajectories (dos Santos et al., 2021).

PART III
CITY
CHAPTER 5
MAKING CITY

This chapter examines the urban manufacturing system moving from the Industrial Districts to creative neighborhoods, which involves specialized small and medium-sized independent enterprises. The territorial logic behind this system enables better Administration and production management, and it is also crucial for the quality of production, as it is based on specializations, processes, and components linked to the territory of origin.

However, this system faces challenges related to globalization and digitization, which have led to the emergence of urban production, a response to these challenges. Urban production has created a new landscape for production by allowing goods and services to be produced and distributed more efficiently across the globe.

The significance of the maker economy is becoming more relevant at the European level, but its impact on national policies is more noticeable in smaller territorial areas, mainly at the urban or metropolitan scale. Public administrations at the local, provincial, and regional levels play a critical role in promoting the maker economy by intervening with policies and programs to strengthen existing communities or by establishing makerspaces or regional networks. This chapter focuses on investigating the complexity and inclusion of makerspace ecosystems viewed from an economic, ecological, and social perspective.

The Research highlights the varied realities within the urban landscape, from urbanized and empowered cities, where makerspaces complement a rich entrepreneurial and design culture, to less urbanized regions where innovation is a cultural challenge. The chapter concludes that makerspaces have the potential to create inclusive and sustainable economic development and that public administrations should play an active role in promoting and supporting these spaces to ensure their success.

This specific context is defined by the temporary communities of the city of Rome, where groups of people set up activities related to their interests or simply to their culture. In this sense, Rome becomes an ideal field of investigation. Over the years, the city has in fact become a multicultural and multi-ethnic city. Rome has considerably increased its reception in past decades, precisely between 2000 and 2015, and shown an increase in the number of foreigners registered in the registry around 115% (Censis, 2015). This fact has consequently increased the constitution of temporary communities thus becoming an adequate experimentation field for this Research. Cellamare considers Rome as a paradigmatic case of this great process of retreat of the welfare state by insisting on the widespread and consolidated presence of alternative cultures and social experiences. Rome, as a "self-produced city" (Cellamare, 2014), constitutes an interesting context for developing reflections on redevelopment processes and forms of self-organization seen as a structural fact of contemporary cities. In Rome, a multicultural and cosmopolitan city, numerous urban realities and particular local actions were born; different forms of appropriation and reappropriation of the city and collective and organized urban practices, as forms of latent planning, are in search of new conditions of mutualism. Public space and common goods, in a context that thrives on the delicate relationship between lawful and illegal, become informal places of change and innovation. Urban regeneration is a panacea for those solutions from above which over time have proved to be inefficient or deleterious, generating on the other hand a commodification of social life (Cellamare, 2018) which is accompanied by processes of gentrification (Semi, 2015) and disintegration of local cultures (Uitermark et al., 2007).

5.1 From industrial districts to creative neighborhoods

The organizational design of Italian manufacturing is based on an articulated subdivision of production which involves highly specialized small and medium-sized independent enterprises. Each of them focuses on a single activity or on a series of small and consequential tasks that diminished a specific process phase. This collaborative structure is better known under the name of "Industrial Districts" and allows the entire production of the artefact to be covered thanks to the territorial proximity between the companies. Rullani (2009) describes industrial districts as geographical areas where a concentration of ecological and cognitive clusters operates in a specific industry. These industries have frequent interactions and close ties with each other, which can include sharing of suppliers, customers, and knowledge. Industrial districts are characterized by high specialization, collaboration, and innovation, which can lead to increased efficiency and competitiveness. Additionally, the presence of a wide network of relationships and a shared culture helps to create an atmosphere of trust and knowledge exchange among companies, which in turn fosters the development of new business opportunities.

Bonomi also argues that industrial districts are important for economic development, as they can support the growth and competitiveness of the firms operating there, as well as promote job creation and a more diversified economy. This proximity facilitates direct interaction between the actors involved, allowing a production capable of transferring the cultural aspects of the territory onto a product with a strong aesthetic value for the final consumer (Morace and Lanzone, 2010). This is the most widespread form of relationship between companies in Italy and sees the realities involved concentrated on production for third parties, which manages to virtuously manage the financial, operational, and temporal aspects to start production and the acquisition of raw materials. This model is the basis of the modern Italian industrial system which developed starting from the 1950s and saw its complete diffusion during the 1990s. This system has been built and developed thanks to the growth of small and medium-sized enterprises which have not focused on the managerial and strategic capacity of the individual craftsman or small entrepreneur, but on the strength of their interaction (Micelli, 2011). In fact, independent companies operate in a single district, integrated in a network of informal and long-term cooperation relationships which allows an intense interdependence of their production cycles and precise mutual collaboration: production orders are distributed; they carry out services together; they share knowledge and develop technological innovation together (Ricciardi, 2018).

The Industrial District is therefore the typical organizational model of the local economy which takes the form of an aggregation of small and medium-sized industrial enterprises with a high production specialization, concentrated and integrated with the local socio-economic environment that hosts them. Such a complex model therefore requires strong coordination, generally carried out by SMEs taking care of the planning, organization, logistics and trade phases. This is possible thanks to the territorial logic behind this system, which allows for better administration and production management. The territorial logic is also essential for the quality of the production since it is based on the use of specializations, processes and components expressly linked to the territory of origin, and which are based on the values and production techniques of a high historicized craftsmanship, capable but to dialogue with the design project (Fusco, 2009). The territorial aspect thus influences the process but also the production practices linked to the concept of craftsmanship, which implies the ability to produce, consciousness of material transformation and processes linked to the territory (Follesa, 2017). However, also those industrial realities have to deal with challenges related to the loss of competitiveness due to globalization and digitization. has been a key driver in the emergence of urban production. The global economy has become increasingly integrated, leading to the development of large-scale, highly interconnected urban areas. These areas are home to a wide range of manufacturing, service, and knowledge-based industries, creating a new landscape for production. The rise of urban production has also been facilitated by advances in technology and transportation, allowing goods and services to be produced and distributed more efficiently across the globe (Scott, 2001).

5.2 Towards citizen-driven urban models

There are various realities that dot the urban panorama, and which allow the citizen, both inside and outside the city, to redesign the space and define work and cooperation dynamics. Reality which, as we will see later, becomes physical and intangible at the same time. These places of training, creation, sharing and, more generally, strengthening of citizens who promote innovation, be it technological or social, have the particularity of assuming different forms based on the place where they are positioned, giving life to that one movement that over time has consolidated under the term Maker. These places are the aggregation centers of a counter-culture that aims to formulate the foundations of new processes of technological and productive innovation that start from the bottom of urban and rural contexts. A first question therefore arises linked precisely to the scale of impact of these spaces which is provided by Guallart (2014) who, based on the canonical definitions of the urban model, defines the urban scale based on population density. On this principle, city models are defined by the extent and accessibility of the structures used to satisfy the needs of citizens, which determine the degree of mobility, density and define the network of social interactions.

The goal of the network is the exchange of information where the city takes the form of a constant overlapping of material and social structures that organize dynamisms and coexistence policies based on this information. With the advent of the information age, interactions have increased exponentially thanks to the potential dictated by the awareness of such data. This awareness is what laid the foundations for defining the self-sufficiency and sustainability of connected systems.

The Neighborhood scale value expressed by Guallart is an innovative approach to urban design that is based on creating autonomous and resilient communities. Its goal is to promote sustainable urban development that meets the needs of the population and the environment. Neighborhoods should be designed as closed systems that can generate their own energy, water, and food through the use of sustainable technologies (Guallart, 2014). In this way, neighborhoods would become more autonomous and able to withstand climate change and economic crises. This model concept

The urban model scale defined by Guallart is defined by the number of inhabitants and divided as such:
- 1 Dwelling
- 10 Floor
- 100 Building
- 1K City Block
- 10K Neighborhood
- 100K District
- 1M City
- 10M Region
- 100M Country
- 1BN Continent
- 10BN Planet

is based on the creation of green spaces, the promotion of sustainable mobility, and the construction of energy-efficient buildings. It also focuses on creating active and engaged communities where the population can participate in the management of the neighborhood and the decisions that affect it

In this model, the infrastructure is designed to meet the needs of the neighborhood, not vice versa, and technology is used as a tool to create a more resilient and sustainable community. The Guallart neighborhood concept is therefore a model of urban development that seeks to balance the needs of society and the environment through the creation of autonomous and sustainable communities. In summary, this approach enables urban design that seeks to promote sustainable development based on creating autonomous and resilient communities through the use of sustainable technologies.

The current era is marked by a new phase in which the territory plays a central role in the ongoing critical process initiated by the 2008 financial crisis and accelerated by the COVID-19 pandemic. The territory is a space of dialectics and ambiguity and is therefore open to multiple influences. Bonomi (2021) identifies two main aspects that is at least contributing to this dynamic: on one hand, algorithmic capitalism is eroding the power of traditional roots, leading to a continued process of splitting and joining social relations; on the other hand, there is a new anthropological and political dimension, which brings together different logics and forces and results in an artificial combination of cultures and practices that can range from care to conflict to industriousness.

Having a clear a punctual map of this weaving is essential to understand the impact of flows on both industry and daily life to identify potential new forms of organization and community. The direction and the range of these aspects are still unclear, but it is important to start by examining some of the drivers of this process. One of the first factors considered crucial is the awareness of being entered in a neo-industrial time (Gallino, 1987) which led to an analytical shift that is more political than just industrial.

Over thirty years, different statistics in the international panorama show that the decreasing number of manufacturing industry workers, although there are some territories where this is not the case. The shift from a narrow notion of industry limited to manufacturing factories to a broad notion of intensifying industrial processes and relationships (that permeate all aspects of social life) can often be misunderstood as deindustrialization. The pandemic has accelerated a general neo-industrialization, where the social and personal spheres, daily life, and collective infrastructure are all being transformed by industrial processes. The technological advancement reinforces this process, as digital and algorithms provide the language and cognitive infrastructure to support its grammar and make every social relationship potentially 'industrializable' and productive. This transformation is not a random flow, but it is characterized by different forms of production, social composition, and geographical patterns of development and socialization (Bonomi, 2021).

We all produce something in city: the market of information

This neo-industrialization process not only affects the reorganization of territorialized production chains, but also the emergence of new industries that incorporate the sphere of social and human reproduction into value networks. It is transforming urban economies and creating integrated and transversal value chains that link city production and the reproduction of urban and social life.

> *"The new urban factories are universities, hospitals, utilities, fairs, platforms, large urban regeneration projects, etc., clusters where the conditions of social and personal life are reproduced, of the organization of consumption, which then trigger production by going back upstream traditional of goods. This is the real legacy of the pandemic acceleration." (Bonomi, 2021, p. 19)*

Urban industries focus on four key aspects of social and human life: health, nature, dwelling, and knowledge, to create a new sense of rootedness and social involvement. Cities drive an economy that produces value by applying industrial and technological knowledge to reproduction, becoming engines of the rise of platform capitalism (Benasayag and Meyran, 2020; Murzio et al., 2019). Zuboff (2015) states that since any companies are increasingly becoming technologically evolved, or at least they are implementing 'digital' information as a valuable flow in their business, their goal is not to create products or services based on user needs.

Nowadays, they aim to build co-production platforms where consumers are free to move within certain conditions, and to 'pay' a fee through different types of currencies (from micro-transactions to data of interest to the creator of the platform). In other words, their business model is based on the value of information, with the aim of acquiring it as much as possible. The "surveillance capitalism" of Zuboff (2019), which is often referring to large companies (and therefore with an influential weight) such as Amazon or Google, is a radical challenge to the very concept of entrepreneurial capitalism which sees entrepreneurship capable of predicting, clustering everything, determining demand and predetermining the 'offer through a capillarity of 'surveillance' and data. The elimination of risk therefore weakens social legitimacy, replaced by the algorithm, which has historically overseen managing it, replaced by artificial intelligence. Beyond the critique of pragmatism that sees data as a primary good, a landscape emerges in which the dynamics of this "dissocialized Fordism" (Bonomi, 2021) will have common feedback and goals. The ultimate goal is to commercialize this information through other ways or 'currencies', which defines the constant experimentation of digital marketing such as the advent of what she calls as 'reality mining', which could be identified as the real threat to reality (Zwick and Denegri-Knott, 2009). Through constant manipulations by marketing initiatives, the boundary between digital and real is getting lost and with it the "whole worlds of capital life" are being reprogrammed (Lazzarato, 2004).

Design, build, destroy, repeat

Since the latest analysis developed by UN-Habitat (2020) related to sustainable urbanization urban economies are seen as accelerators of an economic growth – if SDGs and Recovering Plans from recent health crisis are taken into account – driving the performance on national scale. At the same time urbanization does not need to be intended as an intrinsic threat to the natural environment that will continue to be the driving force for global growth. This strengthening of urban productive capacities becomes a need for Public Administrations from local up to national scale, that therefore need a paradigm shift in how urban planning and governance frameworks view the informal economy. By doing so, Governments would recognize the urban commons as socio-ecological assets, allowing cities to build economies around culture and creative industries in which open and transparent data, would more likely bring creative industries to emerge.

If we consider real smart cities as people-oriented cities, participatory planning needs to be considered while designing or supporting sustainable urban transformation. By forecasting the growth of cities that still confirms a 60% of population expected to live in cities by 2030 (UN-Habitat, 2020), 33% will live in cities with at least half a million inhabitants (UN Population Division, 2016).

"The value of sustainable urbanization is the totality of a city's economic, environmental, social and intangible conditions that have the potential to improve the quality of life of residents in meaningful, visible and concrete ways." (UN-Habitat, 2020, p. 44)

Cities are required to reform legal and regulatory frameworks, providing solutions that enable a safer work environment – especially around those informal economies – if they want to boost their own productive capacities. Those solution must be intended by development countries as leading paths for those activities that would more likely go from an informal economy to a formal one pursuing sustainable and inclusive urban development goals. Technological progress such as car advent opened to a variety of achievements enabling the world to foresee further developments in terms of mobility, transportation, and trading. Nonetheless, it had and still have well-known socio-economic negative impacts by changing radically the urban planning dynamics and its sprawl consequently impacting on biodiversity or financially speaking on households' burdens (Moreno et al., 2021).

Since Le Corbusier's blueprint for urban sprawl that up to then were for him not sustainable enough – where the only and "most dramatic idea" (Jacobs, 1961) was to demolish, re-plan and rebuild – urban environments has been planned to welcome car mobility prompting the demand for vehicular-dependent cites. Years later those principles, in line with industrialization and oil dependency global agenda, nowadays it is possible to recognize the impact that had on climate change due to the emissions. Cities are the engines of growth and development in many countries, and their ability to attract businesses, create jobs, and generate economic growth is key to their success.

However, with the increasing prevalence of informal economies in cities around the world, legal and regulatory frameworks must be reformed to ensure a safer work environment for those engaged in such activities. This is especially relevant in developing communities (such as developing countries), where informal economies are often the only means of income for many individuals. To facilitate sustainable and inclusive urban development goals, cities must provide solutions that encourage the transition from informal to formal economies. This can include the provision of training, education, and financial assistance for those who wish to formalize their businesses. By providing a safer work environment and better access to resources, cities can boost their own productive capacities while also helping to improve the lives of their citizens.

5.3 Proximity and chrono-urbanism

This dependency has become our urban planning legacy, in which deep-rooted inequalities, especially in the social and economic spheres, are (only) now recognized as unsustainable practices.

Recent pandemic broke into a crisis process already underway and dramatically accelerated its time, forcing policy makers to review urban policies providing proximity-based services to inhabitants, and accommodating soft-mobility demands as permanent solutions. Above all, there is a substantial step back from those large infrastructural projects, localizing their attention to local public needs and wills, getting closer to pursuing a "15-minutes City" concept (Sala et al., 2020). With this regard, there are already virtuous examples which enhanced social cohesion and interaction opening to sustainable urban ecosystems, such as the one led by Paris' Mayor Anne Hidalgo; the "15-minutes" concept, since its first appearance around 2016 spread out rapidly leading to global discussion between cities about "chrono-urbanism" philosophy (Moreno et al., 2021). This approach takes into account the relevance of urban rhythms (Mulíček et al., 2015; Neuhaus, 2013) putting space and time as factors to evaluate the quality of life in urban context: *"the quality of urban life is inversely proportional to the amount of time invested in transportation, more so through the use of automobiles"* (Moreno et al., 2021, p. 100).

To briefly give an overview of the "15-minutes", it is a holistic approach to urban design that seeks to create cities that prioritize the needs of their residents and prioritize sustainability, livability, and community. By implementing this concept, cities can create more vibrant, healthy, and equitable communities that support the well-being of all their residents. The "15 minutes" city concept is a vision for urban design that aims to create cities where all daily necessities can be reached within a "15-minutes" walk or bike ride from one's home. This concept is based on the idea that cities should prioritize the needs of their residents over those of cars and other forms of transportation. The "15 minutes" city therefore prioritizes walkability, bike-friendliness, and public transportation to make it easier for residents to access essential services like grocery stores, schools, parks, and healthcare facilities. This concept also emphasizes the need for diverse and affordable housing options, as well as the creation of green spaces and public squares to encourage community interaction and social cohesion. There are of course numerous aspects that this approach brings with it; those walkable neighborhoods (Weng et al., 2019) have positive influence as much on the environment as on people health – for instance with those residents that could struggle with obesity issues. It needs nevertheless, to consider those residents such as elderly people, with mobility issues or economic problems that should not be disadvantaged by socioeconomic status or age. In a city like Shanghai, close to those Le Corbusier principles cited above, most of the amenities are centralized in the inner city and distributed without a proper logic in the outer parts, forcing residents to a car-dependency if interested in those amenities. Cities are called to action to "repair" urban and social fragments literally affected by this modernist approaches. In the concept of "15-Minutes City" urban context allows access to every essential service at distances that would not take residents more than fifteen minutes by foot or by bicycle.

Those essential services or, even better, urban functions, that should therefore define the quality of urban life depending on their reachability and availability, include living, working, commerce, healthcare, education, and entertainment. If the concept is respected, every citizen should be able to access those functions within that maximum time. Moreover, the time saved from mobility has been recognized as a critical factor for citizens that would save during commuting as well as degrade their life. Never than before, the 2019 pandemic crisis, as highlight by the C40 Organization (Sala et al., 2020), confirmed the relevance that the localization of public services has while demonstrating also how our behaviors could change and self-adapt to proximity values. Based on simple principles, we have to consider that: each resident needs to have easily access to every good or service (in particular related to fresh food and health assistance); each quarter must have a variety of households in order to welcome different typologies of families; each resident must have clean air, green areas and be far enough from polluted areas; there should be enough spaces for offices, coworking or considering "work from home" as an alternative.

> *"All city residents will have access to resilient, sustainable public services, especially our most vulnerable. Fundamental to this will be sustainable, efficient, and safe mass transit systems that keep our cities moving and our economies running, while leaving our streets car-free, air clean and skies blue. All residents will live in '15-minute cities', where shops, workspaces and essential services are easily reached within a short cycle or walk, surrounded by plenty of green spaces where they can relax, exercise and play" (Sala et al., 2020, p. 9)*

Pillars of the 15-minutes city

Last century cities were built around an idea of efficiency based on specialization and on the economy of scale in which some areas of the city have specialized and where specific type of activities and services has been concentrated over time. Saying so, a 15-minutes solution has come in help of those citizens that to achieve a better standard of life would then share a common bottom-up vision for social innovation, while receiving top-down redesign solutions for those physical and social infrastructure of the city itself (Sennett, 2019).

Moreover, proximity-based analysis would provide better indications on how to catalyze and coordinate the necessary social, political and economic resources. None of this effect would be possible without a governance capable of stimulating and supporting the resources available to the city, along with an active and collaborative participation of citizens with their various forms of aggregation. For this to happen, a new wave of innovations must emerge which, from the outset, are the result of the convergence of social, technical, cultural and institutional innovation (Harvey, 2019).

Within this concept, it becomes more relevant the role that technology has in tightening the nodes of the community network within the cities (Cocchia, 2014), in which dimensions such as 1) density, 2) proximity, 3) diversity and 4) digitalization has been defined by Moreno (2021) as pillars capable to establish and allowing continuity of those cities that aims to a Smart City framework;

1. Density: as crucial dimension of the city and its built environment. This factor has direct influences on the sustainability of moving around the city as well as for consequent variety of plans that the city councils have to deal with in terms of urban services distribution (Cervero and Kockelman, 1997; Ewing and Cervero, 2010). Therefore, it is possible to highlight that sustainable density is allowed when socio-economic and environmental aspects are taken into consideration,

2. Proximity: a critical dimension that, above the time-saving positive effect, influence all the environmental and economic impacts moving around the city (Marquet and Miralles-Guasch, 2015). It helps in determining social impact indicators, promoting social interactions (Alexander, 2002; Duany et al., 2010; Jacobs, 1961). Outstanding as a coupling of spatial and temporal dimensions, through this dimension the city can be seen from a time-based perspective.

3. Diversity: this dimension has a two-side effect: on one side it influences commercial and entertaining component of the neighborhoods while, one the other, influence the culture of the residents (DeLisle and Grissom, 2013) and promote inclusivity as well as sustainable practices (Toker & Pontikis, 2011). Moreover, vibrant surroundings often times opens to an attractive urban landscape for visitors, thus promoting tourism and other related businesses which are essential in creating activities (Nabil and Eldayem, 2015). This dimension leads to what Bauman defines as "a cohabitation of strangers" (Bauman, 2003, p. 5)

4. Digitalization: This fourth dimension has direct repercussion on the previous three since, relying on the Smart City concept, factors such as inclusivity, resident participation and real-time delivery of services are encouraged through varying digital platforms and devices (Dembski et al., 2020; Kamel Boulos et al., 2015). Moreover, the deployment of digital solutions ensures "15-Minutes Cities" resilience facing challenges such as climate change through declining emissions, linked to a reduction in automobile use and resources consumption (Allam, 2020).

Regarding these aspects, amenities distribution as well as the services accessibility could be considered the core of urban planning practice that adopt technologically advanced solution to reply to SDGs that aim to improve the quality of life in a sustainable, resilient, and inclusive way.

In fact, it is possible to notice that to achieve in a proper way those goals, a city should: promote social inclusion, adapt the infrastructure to actual lifestyle changes, rely on digital revolution, consider environmental issues as well as climate change challenges. The four pillars cited above do not have impact only on managing but on encouraging building sectors as well as design – in each of its multiple facets – to advocate green and civic factors in their approaches, pursuing human interaction and participatory processes at various scales.

Another relevant aspect that is required to be highlighted is that all those pillars do not have relevance (or anyway would have the same beneficial effect) if they are not put together in place and taken into the same consideration. While on the one hand the pre-pandemic scenario has been characterized by a global trend toward neoliberal globalization generating a *"reacting anti-globalism"* and *"altering globalism for sustainability"* (Manzini and Menichinelli, 2021), on the other hand, the latter has been fostering the large wave of social innovation from the reinforced social role of technology in supporting hybrid communities in the physical space after the heavy waves of the pandemic. Such hybridization requires focusing on replacing technologies that create or reinforce the connections between people and physical places thanks to digital spaces versus a displacing one that moves people and their relationships out of physical places towards only digital spaces. Social resilience requires the existence of groups of people who interact and collaborate in a physical context in which they could self-organize and provide solutions.

It is possible to notice how the many different theories are providing also alternatives and updating models to the "15-Minutes City", suggesting different perspective related more to the accessibility rather than transportation, questioning more the infrastructures rather than viability, aiming instead to a "20-Minute City" model (Capasso Da Silva et al., 2020). After more than fifteen years of grassroots and small groups experiments, now social innovation is moving to larger scale of services at city scale, and here the 15-Minutes City model aims at supporting relationships based on a renewed idea of care orientated to people, places, and the environment.

Recent research identifies eight principles which should be taken into consideration while designing the 15-Minutes City (Büttner et al., 2022): proximity to essential services; proximity to public transport; density; mixed land use; walkable and cyclable streets; livable public spaces and placemaking; inclusiveness; ubiquity. It is therefore necessary to highlight the role that technology has when considering the applications and possible implications of adopting a model as such.

Network reliability

Digital manufacturing (in all its various form of production, distribution and consumption), on the other hand, severs this connection, relying on comparable digital manufacturing tools but up to now never fully trustable at a distance.

A physical product design that is created and distributed purely in the digital environment but must be physically realized in an uncontrollable situation: this presents new challenges in terms of impact measurement (on different scales of retribution, success, and infrastructures requirements). We could shift therefore the focus of the problem from the technological one, which constitutes now the simplest part of a path towards a true industrial revolution, to an economical one (Greenfield, 2018). To become as valuable as mass production, generating a real radical revolution, Distributed systems as such are required to have a lasting and concrete strategy of sustenance and development set behind them. A specific meaning of the products that float in the system and to understand how the practice of Open Design shifts not only the creative context, but also the distribution ones. The methods and channels of creation are as open as those of distribution (Malakuczi and D'Elia, 2020). Therefore, they cannot refer to a traditional system, nor to a dead-end system of sale and purchase, but to insert themselves in an open framework that allows the traceability, participation, and identification of individual participants in their actions (creation, sale, acquisition, modification, resale, and so on). The relevance and importance of valuable network is not merely related to a reliability of monetizing system of the movement, which is in any case widely recognized as common ground for Public Administrations competitiveness at the national level. As Denning & Hayes-Roth (2006) pointed out to accelerate development of effective modern organizations we will need a change of perspective about "network" relying on a value-based distribution system. Traditional organizations often have years to learn what information is valuable and how to make it flow.

The current urban condition in Lazio (as shown in the previous chapter) is still based on capitalism and a neoliberal model (Kempf, 2014; Klein, 2015) progressively transforming the social models known up to now, favoring other social models, such as the commons, which veer towards a post-capitalist economy (Dardot and Laval, 2014; Hardt et al., 2010; Ostrom, 1990). Urban capitalism (Smiley and Emerson, 2020) thus becomes both the cause of the fall of a capitalist model and the point of origin of the spontaneous growth of collaborative production through network technology. In fact, technology has facilitated the formation of this model since, as Mason (2016) states, it has given the educated and connected human being the possibility of acting as a new agent of changing, following the footsteps of Cosmopolitan Localism (Manzini, 2015), the interregional and planetary networking of place-based communities that share knowledge, technology and resources (Moreno et al., 2021).

5.4 Urban Design and Maker practices

After about fifteen years of experimentation grassroots and small groups, now social innovation is moving to larger scale of services at city scale, in which the 15-minutes city resemble a second-level cover of the city: in contrast to the dominant trends, those who participate in it seek and produce relationships based on a renewed idea of care orientated to people, places and the environment. The vision is that of a polycentric city that fulfils the promise of the city in fifteen minutes over its entire extension. The first of the steps to take to achieve it consists in operating on mobility and the distribution of services and, in parallel, operating in proximity, to reorient and coordinate the various urban functions: kindergartens, schools, social and health assistance centers, and provision of greenery and public spaces. An entire generation of services and places of service must be re-designed, and new urban commons must emerge.

Within this scenario, a wide network of short-distance connections spreads and links to the long-distances ones which connect the single nodes to the rest of the world. This "spread and link" chain of reaction is what makes this proxemic relations a fertile ground in which cultural production, creativity and design can emerge and proliferate. Cosmopolitan localism could be seen as a balance between what keep us embedded in a place, in a culture, in a community, in what lets us be open to new flows of international, intercultural approaches, knowledge things and profits (Manzini, 2021). From a design perspective, those places, so far identified as nodes, are not isolated at all: they generate and regenerate the local socio-economic fabric and the long networks that connect a particular community and a particular place to the rest of the world, merging this idea of Cosmopolitan Localism with distributed system. Therefore, the latter become the infrastructures in which the Cosmopolitan Localism can give precise directions to those decision makers that handle cultural, political, and environmental topics.

Maker-based urban models

Within those nodes, these small-scale production units are organized as multiple providers to the same order, forming a much more resilient network (if we take for example the cooperatives systems). These nodes get therefore in contact and in strict relation with nearby networks, expanding to a so-called network of networks, or a Distributed Economy Network (dos Santos et al., 2021). If properly designed taking sustainability principles into account, they have potential to promote locally based sustainability, sharing various forms of local resources, including skills, knowledge, and manufacturing/service capabilities such as those good design practices. Thanks to digital technologies such as Open Design and crowd-design (Dickie, 2018), designers engage a wide variety of competence and directly contribute themselves stimulating new configurations of the system in which they operate.

This production of products and services can be done by laypeople, prosumers, producers, creative communities, experts in various fields, designers and companies, or even by the hybridization of all of these actors (de Vere, 2013). It is important to notice how here is not only the digital empowerment that cover a central role to aggregate those nodes; spaces such as makerspaces, Fab Labs and other creative spots becoming central in defining the dynamics and the practical terms of those activities (C. Costa and Pelegrini, 2019). It becomes therefore relevant for the system to work that each node can make use of a proper infrastructure in which the network can proliferate.

Up to now, is it possible to see how cities and even rural area are updating themselves to welcome and scale up the potential of the network, but the infrastructures needed to distribute the power to create physical things seems to be still latent in many places (Lamb and Schack, 2021). The urban context become fertile ground for those community projects, sharing the same values and objectives and providing solutions locally on a proper small scale. However, considering the plurality of skills and backgrounds of the individuals usually involved in relevant processes, this design embedded sustainability in open hardware solutions is perceived and implemented differently by industry-minded individuals and by small, under-resourced communities.

Fabrication cities

Since this localism can count mainly on local resources, the community is therefore more aware of the dependence it has with the environment and its goods. A self-sufficiency concept comes in place at multiple layers of the management of the city as a habitat capable of optimizing both infrastructural and ecological resources (Micelli, 2016). Although the concept of self-sufficiency alludes to a certain level of productive independence (capacity of non-dependent production) at the same time, this independency arises from cross-fertilization of exchange of supply(s) and knowledge(s). It is therefore necessary to point out that self-sufficiency requires that its environment to be interconnected, interrelated and open to exchange.

At first glance, it seems a contradiction between autonomy and interaction (between independence and interdependence), but the empowerment (social, ecological, and economic) along with the awareness are two of the most promising frameworks for understanding the dynamics and contexts of youth civic development (Christens et al., 2016). These factors draw attention to the capacity of institutions and communities to critically analyze social issues, identify solutions and carry-on best practices for design, production, distribution, consumption, and management (Guallart, 2014).

Since the introduction in Barcelonian envision by Guallart, although it was superseded by subsequent city administrations, the "self-sufficiency" concept recognized the civic role of digital manufacturing laboratories that has been compared to services such as public libraries while putting the bases for the "Fab City" concept, a transnational program that is proposed as a natural evolution of the Smart City towards a more resilient and decentralized model of sustainable development of the whole cities partnered.

The combination of makerspaces and libraries is a well-established reality, made necessary by the shift from a "passive knowledge-consumption model to an active knowledge-production model" (Caso, 2019) and the renewed relationship with cultural sharing tools. With the migration of culture to digital support, and especially with widespread access to the internet, one of the main functions of libraries, to host and make culture available to the public through physical support, is in fact diminishing. However, the challenge remains to reconnect libraries with new generations, native digital users, which has been successfully addressed by incorporating new spaces for sharing, where physical aspects of culture referencing the internet as an encyclopedic source can be poured out. These new learning spaces are, in fact, makerspaces, places where new forms of learning are experimented with, and the experience and learning by doing is utilized. Makerspaces and libraries have become part of the "third places" according to sociologist Ray Oldenburg's definition (Houpert, 2019), social gathering places where the pleasure of making culture is shared through physical creation (Sennett, 2008).

Self-sufficiency all-round in this way can be implemented successfully in many sectors (even if partially) as a valid alternative model to economic developmentalism accepted since the second half of the twentieth century as a corollary of the material, industrial progress, or capital form. Within this scenario it is possible then to define the role that its player has in the production system. Citizens as producers (or makers) of their own life world. We already pointed out how the urban 'maker culture' adopts a wide variety of digital tools, like computers, semi-professional software, and 3D printers, to design and develop products and services. Design becomes a strategic tool in triggering, supporting and enhancing social innovation, while putting designers as infrastructures to support initiatives for autonomous and self-established communities (Morelli and Sbordone, 2018). These dynamic and citizen-centered places allow the variety of communities to find solutions through bottom-up interventions, starting by an innovation process that no longer passes through institutions or authorities (top-down). In a broader perspective, design supports communities by proposing solutions to problems that open to a wider disciplinary field that goes beyond productivity, technology, and the market (Villari, 2012). In a highly self-organized context, design play a central role in understanding and developing social innovation by mediating public and private needs.

An interesting semi-institutionalized intermediate form in those urban labs, or otherwise called living labs, in one such as the Buiksloterham district in Amsterdam North, where home buyers could purchase their own lots and develop their own sustainable living space (de Lange et al., 2019). Resources and building materials requirements raise the issue of possible geopolitical implications where countries start to compete to gain access to cheap resources, questioning therefore the sustainability and democratization aspects of these technologies easily accessed by wealthier countries without any limits (Fleischmann et al., 2016).

If, as it has been stated above, the issue related to distributed manufacturing is not related to technological matters but to economical ones, also here the main obstacle should not be addressed with a techno-centric approach, questioning the efficiency of the digital systems, but to a with a sociological and participative approach. To give a proper response to the evolutions in place, it is necessary to have a deeper understanding of the identity of what is "4.0" when relating to technologies, cities, industries, and societies. While the potential of those concept is often represented by the offer of digital platform as a digital twin (He & Bai, 2021) of a productive society, those concepts are at the origins of many good practices in the industrial and scientific production environment.

The Fab City Full Stack
Schematic representation of the full stack Fab City approach.
Image retrieved on 2nd March 2023 from https://blog.fab.city/the-fab-city-full-stack-a17028b2a477

Many cities are nowadays developing unique ecosystems, prototyping new forms of urban production – in cities such as Barcelona, Paris, Santiago, Amsterdam, Shenzhen or Detroit, or in countries like Bhutan and Georgia. The Fab City concept is finding different declinations while networking and exchanging experiences within those city partners as part of a global community for building a new productive and economic model for the future. In a new iteration of democracy, participation should not be merely about giving an opinion or delegating power to elected representatives, but about co-creating and co-building neighborhoods and cities. With this regard, the Fab Lab community replicate a Full Stack approach, often associated with the software developer profession (Bratton, 2016), relying on the ability to provide and monitor the development of technologies for urban regeneration which implies an extended and comprehensive understanding of technical, political social and economic matters (Diez Ladera et al., 2022). The Fab City Foundation is a collective of individuals and organizations from different countries, focused on the development and promotion of the Fab City concept.

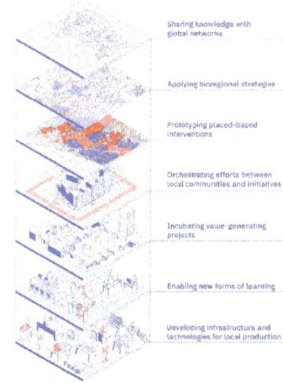

The initiative aims to enable entities to promote common strategies that can be implemented within the Fab City concept, which is not directly set by the Foundation. The Foundation seeks to promote active participation and facilitate the process of getting involved in the Fab City concept for new members. The Foundation does not have a procedural process to have an idea of the Fab City, rather it is a tool of inspiration for the city, which can find different meanings in each layer. At the very beginning of the initiative, public administration was not involved. The Foundation has grown in numbers and is identifying the possible limits of its area of action and is now working to prepare guidelines for active participation to create opportunities for each new member to get involved in the Fab City concept. The Fab City Foundation aims to be an enabler of other entities and not be related to a specific local context or thematic area. The role of the Foundation is to systematize information and needs and bring together different people from different areas to promote common strategies that can be implemented within the Fab City concept. The Foundation has expanded rapidly, and its members are already working on specific themes, such as business models. The Foundation seeks to overlook the connection and link the experiences of its actors.

> *"[…] one of the challenges that Fab Labs and Fab Cities face is to create a support program to incentivize and help develop projects from their global networks and become part of global repositories of solutions to some of the critical issues many communities face locally." (Diez Ladera et al., 2022, p. 10)*

The Full Stack is therefore not a ready-to-use plan but a tool of inspiration for cities, which can find different meanings in each layer, but aims to help to systematize the knowledge to understand "*what to do*" and each city would develop its own strategy that will be implemented in the Full Stack (Diez Ladera et al., 2022). The Foundation has more recently worked on guidelines for active participation to create opportunities for each new member to get involved in the Fab City concept. The Full Stack Implementation Guide has been made to assist members of the Fab City Network in implementing the Full Stack framework locally, by providing recommendations on objectives, key actions, and knowledge-capturing strategies for each of the seven Full Stack layers.

In this sense, each Full Stack layer offers guidance on how to map and research local resources, experiment through community activation, events, and co-creation activities, and rethink local processes and strategies. Through this set of tools, the Foundation aims to facilitate the process of getting involved, since also the knowledge (available for everyone through the Full Stack layers) is quite exhaustive and complex. The Foundation has also worked to adapt to local policy dynamics and understand the current state of each city.

5.5 Innovation through collaborative spaces

The evolution of Hackerspaces, from places of diffusion of an active technological culture to Makerspaces as potential places of widespread production in the territory (Menichinelli, 2016) has brought the traditionally informal spaces of design and production to the center of a new debate on the resilient city. Taking for example the case of Dwarka (Ghawana and Zlatanova, 2013), a subcity of Delhi, where 3D printing technologies and a Geographic Information System (GIS) approach has been applied to the overall urban planning structure, in order to let the Governments and designers involved understand and redesign specific methods and services for the targets highlighted. The example showed that it was possible to adopt 3D printing applications for local scale urban planning even in big metro cities like Delhi. Depending on the need for discussions and area coverage to be considered, it could advocate a participatory approach for urban / city planning.

Maker cities

Other virtuous examples such as the one by Vicente Guallart, city planning councilor of the city of Barcelona, who in 2011 founded the first European Fab Lab in response to a crisis scenario that saw youth unemployment exceed 50 percent, proposed a new model of the city. Production was based on digital manufacturing of the DIDO (*data-in, data-out*) type, to be contrasted with the traditional idea of the city as a place of consumption PITO (*products-in, thrash-out*) (Gershenfeld et al., 2017).

This model was promoted for the 2014 Barcelona Smart City plan (Ferrer, 2017), although it was superseded by subsequent city Administrations, and had a double effect by recognizing the civic role of digital manufacturing laboratories, that has been compared to services such as public libraries, and by placing the bases for the "Fab City Pledge", a transnational program that is proposed as a natural evolution of the Smart City towards a more resilient and decentralized model of sustainable development of the city itself. The distribution of makerspaces or other virtuous examples such as

ATENEU DE FABRICACIÓ

Logo of Ateneu de Fabricació

the *Ateneu de Fabricació*[1] (which will be discussed in the next chapter) in each district was included ten years later in the current plan of "Barcelona Ciudad Digital"[2], implementing the transformation of an informal network of self-managed bottom-up spaces to a new top-down cultural infrastructure (Capdevila, 2014).

[1] https://ajuntament.barcelona.cat/ateneusdefabricacio/en/
[2] https://ajuntament.barcelona.cat/digital/es

Those virtuous examples demonstrated the role of makerspaces transcends mere production for self-consumption, as well as local production, opening to the involvement of citizens in public affairs to "manufacture" more resilient cities (Menichinelli and Schmidt, 2019). From the governments perspective, Zaragoza municipality and Aragon Region (Spain) constitute an interesting, but maybe undervalued, case study, of top-down approach in favor of open innovation and social technologic empowerment. The urban and social context of Zaragoza was characterized by only three open Maker laboratories, facing a community strongly committed to the principles of maker culture. Zaragoza's Administrations have been promoting since 2016 a series of calls for community-based initiatives with hybrid crowdfunding and public funding, aimed supporting bottom-up initiatives of social innovation based on maker practices. Among the virtuous and successful examples, the project "¿Como esta el patio?"[1] represents an efficient case under different aspects: an association of parents committed to learn CNC machining techniques for the construction of structures for the reconditioning of their neighborhoods' school patio. This experience, becoming a format for schools called *Imagina tu patio*"[2] has proved how social innovation does not reside exclusively in the use of technology but more in the new relationship generated between Governments and citizens. The latter recognize in the practice of community action and self-construction applied to public space a potential field of action for social innovation, guiding citizens beyond social appropriation to *res publica*.

Barcelona calling

During the time of the doctoral experience the Research moved for a while in Barcelona as a Visiting Research at the Elisava University, Barcelona School of Design and Engineering (UVic-UCC) hosted by prof. Massimo Menichinelli. The Research was able to explore several specifically selected laboratories in order to provide a picture as clear as possible of the vast offering of creation and digital manufacturing spaces in one of the emblematic cities of digital change from the bottom-up at the European (and maybe global) level.

During the visit it was perceived a general consideration of the relevance of skills and the exchange of knowledge between different disciplines. The city is known for its diverse population, which contributes to the exchange of knowledge and skills. This exchange is facilitated by the presence of different learning spaces in the city, such as museums, libraries, and universities. These spaces provide opportunities for people to learn from each other and exchange skills and knowledge. Barcelona recognizes the need for technological learning places rather than technological empowerment. It was observed that the city has several spaces that provide access to technology and digital tools for people to learn and develop their skills.

[1] https://www.rtve.es/play/videos/la-aventura-del-saber/como-esta-el-patio/5662539/
[2] http://www.imaginatupatio.com/

3D scanning of our visiting team made via architectural photogrammetry system at the UAB.

These spaces are designed to empower individuals to use technology to create, learn and innovate. They provide an opportunity for people to develop their digital skills and stay ahead of the technological curve. Another observation made during the visit was the need to select a precise target to offer specific services and the ability to identify these targets directly in the local neighborhood area. The city recognizes that the needs of the community vary depending on the location and the demographics of the area. Therefore, it is important to identify the specific needs of the community to offer services that are relevant and effective. By identifying these needs directly in the local neighborhood area, it is possible to offer services that are tailored to the needs of the community.

Barcelona also recognizes the need to confront the pragmatic dimension of the market and the prompt response to the needs of citizens rather than generating needs to open new markets. The city understands that the needs of the market are constantly changing, and it is important to respond to these needs in a timely and effective manner. This requires a deep understanding of the market and a commitment to meeting the needs of the community. Another observation made during the visit was the relevance and the specific acceptance that Catalonian Makers has of the concept of error as a basic form of knowledge and the need for a useful "recipe book" for replication. Barcelona recognizes that failure is an important part of the learning process and that it is important to learn from mistakes to improve. The city also recognizes the importance of documenting successful projects and programs to replicate them in other areas.

Finally, it was observed that there is a need for certain spaces to generate "economies" of exchange of skills and knowledge. The city recognizes that there are benefits to bringing people with different skills and knowledge together to exchange ideas and collaborate on projects. By creating spaces that facilitate this exchange, the city can promote innovation and creativity. Among various international experiences, also in Italy new forms of making have been identified (Maffei et al., 2015) which have gradually opened to new policies in favor of hybridization or the shift between professional and productive activity, looking at the dual nature of independent innovators and manufacturers (Maffei and Bianchini, 2014). While the weight of the maker economy is increasingly relevant at the European level, the effect of makerspaces on national policies is more noticeable as one goes down to smaller territorial areas, mainly at the urban or metropolitan scale, and among people who have an interest and means to contribute to their own territory. In the urban landscape (as it has been possible to understand from the mapping results), there are extremely diverse realities, from Milan where makerspaces complement a rich entrepreneurial fabric and widespread design culture, to much less urbanized regions where the spontaneous emergence of makerspaces is more difficult, and innovation is a cultural challenge.

It is the local, provincial, and regional Public Administrations that take on the role of promoting the new maker economy by intervening with policies and programs aimed at strengthening existing communities born from the bottom up, or in less consolidated contexts, by acting in a foundational way by establishing individual makerspaces or entire regional networks with a top-down approach.

Based on the considerations made in the first mapping analysis, and following the reflections outlined above, the Research, as will be illustrated in the next chapter, focused on the second level of investigation, identifying among the elements of the mapping those that are the most complete or diverse, investigating the level of complexity and inclusion within an ecosystem that is viewed from an economic, ecological, and social perspective. In the next chapter, the profiling activities conducted in the Field Research phase regarding the present level of investigation are described. It is worth anticipating that such investigations have further narrowed the focus to the urban level, concentrating on the city of Rome.

PART III
CITY
CHAPTER 6
CITY IN PRACTICE

This chapter presents introduces the actions carried on that start from the mapped realities and it is intended to deepen the investigation into policies and urban development in relation to government and communities outside of individual metropolitan areas.

The Research carries on this investigation establishing direct interviews with experts and entrepreneurs to better understand production realities and the regional economy network. The objectives of the study aimed to understand the evolution of makers into industry, the role of design, and the concept of the maker figure.

Findings of the study show that Makers in Rome present an heterogeneous and complementary set of skills and peculiar identities, which can be identified through direct contact with expert individuals. The study suggests that makers should never define themselves as a separate role but should continue to draw from different sectors in which they operate in order to maintain their cross-cutting skills and identities.

It is therefore important for Makers and Designers to remain flexible and adaptable in their roles, and to continuously draw from different sectors to stay relevant and innovative. Overall, the community analysis approach starting from mapping provides valuable insights into the evolution of urban Makers in Rome and their roles in Capitoline society, which can also provide insights for future Research and practice in this field.

6.1 Zoom in Rome: a snapshot of metropolitan Maker ecosystem

After the map developed and described in the fifth chapter, six entities, covering private and public sector, were selected which seemed to best represent the digital fabrication laboratories across the Lazio region and adequate to evaluate its social value, skills, and local impact. Those entities were: a national foundation, a regional network of Maker labs, a local Fab Lab, a startup related to digital fabrication, a 3D printing filament producer, and a 3D printing service. A campaign of low structured interviews has been conducted, according to a Grounded Theory approach[1] - giving the opportunity to reach a topic throughout conversations as well as an holistic evaluation. These interviews were conducted during the late first strike of the pandemic and during the first lockdown in Italy, together with the doctoral student at the University of Zaragoza Lina Monaco, who in addition to being a Maker was also the manager of the Fab Lab of Zaragoza, and therefore extremely familiar with the historical network of public laboratories. The interviewers gradually led the responders to tackle some aspects of their activities, the perception they have regarding the relationship with Public Administration and above all questioning their role within the social and economic context they profile into. From those interviews it has been possible to have an overall understanding on topics such as their economic model, user profiling, openness, and Government involvement.

The following paragraphs report the interviews held with the individual interviewee who, as anticipated, answered the questions through an open dialogue which generally started from a general presentation of their reality and professional background and progressively led to deal with the aforementioned topics of interest. Little by little, the responders have been led to talk about their challenges and think aloud about potential solutions and evolutions of their reality and their work, a method not too dissimilar from protocol analysis for the study of behavior (Austin and Delaney, 1998). Respondents were interviewed aware of being registered (obviously offering their consent to the registration).

Personal and informal contact has allowed the achievement of a sincere involvement with respect to more complex topics, but, doing so, leading the content of the recordings to be slightly more fragmented than a binary "question and response" conversation.

---

[1] Grounded Theory is a research methodology that originated in the field of sociology, inspired by the so-called "interpretive paradigm," with the aim of interpreting the processes underlying a particular phenomenon through data analysis. According to Grounded Theory, observation and theoretical elaboration proceed in parallel, in continuous interaction. The researcher discovers the theory during empirical research and should preferably ignore the pre-existing literature on the subject to avoid being influenced by it. This technique places emphasis on data rather than theories, which are directly derived from the analysis of local and contextual data. Therefore, it is a different methodology compared to Survey Research, which was adopted during the mapping process.

Therefore, the following reports are to be considered the result of a careful analysis and selection of only those parts related to the questions posed to the interviewees, in which more sociable and verbose dialogues have been omitted (also out of respect for the latter), which could shift also the attention from the focus of the interviews itself - yet still retaining those parts that were key to responders to reach a particular conclusion.

Digital manufacturing tools have already established their role in product design innovation processes, and they are being consolidated also as viable production technologies, which implies a rising recognition in the social, economic, and political sphere. The adoption of digital manufacturing processes always promises to industry the achievement of great advantages in productivity, sustainability, and design, while delivering new opportunities in the market. Those spaces that contain the technologies are so defined in a workflow that relies on a seamless conversion of design and engineering data into digital code to control manufacturing devices (Gershenfeld et al., 2017).

6.2 Profiling local Makers

Since its diffusion, even if the community of makers was widespread all over the world, if we consider that only approximately 135 million adults are, thanks to the increasing accessibility of the technologies as well as for the space, proper figures within activities that could lead these practices along productivity lines are very few. Those technologies are currently developed worldwide in Research centers, but these are often in pre-commercial development stages (e.g., in demonstrators or exploratory pilot projects). Overall adoption of advanced technologies by industry is lagging due to challenges with technology transfer from research to industry. For firms in search of innovative technologies to bring to market, the diversity of potential solutions presents a challenge (Graser et al., 2021). Companies with interest in involving digital manufacturing processes within their workflow lack an overview of proper technicians as well as an overall comprehension about technological use potential to evaluate their match with the own needs and business interests.

After phases of high-tech prototyping equipment and rapid democratization in the 2010's, digital manufacturing is looking for methods of doing business around the technologies adopted, the processes involved, and skills so far developed. While the weight of the maker economy is increasingly relevant at a European level, on the level of national policies the effect of makerspaces is more noticeable when one descends into more restricted territorial areas, mainly on an urban or metropolitan scale, and between people who have interest and way of contributing to one's own territory (Lange et al., 2019).

Citizen-centered Economies

Interviews highlighted two main aspects of the different disciplines within those places:

1. Firstly, a sentence that became recurring during the interviews defined the Maker and its role in and out of urban context: this competence is 'transversal', and it is what truly identify the Maker in the work environment, in which, to be as much effective as it is and it will be in the future, it should never be identified as a standalone profession.

2. Secondly, it becomes evident from the profiling of the figures identified within each laboratory how the figure of the Designer and the discipline of Design is considered central to the accompaniment of projects and the development of new projects, however not covering a central role in the development of the spaces themselves or to the establishment of policies that open to these projects.

Like machinery, in almost all these spaces, the Designer is a tool, moved by the will of another 'nature.' Most of the backgrounds found come from sectors mainly related to the world of engineering or architecture, which however are always guided by the hard science of economics. What emerges, as anticipated in the previous paragraphs, is that the contamination of all these figures makes it possible to generate hybrid disciplines capable of having a transversal look at the different and potential results of Research and Innovation. This value is highly recognized both by its actors and by outsiders of the PA, who, especially the latter, recognize the primary role of a Design-based approach to identify and coordinate those 'best practices' capable of generating truly usable results.

To a greater extent, the analysis has brought out needs and potential resources that if put in a systematic and taxonomic way to understand them could benefit from the network of competencies the Research aims to build. Design as discipline becomes a transversal and transgenerational tool capable of, and therefore responsible for, educating citizens that assume the role of *prosumer*, capable of finding and producing solutions for society itself. To do so, in the wide market of tools, skills, and competence originated inside the urban context, the need for a systematic and taxonomic way to understand the potential on which to design those solutions becomes clearer.

Local digital businesses growth inquiry

By these premises, the meanings of those products that float in the system should deserve a better analysis in these terms to understand how the practice of Open Design shifts not only the creative context, but also the distribution one.

If the methods and channels of creation are as open as those of distribution (Malakuczi et al., 2020), they cannot refer to a traditional system, nor to a dead-end system of sale and purchase, but to insert themselves in an open framework that promotes traceability, participation, and identification of individual participants in their actions (creation, sale, acquisition, modification, resale, and so on), therefore questioning how digital manufacturing-based enterprises have set up their own commercial assets and what kind of local variations emerge. Moreover, this part of the Research focused on how much the assets of those activities are influenced by local or regional matters when their products are referred to a web-based clientele.

A highly variable resilience of the individual spaces corresponds to the growth phase of the global networks of laboratories encouraged by the Governments, which is leading to the contraction of the absolute number of the same. Having perceived this problem in Italy and throughout Europe, it was proposed to work directly and targeted on the operational policies of makerspaces, and the methodology described, to consolidate virtuous contexts capable of self-nurturing their growth by configuring an environment favorable to bottom-up innovation, even in contexts and networks of laboratories established with public investments and a top-down attitude.

Over time, several studies have monitored the impact of the Maker activity at different amplitudes (Maffei et al., 2015; Menichinelli, 2020) always identifying a hybrid, ever-predetermined mutable form of manufacturers, which prove to be extremely adaptive in time passing from production companies, to consulting, to training with simplicity. These three aspects seem nevertheless to be a common ground in which various initiatives linked to the world of "digital making" revolve and in which it is possible to recognize (at least as regards the scenario Lazio region) the following degrees of impact strictly related to time reaction by the selected companies:

- *Short-term impact*: a first level of impact seeks an immediate economic return, and this is the authenticity of those initiatives that have based their business on the sale of products (which in the case of digital manufacturing we could consider tailor-made;

- *Mid-term impact*: a second level of impact looks at those companies that instead base the activity of their technological system on the basis of the request of those individuals, companies or other startups that outsource certain processes for the realization of their own prototypes or small / medium productions;

- *Long-term impact*: a third level of impact glimpse within the networks and the competence of a more profitable solution to sustain this manufacturing system, aiming to a future that considers not only the business itself at its center, but the people distributed in a massive and inclusive production system.

In the following paragraphs, the Research questioned the role of citizens within Open economy environment to underline how digital manufacturing spread through a distributed system of local small entrepreneurial initiatives.

The latter has been consequently investigated through a qualitative research approach described in the methodology paragraph that defined a clearer picture of the status of regional production capacity which has been deeper investigated through a series of action as direct interviews that lead to a SWOT analysis and the results. Starting from the reflections exposed in the fourth chapter which dealt with the different business models of design for distributed manufacturing (Malakuczi and D'Elia, 2020), the Research aims to further investigate the sphere of "doing business" around digital manufacturing system: to do this, it has been understood over time that the process and the forces involved in the production systems, instead of the final product, looking directly to a customer who is its producer as well.

Interviews SWOT analysis

While the presence and productivity of the maker economy is increasingly relevant at a European level, on the level of national policies the effect of makerspaces becomes more relevant the more it gets into more restricted territorial areas, mainly at urban or metropolitan scale, between people who have interest and way of contributing to their own territory.

This phase is therefore to be intended as a Qualitative Content Analysis, in which the method of qualitative data analysis is deemed appropriate for examining the current local scenario. The main focus of the research and analysis of those data has been developed through a categorizing system which could be able to describe and validate the qualitative aspect of the information retrieved (Kuckartz, 2019). It is important to notice how, within this approach, it could be possible to identify two main variants (Graser et al., 2021): a deductive one, in which the literature and previous knowledge could affect the "reading" of the data, and an inductive one, which could come from the content of the data itself.

The Research used an *Inductive Category Development* approach (Kohlbacher, 2006) to categorize the subjects of the mapping part: it summarizes categories derived from the entire collected data aiming to understand "without bias owing to the preconceptions of the researcher" (Mayring, 2014). This approach finds similarities with the "open coding" process of Grounded Theory (Corbin & Strauss, 2008) described above, aa a reiterative process relying on the constant evolution of those individuated activities based on the analysis and categorization of qualitative data, such as interviews, notes, and observations. Nonetheless the approach relies less on interpretative transformation and theory-building, keeping the analysis of the data collected as much away as possible from precognition (Sandelowski, 2000).

In this way the targeted collection of additional data enables the research to focus the inquiry on data that has relevance in the field of study as the theory develops (Eisenhardt, 1989). This reiterative approach has been applied due the variability and hybrid nature of the Maker within the Italian scenario (without considering the instability of the entrepreneurial initiatives after the recent health crisis).

While the pre-pandemic scenario has been characterized by a global trend toward neoliberal globalization, generating both a reacting anti-globalism and an altering globalism for sustainability, this last altering-globalism movement has reinforced the social role of technology supporting those hybrid communities in the physical space. Such hybridization requires focusing on replacing technologies.

Fab Labs are spaces for prototyping and where members can start a business from the activities taking place within it (Capdevila, 2014). However, according to the Fab Charter, commercial activities can be prototyped and incubated in a Fab Lab, but they must not conflict with other uses, they should grow beyond rather than within the lab, and they are expected to benefit the inventors, labs, and networks that contribute to their success. Therefore, places such as the Fab Labs are not spaces to develop commercial projects. The activities focusing on the commercial exploitation of experiment results should be carried out outside the labs, or at least it should be.

The Research, in this sense, is not pointing at the potential projects and startups that could be born in those public spaces (as its potential to lead and stimulate the birth of initiatives has been recognized by time). Indeed, it is the local, provincial, and regional aspects, in the role of Governments selected based on the heterogeneity of their technological asset, value proposition and service provided. Semi-structured interviews, that averagely last two hours each, have been carried on according to anthropological investigation methods, and ground theory, characterized by low structured questions, giving the opportunity to reach a topic throughout conversations, and holistic evaluation (including non-explicit commented context). From the interviews transcripts, the Research has carried on a SWOT analysis, which stands for Strengths, Weaknesses, Opportunities, Threats, for each of the main categories that resulted from Qualitative Content analysis.

Those interviews highlighted the perception that responders have regarding the actual impact of digital manufacturing on the public (whether there are actual clients or potential ones) along with the attention paid by the institutions towards them.

(Short-term impact) those who offer the product

Completely internalizing the production line, these business assets offer different kinds of product based on clientele needs. In this case, the type of impact is totally based on the reliability of the design and the technology adopted within the activity. From the data retrieved, available online and via direct chat the Research gave a first frame of the overall products available on the market at local level.

Strengths

Their strengths rely mainly on the democratization aspect of digital manufacturing. This is a common thought related to digital manufacturing technologies which are going time by time and with exponential rapidity more accessible and user friendly. It has been possible to see a sort of romantic view from private business sites that are still thankful for the power that has been given to them via desktop technologies and the openness of the knowledge behind it.

Weaknesses

On the other hand, innovative startups in Lazio seem to have to face a general mis-understanding from PAs which does not consider, or not enough for their needs, the immaterial necessities which their activities have. Those necessities comprehended mainly communications solutions and staff management. The latter especially is affected, for them, by a low alphabetization regarding new technologies in schools and universities.

Opportunities

Digital manufacturing network is one of the main bases which most digital manu-facturing related initiatives (if not all of them) rely on. Especially in the last five to ten years, the internet, the Open concept and its derivations, peer-to-peer interac-tions has empowered the private and enhanced the ability to participate and distrib-ute tasks and activities.

Threats

However, it has been reported from the interviews how in Italy and especially in the Lazio region the relation with local Administration is affected by a lack of respon-siveness does not match with the entrepreneurial frenzy and objective needs. This slowness, which in some cases became an anachronistic delay, results in large part misunderstanding general of "innovation" meaning (without denying that could be from both sides a general confused perception of the role they may have in the system).

This led the responders (and we will see it also in the next paragraphs) to also ques-tion their role as "innovators" which seems to them to be not recognized enough (or at all in some cases) by the institutions.

(Mid-term impact) those who offer the technologies

As public services activities are accepting to print third parties projects, the impact of their activity is based on the request and the complexity of the final product. From the information retrieved, it is possible to notice how the intrinsic value of the activities is developed around the network and each specific know-how.

Strengths

To improve the quality of the service provided, the businesses that put on the market their technological implant usually have to deal with the necessity to update their staff to the use of specific technologies with other specific techniques. Usually, the machines those services use are desktop or built on the spot, not to mention the well-known DIY and hacking approach that most of the Makers have within this phenomenon. Therefore, it is necessary to always have a proper formation to the use of them to provide the best quality. This know-how is most implemented in the maintenance of the machines and the assistance to the makers, since inner policies most of the time do not let this knowledge get out of the business.

Weaknesses

As for previous cases, also for this asset the perception of a general misunderstanding of the digital manufacturing seems to be extremely relevant, both from the clientele perspective, which still suffer from a misconception of digital manufacturing especially related to 3D printing technologies, and from the Governments perspective, which does not recognize at official levels the role of manufacturers within these activities that are officially enrolled in the Chamber of Commerce as "Fashion studio" or "Digital/Marketing service." Indeed, businesses that provide privately these kinds of services, perceive that their Ateco[1] code would represent more the product instead of the whole production system.

Opportunities

For these types of services as well, most of these activities rely on a network of partners that most of the time are developed around complementary principles: those machines that for economic reasons or regulation limits are not possible to be internalized are then distributed.

Threats

In fact, this network is for them a precious value which is in some cases jealousy preserved by the owners, since it is considered the actual resource in which they evaluate their impact based on the variety of technologies they can access (and therefore that can resell to their clientele).

[1] In Italy, the Ateco stands for ATTività ECOnomica (Economical Activity) and it is an alfa-numeric code allocated to a business on registration and start-up, and it is used for statistics by the tax authorities for tax reference and for social security contributions. The full code specifies the type of activity and governs its eligibility for specific bonuses, ensuring compliance with required duties.

(Long-term impact) those who offer the competence

This includes those private design studios and labs who offer their skills to put in place those best practices aiming to exploit the full potential of distributed production.

From the information retrieved, it is possible to notice that also for this case knowledge and know-how are the actual value of these spaces, which however look to a return that has longer-lasting repercussions and that aim at a broader perspective.

Strengths

For many activities that are digital manufacturing based which have struggled especially during the pandemic emergency, the core has shifted to the educational mission directed both to the public (such as schools or private courses) and, for a few more cases, to industry. The perspectives of new user-driven literacy standards strengthen further the confidence of the Public Administrations which often adopts these training services (currently generally entrusted to specific centers such as Fab Labs or other state bodies) for updating and the implementation of structured courses in schools and social recreation centers.

Weaknesses

As per many public laboratories distributed in the Lazio Region, access to the machines is limited and, in some cases, not allowed, leaving the practical part to a conceptualization step or to a digital modelling level. This barrier is sometimes due to poor care of the machines, in other cases to a difficulty in managing spaces. It has been reported that some of the selected projects unfortunately do not look beyond the world of hobbies and a DIY mindset that is still difficult for the business sector to place within a consolidated business plan

Opportunities

The heterogeneity of the profiles participating in the courses or requiring these training services is noted. Some are mainly driven by curiosity (especially when we talk about private individuals where the average age is between twenty and thirty years). In other cases, they are young startups intent on participating in tenders to finance their projects. Training in this sense is very varied and in some cases the background is not considered at the beginning (as it is usually information that emerges along the way), opening it to mutual contamination.

Threats

The local entrepreneurial initiative reported in almost all the responders a sort of mistrust or serious concern about its future, which is perceived as threatened with a short-term end, especially when it is confronted with local companies that suffer or have been crushed from different crises or that require to be supported with great difficulty through projects of lesser impact.

If on the one hand this fear has spurred the businesses in search of greater foresight, on the other hand they cannot help but be afraid for their own stability. The economic models of public labs are shifting their cultural objective in favor of financial booster and project incubator, with an increased focus on intellectual property. This led the latter to be more selective with its audience, shifting from direct alphabetization to mentoring programs and research support offers. Instead, private maker labs, that were founded with educational purposes, have been forced to shift to service practice for economic sustainability (also due to pandemic restrictions). Furthermore, despite the differing opinions on the issue of the role covered as a 'digital manufacturer,' they commonly seem to be still economically indecipherable; in this way, digital manufacturing has not yet found a stable and consolidated economic model within these spaces.

Further considerations: Infrastructures, Community and Policies

Within private Maker labs, networking activities as well as interactions with the users are carried on mainly via traditional channels such as direct contact meeting, events, or door to door activities for SMEs. Regardless of their proximity relations, there is a robust community characterized by strong, interdependent personal and professional relationships that do not correspond to a synergic vision of a new production/distribution short chain model. In fact, among all the interviewed Maker labs, digital manufacturing is still not considered as a relevant alternative for mass production. Regarding their audience, public Maker labs profile their audience under thirty-five-year-old users with an academic background, while private maker labs seem to be not actually interested to profile their customers by age. The Open concept, as well as for sharing activities, has revealed a diffuse misuse of characteristic Open-Source design sharing platforms, especially for SMEs. Public Maker labs affirmed that they do not open the design, sometimes justifying the practice with the necessity of protection of possible patents, while private Maker labs recognize open innovation as a necessity to allow SME development, but don't usually share design anyway for third party interests.

Regarding this, there is a widespread misalignment between digital and physical identities: person to person design development does not correspond with Open-Source design and sharing practices. It is not possible to define a proximity client's environment, even if the commercial network is mostly based on door-to-door relationships. The Government's role has been reported to be simultaneously fundamental for the development of a sustainable management model, but unclear in giving guidelines to calls and funding opportunities in supporting Maker network challenges. To sustain Maker labs as spaces in which the sharing and co-design practices of the consolidated digital community come physically, new governance models should be then considered as undoubtedly necessary.

It has been acknowledged the condition of the evolution of Open projects among the Lazio population, and it is therefore assumed that the respect due to NDAs or business secrets in place within these spaces can instead become a stimulating key to the establishment of projects. Not looking specifically at the products developed and the consulting offered (which therefore characterize the laboratories by competence and qualify them by specialization), it is possible to classify the individual laboratories by topics of interest that can open to connections based on their 'disciplinary areas,' rather than on the equipment and skills. Developing the analysis of the businesses and their categorization it has been possible to glimpse a correlation between their impact with their entrepreneurial asset. With this regard, short-term impact actions, struggling to reply with enough rapidity to their own needs, tends to be referred more to a centralized system organization.

In contrast to the distributed system model, a centralized system is usually characterized by large production units located mainly far from its customers (whether they are individuals or organizations). Its stand-alone production units demand high control of essential activities and, thus, decision making is often centralized.

■ Infrastructures
■ Community
■ Policy

Impact timeframe	SHORT	MID	LONG
Value offered / exchanged	Products	Technologies	Competences
Main characteristics	Internalized production	Interdependent process	Consultancy / training activities
STRENGTHS	Production's	Accessibility	Research / Education
WEAKNESS	Communication bias	Technology missuses	Facilities
OPPORTUNITIES	Public participation	Networking	Clientele diversity
THREATS	Government's responsiveness	Stability	Collaboration

The tables illustrate the results of the SWOT analysis retrieved from the interviews conducted with the individuated initiatives on the time frame with which they have been associated to.

This concentration of decision-making and management power, which over time we could almost define as obsolete in the economic and social transformation we are experiencing, seems to have characterized the birth of some of the most prolific activities in the metropolitan areas which aims for an immediate return of their action. Nonetheless, it presumably came as the fastest response possible at the time of birth of those initiatives (which we have outlined mostly comes from a period that goes from 2015 and 2017). It is therefore possible to notice how the technological transfer has marginally affected those business models which have foreseen a production chain development through a personalization and customization process. It seems that the more those services are closed in competence and technologies, the more the activity itself tends to expand its distribution but nonetheless marginally (if not collaterally) have a social impact.

Getting further on mid-term impact activities, their assets, that could be mistakenly perceived as distributed ones, is closer to a decentralized system organization. A decentralized system is characterized by small-scale production units that deliver their goods and services via light distribution networks, directly to customers, whether individuals, entrepreneurs, or other organizations/institutions, increasing customers' control over essential activities. Thus, the cost and time for implementing or changing them is also variable. It could be possible to notice a completely different impact, if put in comparison with the previous case, where those realities that tend to be more open also tend to be more localized and limited despite the potential.

Getting to the third long-term impact analysis, the research has instead noticed various connections more related to the distributed system organization, while we keep distances from the physical product for immaterial values. While distributed systems involve small-scale productions closer to end-users that have, and that also has control over essential activities, those systems could be translated in many forms of participation such as stand-alone, or peer-to-peer, but always connected to each other to share various forms of goods and services.

Moreover, it is well-known the concept of distributed production when discussing information/knowledge topics, for instance via a computer which is the basic hardware for such production (Powell and Snellman, 2004), located by the end-users or peer-to-peer connected with the end-users, whether individuals, entrepreneurs and/or organizations/institutions. If the knowledge is therefore produced in such a system sharing open information and data, they will be more likely to become what (Honavar et al., 1998) described as a distributed knowledge generation network, which may, therefore, relate to other similar networks. If properly designed, they hold a promise to promote sustainability on a multi-local level.

The broad diversity of the economies born in the city make it challenging to intro-duce a well-defined framework and is not intended to be an overview that could cover an entire globally diffused phenomenon (Ranjbari et al., 2018). In particular, some of the competence put on the market have created controversies about their relationship to basic values that are traditionally associated with the sharing econo-mies concepts (Pouri and Hilty, 2021). The main aim of this very first report is to provide a neutral and inclusive descriptive framework, this part of the Research lays the ground for discussing the normative aspects separately and with explicit reference to normative frameworks such as sustainable development, as we do in other contributions to the discussion.

This part of the Research has been built upon two levels of analysis: the first one is defined by the users' identification and the accessibility to the service infra-structures, while the second is defined by proposition, support, and development involvement in the processes of engagement and commitment of those places. For the first layer, four users' profiles have been defined: Maker, experts, citizen, and governments. While accesses have been intended as a combination of interaction allowed and involvement role, many variables in defining each user profile offered a mutable work base by which it could has been possible image future adaptation. Corresponding to a different degree of involvement for each user's profile, on sec-ond layer, the investigation took under consideration those degrees of open sourc-ing and sharing obligation within Maker networks. With this regard, the research is challenging those definitions of possible interactions of a variety of stakeholder's interest while negotiating to reinforce the identification of proximity-based process. Assuming a long-term scenario in which the local networks of digital manufactur-ing SMEs, makerspaces, and Fab Labs, the proposed solution that will be discussed in the following chapters would act as an infrastructure rooted in the territory, to in-vestigate the current condition of these laboratories within the urban context as an effective network of production. The aim of this third part is to provide useful data for the establishment of guidelines that can be implemented for the coordination of an intrinsic creative potential as a resilient social response capable of stimulating social innovation actions, shared economies, and good daily practices.

To explain how those experts' principles and practice definitions could act locally, and therefore affect the platform participation, it is necessary to set forward the specificity of the Roman scenario: on the one hand, experts' involvement defines specific constraints, such as the openness and the participatory factor of the proj-ects; on the other hand, if pursuing an open design experience getting the project to a globally diffused community, the new scenario should then refer to local commu-nities to find similar cohesion beyond common their necessity, such as in person-to-person relationship and a priori cohesion within specific local identity.

Different realities currently collaborate, design, co-design and produce within the city and the region, but their different visions, knowledge, skill, work attitude and conception keep the individual realities from opening to each other unless previous, dictated most often by personal experience, has not been put in place. Therefore, the goal of the Research is not to assume that it would be possible to create new networks and enable connections but, instead, that it is only necessary to structure a playground for a possible network, that would more likely establish by itself, since the main characteristic of these transformations is that they are unpredictable and spontaneous. The interviews highlight the need for these laboratories to recognize a network they could trust and feel related to, not only for their own production capacity or for the social role associated to the citizens responsiveness to stimulate the connections between these realities different digital tools has been considered to localize individual laboratories. Nonetheless, within this specific local context, it seems that few efforts have been conducted towards those updated models that could efficiently help the infrastructure of productive nodes to connect and produce, aiming to a proximity-based planned actions close to the "15 minute city" model (Manzini, 2021).

Promoting and determining these interactions dictated by proximity and by a type of SLOC activities opens the possibility of supporting the constitution of hybrid communities of producers, which will therefore be able to develop new activities and relationships. As seen in the analysis of the communities, if their practices promote and protect individual identity within public services and policies (Selloni, 2018), it is possible to glimpse the role of design in addressing social issues and in building a resilient culture, distinguishing between experts (design professionals) and a diffused design (people, social groups).

Through the interviews, the evolution of open projects among the Lazio population become clearer despite the barriers imposed by non-disclosure agreements (NDA) or business secrets in place within these spaces that can instead become a stimulating key to the establishment of projects. Therefore, a hypothetical emerging map of projects should not look specifically at the products developed and the consulting offered (which therefore characterize the laboratories by competence and qualify them by specialization).

Instead, it has been pointed out in different occasions the will of those spaces to be identified by topics of interest that can open to conversations defined by disciplinary areas characterized more than from the technological and owned skills. A hypothetical tool would then act as a multi-sided tool for comparison and visualization of collected data, a map with individual nodes representing georeferenced laboratories within the area, linking to each of these one of the values investigated and reported at the end of the map.

Starting from the investigations conducted, the Research has therefore considered the possibility of developing a multi-sided solution that could address the different needs of local stakeholders facilitating the interconnection of these production centers. By adopting different research criterion, this solution would not only give back a clear picture of the technological and disciplinary system of the activity of urban production places but could possibly stimulate the establishment of thematic bridges guided by the identification of specific practices initiated in the individual creative spaces. A "citizen-based" approach that hopefully will be able to open the possibility of setting up community supported projects that hopefully would possibly act as bottom-up response by which community can express specific needs and ask other spaces to participate to the development of specific projects, while allowing the Public Administration, having a clear picture of the potential and the "project trends", to plan specific top-down initiatives for projects specifically designed on community needs.

Assuming a long-term scenario in which the local networks of digital manufacturing SMEs, makerspaces and Fab Labs can act as an homogeneous infrastructure rooted in the territory, the Research considers the current condition of these laboratories within the city as an effective set of production nodes (distributed, but not necessarily linked each other) which could provide useful data to establish guidelines that can be implemented for the coordination of an intrinsic creative potential as a resilient social response capable of stimulating social innovation actions, shared economics and good daily practices. This part of the Research outlined a framework of possible models which could thrive around digital manufacturing, and which will be extensively discussed in the chapter 8.

Introducing the next chapter, the Research took a step back to get an overview of all the three levels of investigation. This phase has been crucial to get an idea of "where we get and where we go" in the Research path, which will be introduced in the next chapter as a summary of the concepts so far outlined: a critical step indeed, which has been made also thanks to the wise guide of prof. Massimo Menichinelli who has also contributed to the writing of the next chapter.

LUCA D'ELIA

MASSIMO MENICHINELLI

PART IV
MAKIN'
CHAPTER 7
PROXIMITY-BASED MAKER SERVICES

Urban planning models are nowadays being questioned with a renewed focus on proximity, walkability (chrono-urbanism) and self-sufficiency. Reconfiguring how cities and their flows and services are organized re-quires not only urban planners and architects but also designers, a topic of research only recently emerging especially thanks to the phenomena of the Maker Movement and of Distributed Economies.

This chapter is dedicated to a reflection made with Massimo Menichinelli, professor at the Elisava, Barcelona School of Design and Engineering (UVic-UCC), on the factors that enable the creative communities of urban manufacturing spaces in becoming a public empowerment service *for* and *by* citizens within chrono-urbanism and proximity urban planning models. Through a literature review, a preliminary framework is then elaborated to build upon the second part, which exposes an investigation toolkit to support the birth of Community-based project based on the following aspects: 1) Maker culture as made of makers, designers, citizens, and maker laboratories which 2) via digital technologies develops into Distributed Economies that 3) interacts with Governments through the interface of proximity-based urban models and governances. Each tool of this set took something learned from previous experiences described in previous chapters.

The promotion of urban economies is considered as one of the main strategies for leaving behind the COVID-19 crisis, for reaching sustainable urbanization, and for improving overall performances at national scale (UN-Habitat, 2020). At the same time, urbanization should not necessarily be considered as an intrinsic threat to the natural environment even if it will continue to be the driving force for global growth. The various form of dependencies we have developed has become our urban planning legacy, in which deep-rooted inequalities, especially in the social and economic spheres, have been recognized as unsustainable practices (Jacobs, 1961).

The COVID-19 pandemic has had an impact on cities' flows and processes, but it has merged into an already existing crisis of urban models, dramatically accelerating it. Policy makers are therefore reviewing urban policies starting from re-configuring mobility around proximity-based models, turning recent ad-hoc and temporary interventions into permanent infrastructures. Many ongoing attempts are now focusing on strengthening social cohesion and interaction opening to sustainable urban ecosystems, where the quality of urban life is inversely proportional to the time spent in the traffic (J. R. Brown et al., 2009). Cities are called in action to repair their social fabrics that during modernist approaches were disrupted from human-scale to car-scale, developing new urban planning models focused on reorganizing cities according to the timing of walking mobility (chrono-urbanism) based on the concept of proximity of interactions (Moreno et al., 2021) and self-sufficiency of resources (Guallart, 2012).

Reconfiguring the organization of cities and of their flows and services requires not only urban planners and architects but also designers, and reflections on their role in this transition have started only very recently (Manzini, 2021) especially within the framework of Distributed Economies (dos Santos et al., 2021). Designers may have a role in such economies through the Maker Movement, as both a way for re-organizing supply chains and manufacturing processes into accessible maker laboratories such as Fab Labs and Makerspaces and for the democratization of design tool and practices towards empowering citizens (Browder et al., 2019; Gershenfeld, 2005; Menichinelli and Gerson Saltiel Schmidt, 2019). This part of the Research investigates the enabling factors of the creative communities of urban manufacturing spaces in becoming a public empowerment service for and by citizens within chrono-urbanism and proximity urban planning models. Following this, the Research reflects on the chrono-urbanism models, the practice and research of designers within Distributed Economies.

The goal of the reflections presented here is to elaborate a preliminary framework for informing future practice and research about the role of design in enabling creative communities of urban manufacturing spaces in becoming a public empowerment service for and by citizens within chrono-urbanism and proximity urban planning models.

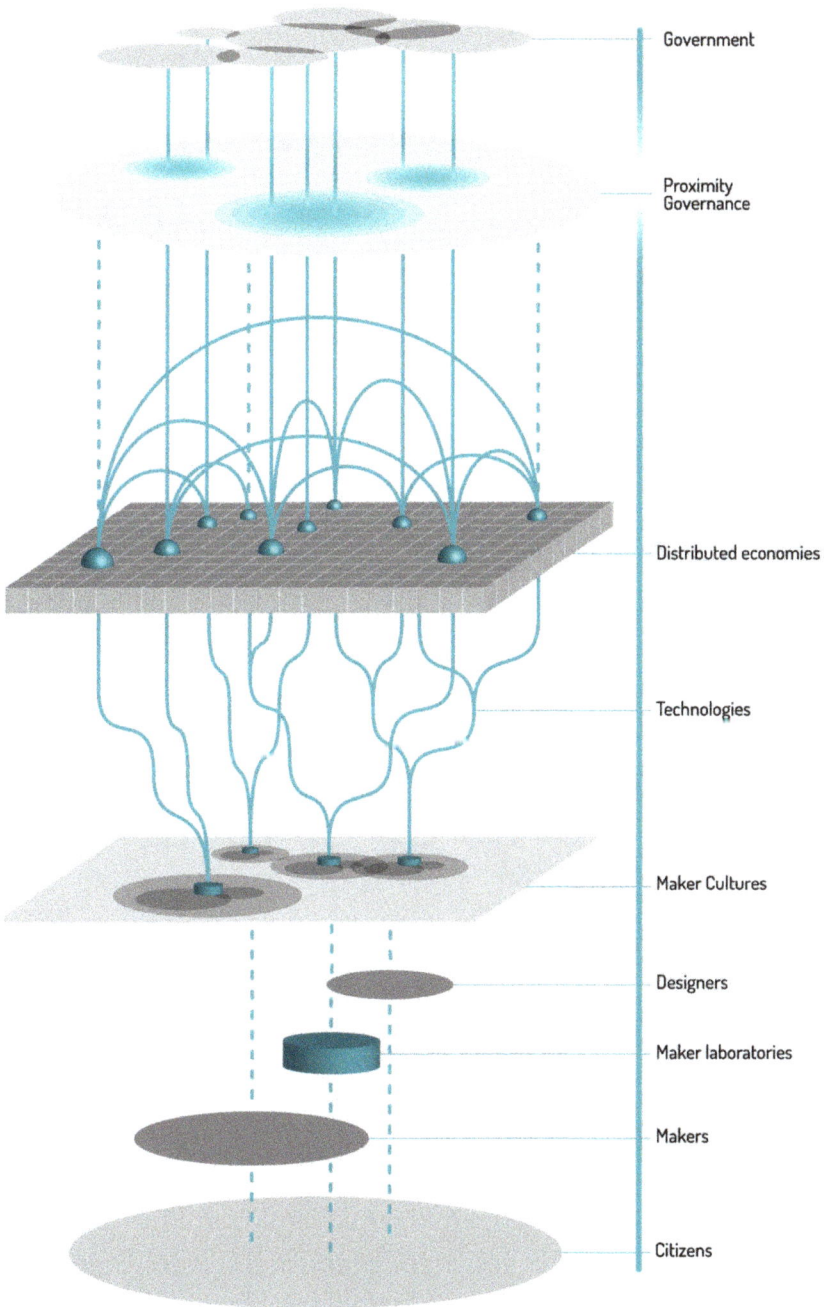

A preliminary framework for the role of design in enabling creative communities of urban manufacturing by and for citizens within chrono-urbanism and proximity urban planning models.

Research adopted an integrative review approach (Snyder, 2019) in order to organize contributions, models, and concepts that we have already encountered in both our research and practice. The resulting framework, as will be seen in the next paragraphs, is structured in three parts:

1) The first one considers the collective practices of makers, designers, and citizens in maker laboratories.

2) The second one, recognizes those technology-enabled economies that are slowly reconfiguring production systems towards proximity.

3) Upon the following reflections, this part of the Research elaborated how Governments develop governances for proximity-based urban planning models that become an encounter point with the distributed economies emerging from empowerment practices of makers, designers, and citizens. The final section closes with a recap of the overall framework while pointing to future research.

7.1 Spaces for Makers, designers, citizens

Maker Cultures have emerged from the encounter of professional designers with non-professionally trained citizens that become makers while accessing and working together in urban manufacturing creative spaces such as Maker laboratories: Fab Labs, makerspaces, hackerspaces and so on (Menichinelli and Gerson Saltiel Schmidt, 2019). Makers can be understood as a portion of creative citizenship enhanced by increasingly made accessible digital fabrication technologies and professionally trained designers here can be especially considered for being able to systematize the best practices and methodologies of design and creation.

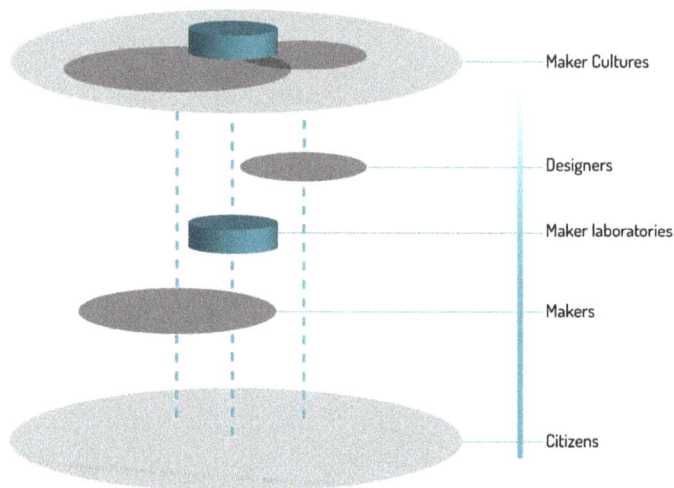

Maker culture: makers, designers, citizens, and maker laboratories

Maker practices have already had a certain impact on social, economic, and institutional levels but they could be still considered marginal because their economic model is still recent and clearly in contrast with current dominant economic models (Holman, 2015). To become as relevant as mass production systems, Maker practices should become more coordinated and integrated in a systematic way by means of open frameworks and platforms that allow traceability, participation, and individual contribution (Malakuczi and D'Elia, 2020).

To have a positive impact, Maker practices should expand their focus from mere technologies to how the latter influence social and political processes in counter intuitive, non-linear, and novel ways (Greenfield, 2018). Best practices in Design can then be triggered between social planning and 'Politics' (Manzini, 2018) overturning rooted political, economic, ideological, and technological foundations (Fry, 2010; Transit, 2017). Within this context, designers cover a political role influencing decision making processes related to social innovation. Makers and designers are thus active participants in urban settings, and Maker laboratories become the place of transformation of citizens into makers by getting in contact with the Design practice and the Maker culture.

As the result of these interactions, Maker cultures could be considered as promising strategies in which Governments can reach citizens. Design is considered strategical in advocating social innovation, and designers act as infrastructures to support initiatives for autonomous, diffuse, and self-organized communities (Manzini, 2015) - where makers and maker laboratories tend to build communities as core value in Maker culture.

7.2 Cultures and technologies towards Distributed Economies

Over time, the Maker culture has evolved, differentiated, and spread thanks to the implementation of ICT and digital fabrication technologies that have allowed a continuous and constant strengthening of networks of locally distributed and globally connected initiatives, generating new Distributed Economies. Thanks to digital technologies, several concepts emerging from digital culture such as openness, peer-to-peer and distributed systems have been integrated into the design discipline giving birth to phenomena such as Open Design and Distributed Manufacturing among several different possibilities (Bakırlıoğlu & Kohtala, 2019; Menichinelli, 2016). Consequently, designers engage in a wide variety of processes, practices, competencies, and skills re-configurations where spaces such as Fab Labs, Makerspaces and other creative maker laboratories become central in defining the dynamics of this transformation.

New forms of knowledge generation and management have led to more fluid, adaptive and sustainable contributions (von Hippel, 2005; Zatsarinnaya et al., 2021) and to a reconfiguration of the living, planning and perception of places between local and global as an open and ongoing foundational political process (Latour, 2017). Within the Design discipline, such reconfiguration has been addressed over the last two decades with at least three concepts that build on each other: Cosmopolitan Localism, Hybrid Communities and Distributed Economies.

Cosmopolitan Localism considers how design can contribute local short-distance networks connecting with global long-distance ones, supporting localities and territories while connecting them which connect the single nodes to the rest of the world (Manzini, 2012). A similar approach, Cosmo-localism, focuses on the dynamic relationship among people that can design within a global infrastructure and project which are shared globally and served locally (Kostakis et al., 2015). We should note that Cosmo-localism aims at a universal community, while Cosmopolitan Localism aims at valorizing local diversities and connecting them globally (Menichinelli, 2020). This network society (Castells, 1996) enables new ways in which communities can meet their needs and express them in creative ways, empowering the single citizen up to question the current systems (Benkler, 2006). It must be acknowledged that this shift to the network society hardly matches with common oriented societies mainly oriented on market requirements, public sector infrastructures improvements and civic priorities, in particular when trying to keep ecological impacts in mind (Mirata et al., 2005).

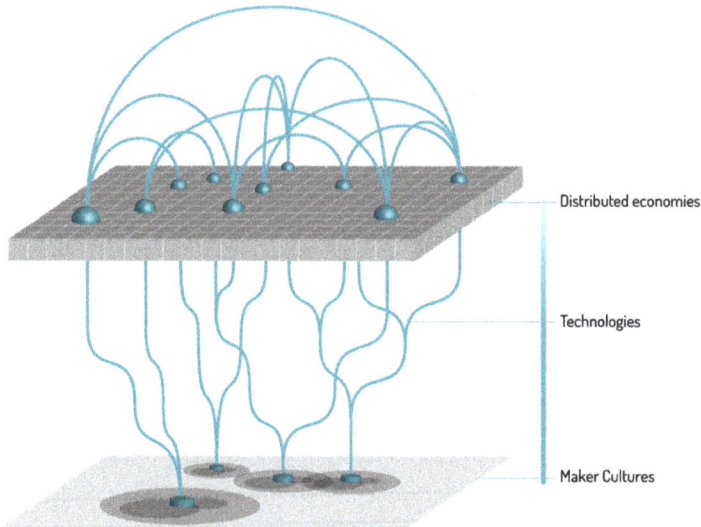

Distributed economies

Technologies

Maker Cultures

Evolution of the Maker culture into Distributed Economies

A pre-pandemic scenario was characterized by a global trend toward neoliberal globalization generating two opposite political reactions: a reactionary anti-globalism on one side and an alter-globalism[1] for sustainability on the other (Manzini and Menichinelli, 2021). The latter has been fostering the large wave of social innovation from the reinforced social role of technology, especially after lockdown experience, by supporting the birth and the thriving of Hybrid Communities in the physical spaces. By inventing and enhancing new socio-cultural and economic activities, creative communities are generating a new sense of place and a new idea of locality, where the role of technology become more relevant in tightening the communities within the cities models that aspire to a Smart City framework.

Within this scenario, production and service distribution are connected and distributed in small-scale production units, within a larger network forming more resilient networks. Those small-scaled connections cover a relevant role in participatory systems, where actors can handle with complex socio-technical systems, enabling individuals to carry out their own personal activities (Manzini and M'Rithaa, 2016) within a system of Distributed Economies where the control is shifted towards the user/client (dos Santos et al., 2021). Networks of services, therefore, provide the potential to promote locally based sustainable solutions, sharing various forms of local resources, including skills, knowledge, and manufacturing/service capabilities such as those good design practices.

7.3 Proximity-based urban models

The expansion of these Distributed Economies has been noticed over time by Governments which, through governance models based on proximity, are active in promoting increasingly precise guidelines and actions that act in favor of local development based on knowledge and innovation. The COVID-19 pandemic crisis confirmed the relevance of the geographical location of processes including public services and how it affects our behaviors, thus moving governments towards proximity-based values and strategies. From cities planned around the 'economy of scale' concept, with specialized and concentrated production areas, now 'chrono-urbanism' approaches such as the '15-minutes city' concept (Manzini, 2021; Sala et al., 2020) are being taken into consideration in order to enable citizens to achieve better standards of life in a more sustainable way. Within this view, communities generate and regenerate the local socio-economic fabric as a node and expand through a wider network that connects communities and places to the rest of the

[1] Intended as social movement that seeks to promote sustainable and equitable solutions to global problems, while challenging the current economic and political system. It aims to create a more democratic and sustainable system that prioritizes the needs and interests of people and the environment over profit and power, often through grassroots activism and social innovation. With this regard, the concept of pro-sustainability is the idea of actively working towards achieving sustainability, rather than just avoiding actions that harm the environment, taking actions that have a positive impact on the environment, society, and economy, both in the short and long term, to ensure a sustainable future.

world, merging the Cosmopolitan Localism, Distributed Economies and Hybrid Communities concepts. The concept of localism implies a deep understanding of the system: the city requires a multiscale analysis in which each scale, from the citizen up to the network of cities, should use the knowledge generated by each layer to promote a self-sufficient production (Guallart, 2012). Although this concept could seem to allude to a certain level of productive independence at the same time, this independence arises from cross-fertilization of exchange of supplies and knowledge. This production could come even from the single citizen but thrives through the cohesive work of those communities, especially when their proximity is reinforced by physical space and geographical nearness defined by the scale of their neighborhood (Guallart, 2012). It is therefore necessary to point out that self-sufficiency requires an interconnected, interrelated, and open environment to advocate the dynamics of civic development (Christens et al., 2016).

Within the Maker culture different approaches are forecasting scenarios of cities as an open lab in which share experiences and make free experiments. One example is the reinvented urban life in the Maker City (Hirshberg et al., 2016), where the attention is paid to traditional practices to empower an educated generation or modern artisans with a renewed interest in a hands-on approach to urban matters. Another example is the Fab City initiative (Diez, 2018) which proposes a 'full stack' approach, adopting a software development metaphor of multiple layers for developing a strategic framework that integrates several different Fab Lab initiatives while networking cities to exchange experiences within a global network.

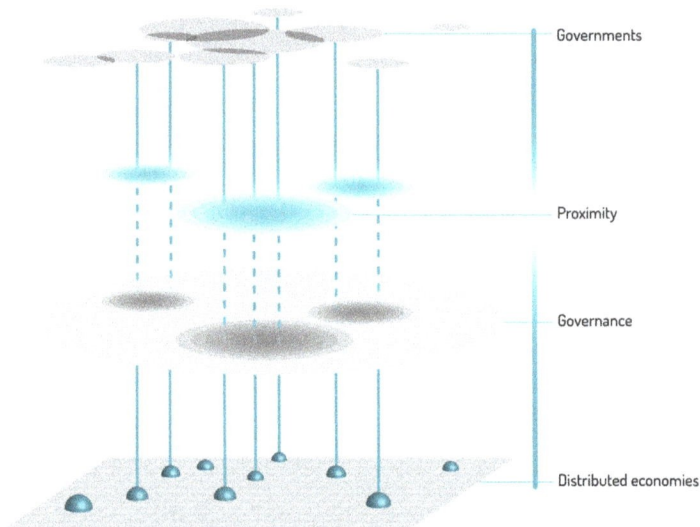

Proximity-based models and governances as the interface between Governments and Distributed Economies

Within their view of a city made of data and service infrastructure they proposed an analysis of the city built upon primarily on the infrastructures for digital fabrication innovation, which enables new forms of learning system, incubators for urban innovation, strategy sharing for local needs adoption, where the latter thrive through a Platform Ecosystem and lastly the City Network which shares the metrics to evaluate the system. This approach relies on the ability of each city to evaluate and monitor which functional layer could be better implemented or updated locally. Another related proposal (Menichinelli, 2020a) aimed at connecting such models considered as experimentation and strategic dimensions with research on cities as commons and collaborative governance together with the Maker Movement, Open Design, Open Hardware, and the Urban/City Manufacturing. Such model focuses on the concept of well-being to evaluate the impact of the Maker Movement on cities and regions as a proxy for impact on overall society, environment, and the economy. All these models contribute to redefining how makers can work at city scale by:

1. moving from the individual to the community to the city scale;

2. redefining proximity-based planning models;

3. creating an interface of negotiation with government for the development of data, services and policies that enable proximity-based strategies.

7.4 Between top-down and bottom-up

Digital technologies have facilitated the birth of new collaboration and organization models that enable educated and connected people to act as a new agent of change towards new economic and social models (Mason, 2016), where the planetary networking of place-based communities share knowledge and resources while acting in a distributed way. Collaboration and distribution of knowledge and practices have influenced the manufacturing industry as well as the Design discipline; both now advocate a strong role of the sustainable and social dimensions, focusing on richer human interactions and more pervasive participatory processes at various scales. The original bottom-up nature of the Maker movement has provided the basis for about fifteen years of social and grassroots experimentations that have been moving towards a larger scale of services at city level, both contributing to and being influenced by chrono-urbanism models. By tracing the evolution of the Maker Movement as a still evolving social movement, this article elaborates a preliminary framework for the role of design in enabling creative communities of urban manufacturing by and for citizens within chrono-urbanism and proximity urban planning models. Such framework is based on three elements: 1) Maker culture as made of makers, designers, citizens, and Maker laboratories which 2) via digital technologies develops into Distributed Economies that 3) interacts with Governments through the interface of proximity-based urban models and governances.

We argued that, to enable creative communities to produce and expand their potential, it is necessary to establish a dialogue between distributed bottom-up practices and proximity-based top-down enabling frameworks. These factors draw attention to the capacity of institutions and communities to critically analyze social issues, to identify the best practices for design, production, distribution, and management. The overall direction of these upcoming models suggests a reiterative process of developing and prototyping empowering tools for, by and with citizens. It is therefore possible to glimpse a double flow of actions which meet in an interstitial space: the effectiveness of the actions and the practices put in place are determined by the mutual ability of the players to interact with each other. This space is the interface between the 'top' and the 'bottom', *"a place where different actors interact and maintain relationships"* (Scolari, 2021, pp. 112–113), where the continuity or discontinuity of the latter are seen as different approaches to the same evolution (Scolari, 2013). If we consider this interstitial place as an interface where 'top' and 'bottom' look at each other and try to interact, it could be possible to assist to an event where both parties will try to emulate each other to comprehend and be comprehended. Scolari's reflections opens to a much clear pathway defining the possibilities offered considering the interaction that could be enabled by a properly designed interface between the actors in place. On the other hand, as Steinberg stated:

> *"Our fundamental problem is that we are organized for an 18th century world, facing 21st century problems. Our academies of learning, our governmental structures, and our professions are siloed by boundaries that do not match the needs of the world we live in"* (Steinberg, 2010)

Despite the fact that through time these considerations may slightly lose (luckily) of validity in modern European policy system, thanks to the informational power of the internet, this empowerment (still sadly not always achievable for everyone) requires constant monitoring and updating to maintain control of the transformations and transitions we are living in and most probably will continue to have.

> *"Public administration embodies a concept about the relationship between government, people and society. As new ideas and new ways of doing things emerge, the old ways become unstuck. This provides an opportunity to modernise public administration and to propel our societies forward."* (Bourgon, 2011, p. 19)

Many scholars, as well as the outcomes of different Research discussed in the pages of this book, agreed on the fact that find an answer to this matter is not something that could be possibly designed to be an "evergreen" solution. Dan Hill (2014) expressed very well the way we could figure out unknown problems and this sort of feeling of uncertainty, which has been compared to a blind man in a dark room looking for a black cat (that is not there): the only possible action is to listen.

Before the road test

As a preliminary framework, this reflection has undergone further iterations and improvement adopted into next chapters of this manuscript that at the same time aims to reflect on it, and in general aim to a validation by confronting it with experts (researchers, governments) and stakeholders (makers, designers, citizens) with interviews, focus groups, surveys and so on. The overall Research and its results described so far, along with the deductions that have arisen from it, have provided the data necessary for the construction of a strategic tool whose purpose is aimed at understanding and applying technologies in a strategic and timely manner with respect to the needs of the real world, which if not properly understood lead to unusable and in some cases even harmful results (Papanek, 1971). The construction of the strategic tool took place through the application of the typical Design Thinking approach (Brown, 2009) aimed at integrating the needs of the reference targets with the technologically and economically feasible possibilities. Each experience so far developed contributed with crucial information and reflections which led to the consolidation of this experimentation: from the Temporary Designer of Clab, to the interviews conducted, up to the experiences in Barcelona. The research has put all the information collected into a system and integrated it to achieve the aims just set. Design-led approaches are promoted for their user-centricity and customer focus (Bailey et al., 2022). However, a proximity-based approach helps SMEs to know more details of their customers and thus this aspect of design-led innovation is less relevant to them (Gulari and Fremantle, 2015). On the other hand, Design Thinking principle of user/customer focus using such tools as customer journey mapping and personas helps to reveal new knowledge to entrepreneurial managers of SMEs (Nielsen et al., 2017).

For designers, using this tool would facilitate the development of customizable and customized products, conceived along with the support of the stakeholders. Furthermore, the articulated format of this tool allows for a holistic comparison of the developed concepts, facilitating the choice between ideas (e.g., the identification of the relative strengths and weaknesses of the project).

Structured as a living lab[1], the tool has been used as a workbook for the MakIN'Rome Synthesis Laboratory, coordinated by prof. Lorenzo Imbesi which saw the involvement of the teaching assistants Lina Monaco, Teodora Ivkov, Sara Muscolo and Francesco Scalera. From the following paragraph, structures and results will be laid out and discussed.

[1] A living lab is a research methodology that involves real-world testing and experimentation of new technologies, products, and services within a controlled environment. It is a user-centered and open innovation approach that aims to bring together researchers, developers, end-users, and other stakeholders to co-create, co-design, and co-evaluate solutions for societal challenges, to facilitate the development and implementation of innovative solutions that are tailored to meet the needs and preferences of end-users.

MAKIN'/ ROMAN LIVING LAB

PART IV
MAKIN'
CHAPTER 8
ROMAN LIVING LAB

This last chapter is a report of the three months experimentation phase, which has been conducted with Design practitioners, Maker laboratories and Roman communities. All of them guided by the MakIN'Rome tool, proposed as results and extreme synthesis of this Research which also gave the name to the whole living lab experience: a twelve cards tool designed to analyze, report and design a series of community-based projects developed around the principles of the 15 minutes city.

While the impact of the projects is the designed product/system itself, evaluated monthly in three main check deliveries (respectively Be Curious, Be Tinkerer and Be Maker), the last paragraph is dedicated to the validation of the tool efficiency from a Design perspective, which has been done through a survey aimed to explore the way Designers felt confident in tackling urban development and social innovation matters. While Makers are more used to work with these subjects, design practitioners may need to confront with Makers practices before the latter may effectively consider the involvement of the Design ones in the establishment of new virtuous practices.

Fab Lab Ostiense
via Ostiense, 92

OZ - Officine Zero
Via Monte Pàtulo, 20

Spazio Attivo Casilina
Via Casilina, 3T

3DZ Roma
Via Filippo Nicolai, 24

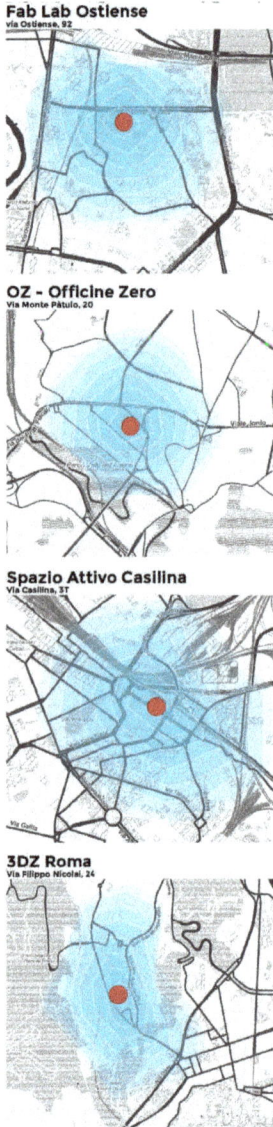

8.1 Prototyping *for* and *with* the city

The Lab takes its cue from the growing phenomenon of digital manufacturing which has entered the urban context as an increasingly accessible form of production, education, and aggregation. A network of services, projects, skills, and machinery capable not only of producing artefacts, but of acting as a distributed system of both technological and social innovations, capable of generating new knowledge and skills sensitive to the use and availability of local resources.

The objective of the experimentation was to generate projects that place digital fabrication at the center of the process, starting a design process structured on the three canonical levels of investigation of this book (which implies technological, social and local factors) and on which the students have structured an initial analysis of the laboratory and its context, which therefore included the technique and the technologies, the community involved and the city knowledge and engagement. Usually, local businesses which aim to innovate would more likely take innovation paths which could possibly hedge financial risk and build managerial controls (Borgelt and Falk, 2007), prioritizing process models such as the phase-gate (or stage-gate) (Cooper, 1990), or discovery-driven planning (McGrath and MacMillan, 1995). Both concepts involve a compartmentalized process where innovations must pass through specific steps to receive support and reach the next "gate".

Those gates has been defined in many disciplines: discover, define, develop, and deliver by the British Council (2000); empathize, define, ideate, prototype, and test by Brown (2009); the build-measure-learn cycle as feedback loop defined by Ries (2011); up to the model of Keeley et al. (2013) which defines the breakthroughs model on three parallel factors for product development which involves customer, technology, and business. The latter found assonance with the stream of work of the Research which has been finalized to developed innovation to respond to those technological, social, environmental needs.

The expected results of the course are therefore a collection of projects that look at these spaces as containers of cultural expression, a production base for products and knowledge, and an aggregation center for local communities.

To test a possible solution in this last Field Research, eight out of the forty-nine previously mapped laboratories were therefore selected and they collaborated in the implementation of the projects. The tool in question therefore took into consideration the physical spaces and their geolocation on the territory (rather than the registered office or belonging to a more extensive corporate network). The laboratories involved were Fab Lab Ostiense, Spazio Chirale, OZ – Officine Zero, Famo Cose, Gulp 3D, Spazio Attivo Casilina, 3DZ Roma. The laboratories were selected based on the traits – to ensure as much heterogeneity among the participants as possible – which also included their legal form. Moreover, the geographical position in the city has been taken in consideration in order to cover the largest possible area, but also to create different perspective based on the local scenario – only in one case were the laboratories considerably close one each due to the fact that the owners were the same (Spazio Chirale and Fab Lab Ostiense), but the different nature of the spaces made quite a crucial difference in the project development. MakIN'Rome is a tool designed to follow the Research and Development phases of a product that could possibly reply to the citizen's needs through the skills of the laboratories located in the urban fabric and accompanied by Design practices, which can become therefore 'empowering' only if adequately aware their impact on the territory. This tool facilitated the identification of the figures and project potential offered by the local context, including on the one hand organizations, businesses and private individuals, maintaining a particular focus on the citizen, identified no longer as a target, but as a figure made up of a name of a surname, already in possession of tools and technical knowledge suitable for enhancing an ongoing process and only looking for potential fields of application.

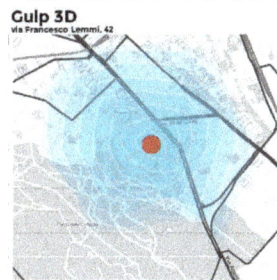

Spazio Chirale
Via Ignazio Persico, 32 /34

FabFactory
Via Giovanni Battista Magnaghi, 59

FamoCose
Via Caltanissetta, 26

Gulp 3D
via Francesco Lemmi, 42

On the other hand, it is addressed to designers, and in the specific case of this experimentation, to students of Design, who will carry out their career in the scenario of a saturated and extremely articulated market; in this context, it is hypothesized that one of the possible ways of being competitive will be to satisfy the particular needs of individuals thanks to the use of ever more powerful and sophisticated technical tools, as well as a renewed wisdom dictated by artisanal and historical practices put at risk by the increasingly complex dynamics of the market. A codesign tool that puts design face to face with the real world made up of individuals, names and surnames, techniques, and technologies.

8.2 MakIN'Rome

The students have been divided into groups of a maximum of three members, and two of those groups has been assigned to each laboratory (three in the case of the Spazio Attivo Casilina which kindly agreed to accept the extra number). To ensure that the students also had a practicable field of action, for each laboratory point assigned to them, a radius of action was delimited that covered fifteen minutes by foot (in line with the principles of '15-minutes city'). From here, each group operated independently, as far as possible given the limited space of some laboratory spaces. Each group therefore worked on different project lines, thus developing the project around different technological and technical tools.

The development of the projects was divided into three main project phases respectively: *Be Curious, Be Tinkerer, Be Maker*. Each phase has been structured in order to give to all participant the possibility to document and report everything they may need to develop their project. The toolkit consists of twelve boards divided into three phases: nine boards in the first phase *Be Curious*, aimed at researching and investigating laboratories, the urban and city dimension; one board in the *Be Tinkerer* phase, intended as a matrix for the reports of Tinkering activities, to be used repeatedly for each activity; two boards in the *Be Maker* phase for finalizing the project. Each phase lasted one month (mandatory) which has been considered enough time for the students to properly set up the data retrieved (in order to receive proper feedback from reviewers) but also not so much to get stuck with the analysis and push them towards development.

The Laboratory portion of each phase, has been carried on through an iterative process of continuous design and redesign of the proposals (Jones, 1983; Tonkinwise, 2004) whereby the researchers and the designers have taken responsibility for its continual evaluation and refinement. For each of these phases, a set of tools has been provided to map, document and analyze the result of this Research work, which is able to respond in an extremely punctual way to the needs of the laboratories together with the needs of its catchment area, which simultaneously considers the potential of the of each other.

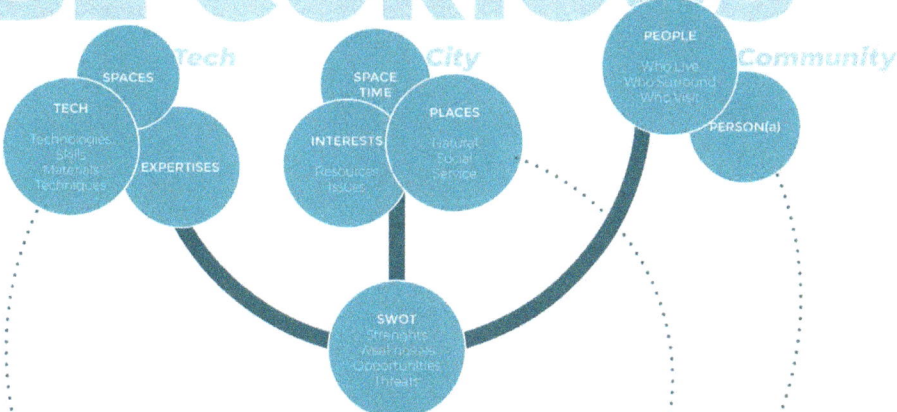

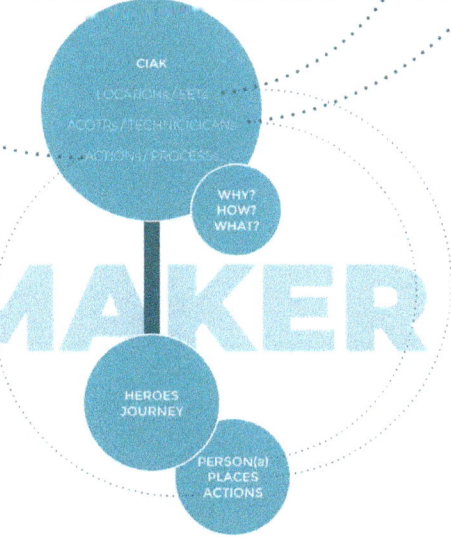

8.3 Be Curious

This first phase is purely research and analysis of the territory. Students investigate the laboratory based on the three aforementioned levels and carry out an analysis that looks inside the laboratory and outside it. In this first phase, more analytical, but with a direct focus on the territory, the first tools were provided which allowed the laboratories and students to analyze the potential of the territory in a hyper-local dimension. These tools are made up of files divided to include different aspects of the laboratories and have been supplied with precise instructions given for each aspect to be filled in.

SPACES

The space map serves to better understand how the laboratory is organized by defining the distribution of special work areas, spaces, and operational dynamics. A plan of the space is drawn (avoiding getting lost in the details) trying to best identify specific work areas such as workbenches, study tables, computer areas, common areas, post-production rooms or ventilated rooms. Whenever possible, a photograph of the space is attached to each area of particular interest. Through this sheet it will therefore be possible to have a clear idea of the predominance of work areas compared to others (thus defining the priority of certain processes), but it will also be possible to draw in future project phases the flows of people who can move in space, thus simulating the dynamics of work on paper.

TECH

The plan divided into four quadrants shows for each the techniques and technologies made available within the laboratory. Respecting the indications for each quadrant, report the information of each quadrant through post-its or printed photos on which you can write or possibly put post-its nearby.

- The *Technologies* quadrant shows all the digital manufacturing technologies and machinery. For each machine it is useful to report the type of processing for the type of materials.

- In the opposite quadrant *Techniques* those manual skills possessed and made available by the people who live in the laboratory space are reported. Refer to all those working practices, even those that use analogical machinery. (e.g., sanding, varnishing/painting, cutting, sculpting, sewing). For each manual skill, indicate how many people share the same skills or interests.

- The *Materials* quadrant shows all the materials present and most used in the laboratory. For each material, indicate how much it is processed by digital manufacturing machinery or is instead used for manual processing.

- The last quadrant *Skills* shows all the design abilities (e.g., 3D sculpting, coding, Mesh/Nurbs modelling, sketching, etc..) and specific affinities (e.g., jewelry design, biomedical design, light design, product design, mechanical complex, etc..) of the figures who dwell the space and are made available in the laboratory.

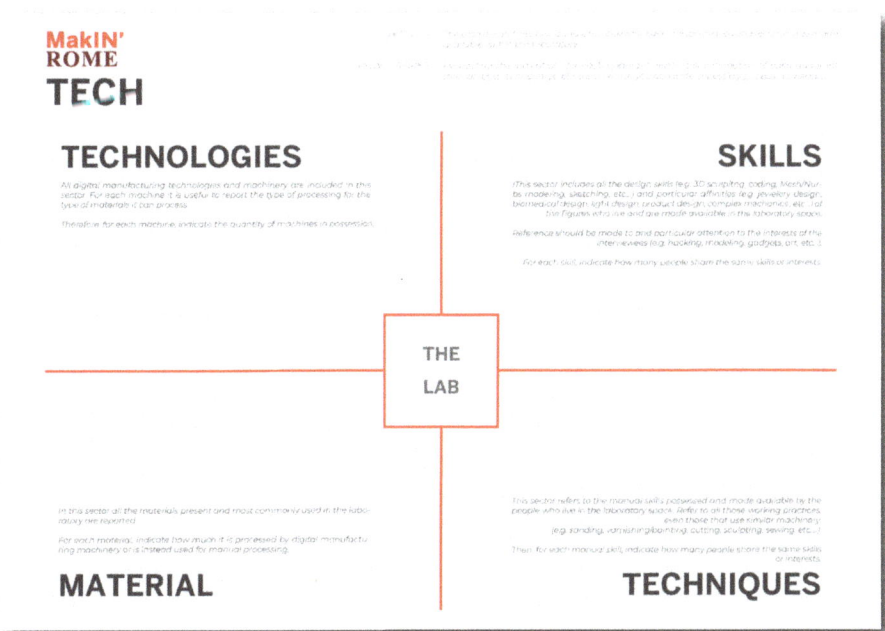

Particular attention should be paid to the interests of the interviewees and personal hobbies considering those who could be strictly related to the work developed inside the lab (e.g., hacking, modelling, gadgets, art, etc.). For each skill, it is required to indicate how many people share the same skills or interests. As an extreme synthesis, at the core of the graph it has been left an empty space to identify the laboratory itself (through photo, a printed image of the logo or a post-it with the name).

EXPERTISE

This model in A4 format is made up, contrary to the previous ones, of a series of files showing a product identified in the laboratory of particular interest which is described according to the following information to be collected. It enables the collection of photographs of the product or prototype and the year of construction. Subsequently, the form requires information of a general nature that is reported through a brief description of 150 words. Other features are defined by pointing out characteristics such as the shape, in case it recalls particular ones (e.g., particular shape, or famous design shape), techniques, technologies, materials and processes of production involved (even not immediately visible if the company is willing to talk about it) and finally personal notes on the matter (free choice of the designer).

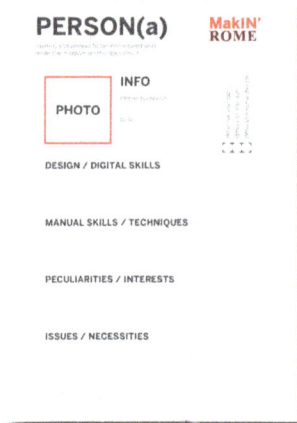

PERSON(a)

Technically speaking, personas are behavioral archetypes, aimed to capture ways of being without expressing a defined personality or socio-demographics (Goodwin and Cooper, 2009; Long, 2009). However, the digital manufacturing processes has no value in the massive market logics that standardize the design and production process (Phillips et al., 2016). Each piece carries with it the fingerprint of his technicians. Therefore, this form is proposed as a useful tool for systematize the real persons identified and subsequently involved in the project, defined by design or digital skills, manual or peculiar techniques, interests, issues or necessities.

PEOPLE

"The more the archetypes assume a realistic feeling (e.g., name, age, household composition, etc.), the more they become real personas, fully expressing the needs, desires, habits and cultural backgrounds of specific groups of users."[1]

Simultaneously with the identification of the figures of interest, the scheme collects and categorizes the people who host the space and who can be found around it. With the laboratory space as a reference, the form is divided into three quadrants that identify categories of users inside and outside the laboratory. Starting from the figures inside it is possible to identify *Who lives the lab* sector, which includes all the people who manage the space and who are vital to its continuity. These people can be the owners, founders of the enterprise, laboratory technicians, associated designers, employees, *Who visits the lab* sector, which includes all the people who visit the laboratory with a certain frequency are reported. These people can be identified as regular customers, space tenants, coworkers, and external consultants. The subjects of interest outside the laboratory are grouped in the *Who surrounds the lab* quadrant. This sector includes all the people who surround the space, but who do not visit it directly or only occasionally. These people can be local entrepreneurs of small/medium businesses such as other manufacturing laboratories (both digital and artisanal), bars/pubs, private studios, workshops.

[1] Description retrieved https://servicedesigntools.org/tools/personas

Groups of people identified as a community (fixed or temporary) can also be entered. The latter plays a more interesting role. Each figure must correspond to a *PERSON(a)* file to refer to which can be inserted in the scheme respecting the indications for each quadrant and reporting the information through post-its or printed photos on which you can write (or possibly put post-it close).

PLACES

Moving outside the laboratory space, information from the local sphere is therefore collected in this file. The plan divided into three quadrants shows the areas of interest, the centers of aggregation and the amenities distributed around the laboratory. These define the degree of interest that the laboratory itself can develop towards the city, and the distribution of resources that the laboratory may possibly have at its disposal. These resources are defined as follows:

- The *Natural* sector includes all amenities related to natural spaces or elements, including green areas including larger ones such as parks, waterways, and any natural basins.

- The *Social* sector shows all the amenities linked to spaces for social aggregation or which host communities (referring to the *PERSON(a)* files). Schools, dog areas, social centers, co-working spaces of other or similar nature can be considered, up to a public meeting point for fixed or temporary communities that characterize a specific place, the latter above all playing a role of greater interest.

- The *Service* sector shows the network of services and small businesses distributed in the area around the laboratory. Small/medium-sized commercial businesses, craft workshops or workshops, bars/pubs, workshops can be considered.

At the bottom of this file, a *Notes* section is maintained for all those aspects which cannot be separated from standard cataloguing, and which are part of the local and personalized culture of the place. In this sector all those qualitative aspects not pertaining to any of the three categories listed above are reported. This part is the one that relies most on the sensitivity and knowledge of the urban area of the laboratory (which could derive from the direct experience of the work group as well as from the interviewees). Small characteristic notes of the place could concern the average age of the citizens perceived by the 'life' of the neighborhood (for example there could be neighborhoods more frequented by young people than others whose attractions are aimed at a more mature public), the viability of the roads in relation to the density of the local population, the presence of other laboratories or particular production districts or neighboring industrial areas.

INTERESTS

The diagram makes it possible to collect and represent the points of greatest interest within the designated area *Resources* and *Issues*.

- In the *Resources* sector the most interesting or potentially useful aspects of the project in the city are reported.

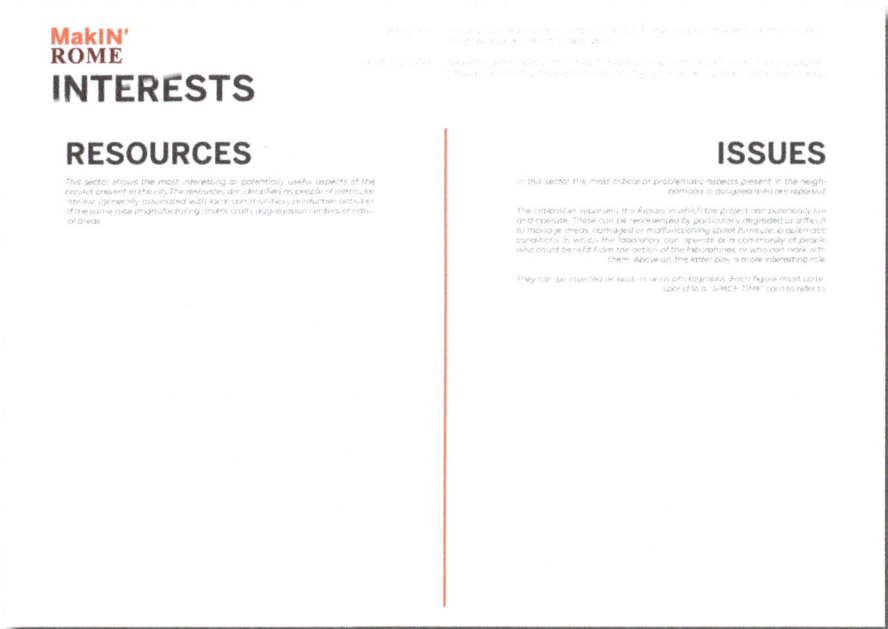

The resources are identified as people of particular interest (generally associated with local communities), productive activities of the same type (manufacturing and/or artisanal), aggregation centers, or natural areas.

- In the *Issues* sector the most critical or problematic aspects present in the district or assigned area are reported. The criticalities represent the factors in which the project can potentially live and operate. These can be represented by particularly degraded or difficult to manage areas; damaged or malfunctioning street furniture; problematic conditions in which the laboratory can operate with a community of people who could benefit from the action of the laboratories, or who can work with them. Above all, the latter play a more interesting role.

SPACE TIME

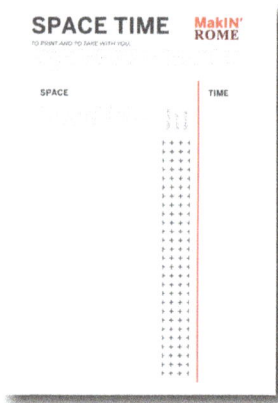

This card is designed in A4 format to be portable when patrolling the '15-minutes city' range. It splits into two columns:

- The *Space* column shows the streets or reference points of particular interest, which are then identified according to the criteria of the *PLACEs* (Natural, Social or Service) file.

- The *Time* column instead shows the timed travel time between the laboratory and the point of interest. It will be useful to understand the time and distance required to complete certain activities in workflows outside the laboratory. At the end of the first phase the students have analyzed in detail the laboratory as a whole, giving feedbacks about technologies, skills, distribution of spaces, possible processes, but more importantly, they have discovered the city as a whole ecosystem of infrastructures and services, delimited by a neighborhood area that can be travelled in fifteen minutes starting from the laboratory itself. Documenting through photos, videos, and notes, they will have to report and catalogue the points of interest and critical issues of the green areas, the social areas and the distribution/condition of the services.

SWOT

SWOT should not be viewed as a static analytical tool with emphasis solely on its output. It should be used as a dynamic part of the management and business development process. (Pickton and Wright, 1998) In order to systematize and synthesize the information gathered so far, the last card of this first phase is translated into a SWOT analysis that focuses on a preliminary 'idea' of the direction that the project may potentially take (Chang and Huang, 2006).

Unlike the previously described case of the CLab project, the IPA tool (Abalo et al., 2007; Martilla and James, 1977) has not been applied as the project's considerations do not involve a priori responses to actual project desires, which may also arise from speculative research, artistic performative operations, and even scenario simulations within a restricted field of investigation.

In the case of the project described, the SWOT analysis can provide valuable insights into the potential strengths and weaknesses of the project, as well as the opportunities and threats it may face:

- The *Strengths* of the project may include the expertise and experience of the team members, the availability of resources, and the unique approach or idea behind the project;

- The *Weaknesses* may include a lack of funding or support, limited resources or time, or a lack of experience or expertise in certain areas;

- The *Opportunities* may include new partnerships, potential funding sources, or emerging technologies that can be leveraged to enhance the project's impact;

- The *Threats* may include changing market conditions, competition from other projects or programs, or regulatory changes that can impact the project's success.

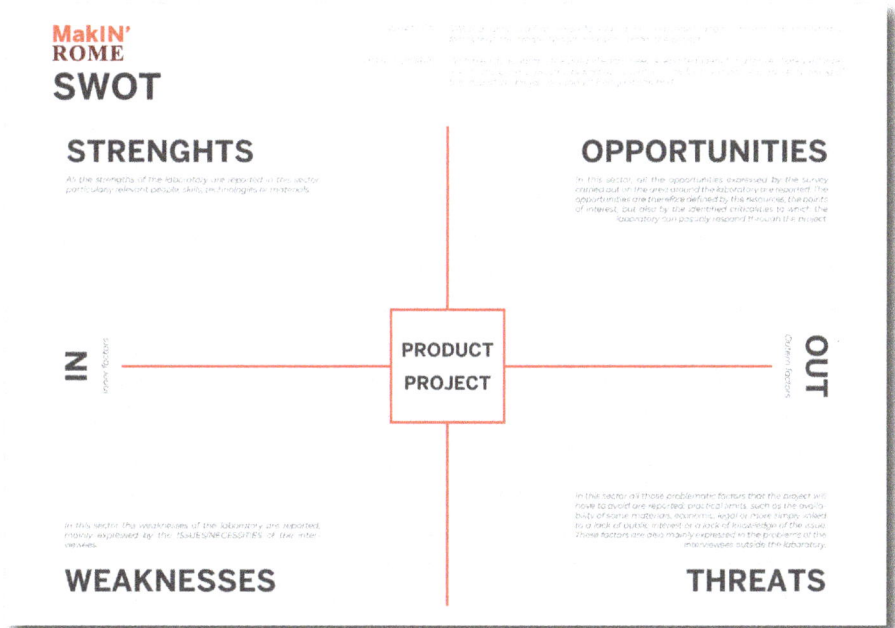

By conducting a thorough SWOT analysis, the project team can gain a better understanding of the current state of the project, identify potential challenges and opportunities, and develop strategies to mitigate risks and capitalize on opportunities. This can help ensure the project's success and enhance its impact, ultimately contributing to the overall success of the organization or community it serves. By identifying the strengths, weaknesses, opportunities, and threats, teams can develop effective strategies to mitigate risks, capitalize on opportunities, and achieve their goals.

8.4 Be Tinkerer

Making, as a form of education, is a revival of earlier, student-centered teaching methods that emphasize inquiry and exploration. These methods have been overshadowed by recent emphasis on accountability in schooling (Porcari et al., 2016; Honey, 2013). A broad range of researchers have documented how these learner-driven practices support student participation, learning, and conceptual understanding (Darlington, 2011; Driver et al., 1985; Minstrell and Zee, 2000; National Research Council, 2000).

Tinkering means being able to transform an initial exploration phase into a "bottom up" activity in which the solution is reached by operating directly on the objects (material or virtual) perceived as real (Resnick, 2007). Born at the Exploratorium of San Francisco[1] this approach allows students to creatively experiment and explore their knowledge in order to find a process rather than a solution. The task is therefore not perceived as imposed and it will be the practitioners themselves who will gradually find a personalized solution. It is possible to define Tinkering as an ability that allows transforming an initial phase of exploration into a finalized activity, just as happens in coding or educational robotics.

The Tinkering activity is especially useful for being able to learn and manipulate a technology right away before the knowledge of the latter can 'spoil' the vision of its use. Simple techniques and basic technological processes are often introduced in a random way and tied together by makeshift, recycled or cannibalized materials from other products to respond to a pre-defined task. The intent will not be to solve the task immediately, but to verify "*what happens if...*" (Taylor, 1993). These practices have the great advantage of immediately developing practical laboratory activities to gradually define an interactive workflow.

In the most established teaching practices of Design, the educational path usually involves a specific request that the student is called upon to respond to through the implementation of a process, so that only at the end of the path do the directions imposed by the teacher become clear.

---

[1] www.exploratorium.edu/tinkering/

As designers advance in their practice, empowered by the skills acquired through their studies, they become able to collect project briefs that are increasingly comprehensive, and are able to identify motivations, criticalities, and potentials, from which they extract the necessary production processes and skills to carry out the project. Tinkering, in this sense, becomes an interesting paradigm shift in the design practice that excludes a predefined end goal and starts with a base material that is not clearly defined but has potential or criticality that can be manipulated in various ways. Through experimentation and the application of various processes, the final product gradually emerges, much like in free building with Lego, where the final object grows as more pieces are added.

It is possible to note that Tinkering, in this sense, overturns the conception of a project that no longer has the end product as its primary objective, but rather the process, which can naturally lead to the potential product. Although originally conceived as an introductory tool, Tinkering is gaining space as a consolidated methodology in various social empowerment practices. It is worth questioning how this practice converges with the discipline of Design, which, as previously introduced, looks at the design approach differently, envisioning a specific objective to be achieved from the outset. Specifically, the evolution of this second tool hinges on the same topics raised also by Sinek (2011) while dealing with the marketing of a product: he theorized a workflow that starts exactly from 'why'. Once it has been exploited the reason, it moves on by wondering 'how' the project could possibly answer the first question – therefore defining the approaches, methods and possible applications – to obtain finally a tangible result that identifies the 'what', the final product and what in the end the project will sell. The goal of the definition of the path is the quantifiable result of the processes and results achieved which are most often finalized in a sort of report or "recipe" of the process. This process is made up of mostly visceral inducements, but which must therefore be introduced into a consolidated and valid system to make the results usable. The Research, in this particular phase, refers to the theories of Norman (2005) of the Emotional Design which defines three interpretations which the design project cannot ignore in order to be successful in the market. Donald Norman's "Emotional Design" categorizes design into three levels: visceral, behavioral, and reflective.

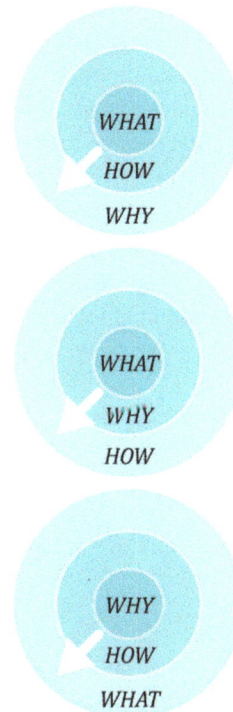

The visceral level refers to the initial emotional response to a product's physical appearance, such as its color, shape, and texture. The behavioral level is concerned with how well the product functions and satisfies its intended purpose. The reflective level involves a person's overall evaluation of a product, considering their past experiences and cultural background. The three levels work together to create a harmonious and satisfying user experience, with emotions playing a crucial role in shaping our perceptions and decision-making.

> *"The success of a product lies not just in its basic utility but in its meaning in the lives of its users"* (Lupton, 2017, p. 63)

From this premise, the Research wanted to provide a lens of investigation of the meaning of their action, which starts from the same question as Norman regarding *WHY* certain emotions are felt, and therefore certain interactions are developed, with a given product. The Research therefore intends to test the efficiencies of the interaction between these two theories within the Tinkering system by proposing a work scheme that allows designers to schematize the results of the work carried out. Given these considerations, the development path of the projects leads the laboratories to develop free creative activities together with the subjects involved without wondering what will come of it, but carefully documenting each step through photos and videos.

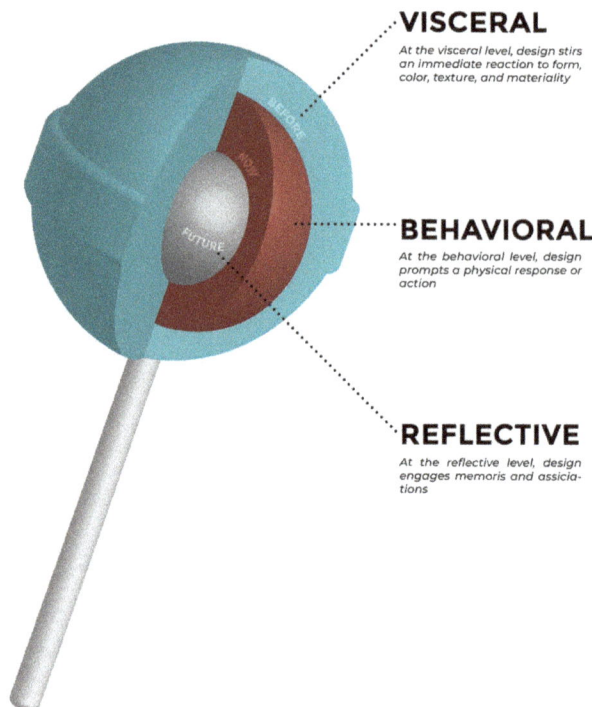

VISCERAL
At the visceral level, design stirs an immediate reaction to form, color, texture, and materiality

BEHAVIORAL
At the behavioral level, design prompts a physical response or action

REFLECTIVE
At the reflective level, design engages memoris and assiciations

CIAK

The file in question therefore appears as a matrix that leads designers to position the elements of their business in a coordinated way by answering the following questions on the abscissa axis:

- In the *ACTORs / TECHNICIANs* sector, the figures involved must be part of the list of *PERSON(a)* created in the previous phase. These could be updated as the activities progress, so you are not necessarily linked to just the people identified, but, if new figures are added, a special form will have to be created for each of these;

- In the *LOCATIONs / SETs* sector, places of interest are highlighted among all those identified during the first phase. There may be new ones based on the needs that emerged during the workshops, but in this case, they will be added to the *PLACEs* file;

- The *ACTIONs / PROCESSes* quadrant represents the intrinsic value of a certain activity (regardless of the result) and analyses the most interesting actions that took place during the workshops.

These elements follows a specific development which starts from the 'visceral' phase (*WHY*) continuing through the video documentation (from which a few crucial frames may be extracted to be reported in the matrix) the 'behavioral' (*HOW*) of the users in the project, the interactions with the spaces and workings of the machinery or techniques adopted, and ends with a 'reflective' moment on the results, the effects they have had on the people, the impact on the environment that hosted them and finally the product that is generated by the activities carried out (*WHAT*).

8.5 Be Maker

The last part of the process envisaged by the tool in question concerns the formalization of the previous design and laboratory phases. The processes are validated with the participation of all the figures involved, who are arranged in a free-format table that takes up the modus operandi of a classic customer journey, which however places the emphasis on the elements identified in the first phase: people, as active actors involved both in the planning and construction phases up to the fruition of the results, the spaces, as physical centers of aggregation of processes and skills, and the processes, in as materialization of the skills, resources and processes deemed most valid.

HEROES JOURNEY

The table in question looks like a classic Cartesian plane with time (t) on the abscissa axis and each *PERSON(a)* involved on the ordinate axis (p). Both the time dimension and the number of participants involved can be customized by the compilers of the form itself who can decide the maximum 'life' time of the process and the number of people (or in any case they will report the number at the end of the project). With a direct reference to the form of the first phase *SPACE TIME*, each moment of the process is also qualified by the presence or physical co-presence of the actors in a certain place, which is then declared through a special tab showing the name of the place where the process shown in the quadrant takes place.

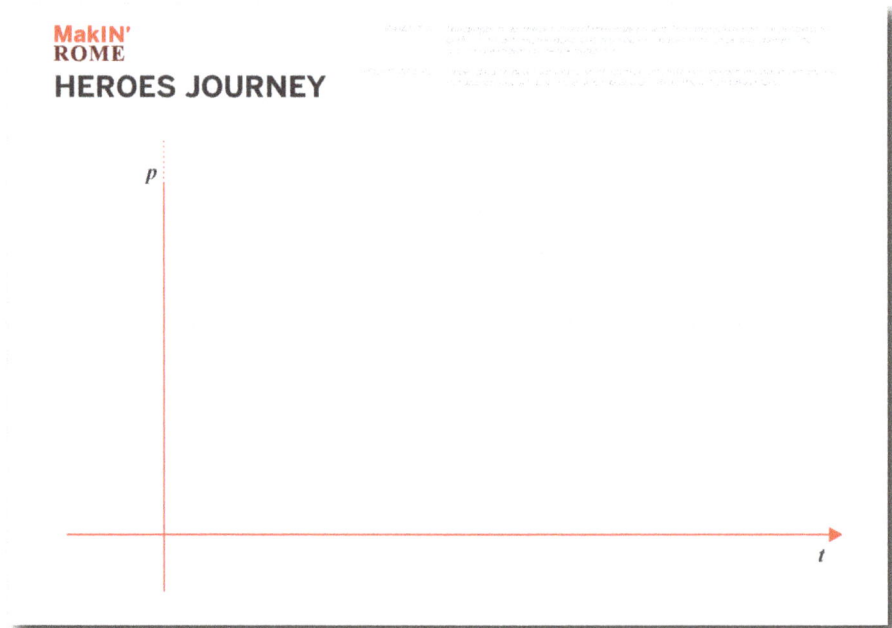

Students are therefore required to report the entire system in the scheme, pointing out places, stakeholders and the specific interactions each of them has with products, spaces, machines, materials and other players of the project.

ACTION

This process will take the name of *ACTION* and will be positioned within the map in correspondence with the place for the abscissas and people for the ordinates.

Each *ACTION* has a title left to the discretion of the compilers which will refer to the reference sheet of the same name in A4 format in which the basic information reported in the *HEROES JOURNEY* sheet is inserted, implementing it with a brief description of the activity carried out of a maximum of 125 words and a detailed list of the materials, technologies and techniques involved aimed at systematizing the requirements required by the process to be implemented in the future within other spaces. Thus, a basic 'recipe' becomes useful for the reproduction and implementation of the process.

These cards were then exhibited and categorized in phases that identified the project's production macro-systems, mainly linking them to the physical dimension in which the actions were carried out. In this way, designers were able to expose the individual development support procedures clearly and precisely for both their project and the individual actions undertaken by the stakeholders involved.

8.6 Community-based projects

This last paragraph is dedicated to some of those projects made the students and laboratories involved: seventeen projects has been designed and successfully produced during the lab, but here will be reported only a portion of those notable that had an immediate impact on the territory and the community even at policy level, engaging policymakers, third sector associations or which have purely worked on the territorial dimension of the neighborhood.

My Garba

Design team: La Penna A., Lucchesi A., Maresi, F.
Lab referent: Tassinari S.

My Garba is an urban furniture product aimed at enriching the public space of the Roman neighborhood of Garbatella, specifically looking at the facades of local businesses. Through a modular system, the exhibitors open up the possibility of setting up "vertical green zones" potentially accompanied by coordinated elements of various functions chosen by the merchant. The goal of the project is to give greater visibility to the participating businesses, while at the same time demonstrating a real and concrete commitment to the care of the neighborhood, communicating their values and attachment to the local community. Each module is designed to encourage interaction between passersby and potential customers of the local, looking at the wide range of actions possible by those who daily live in the spaces and of any passersby. My Garba is a product created in collaboration with the FabFactory laboratory, and customized by the companies that directly experimented and personalized the modules. Among the companies that participated in the simulation, the local tire dealer Paparusso[1] and the local Garbatella Entrepreneurship Association[2]. By involving these stakeholders, the project ensures its sustainability and effectiveness in the long

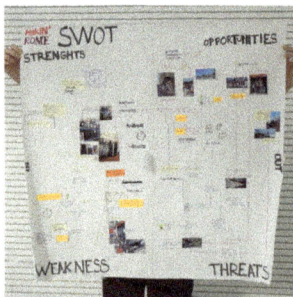

run. The project's focus on creating a green area also aligns with larger environmental initiatives, such as promoting sustainability and reducing carbon emissions. By utilizing technology to create these green spaces, the project can contribute to a larger movement towards a greener future. The project was then presented to Marco Paparusso's car workshop, immediately arousing great interest and inspiring some of the stakeholders involved to

[1] www.paparussopneumatici.it
[2] www.facebook.com/AssociazioneImpreseGarbatella

MyGarba

Prodotto di arredo urbano sviluppato in collaborazione con Fab Factory.
Grazie al prodotto si arricchisce l'esterno dei locali attraverso un sistema di verde verticalizzato con l'aggiunta di elementi coordinati di varia funzione scelti dal commerciante. Ogni modulo è pensato per suscitare interazione ed interesse sia in chi vive quotidianamente gli spazi sia in chi è di passaggio.
Le imprese che adotteranno MyGarba non solo potranno dare maggior visibilità alla loro attività, ma dimostreranno un impegno reale e concreto nella cura del quartiere, comunicando i loro valori e il loro attaccamento alla comunità territoriale.

Studenti: Alessandra La Penna, Andrea Lucchesi, Federico Maresi
Laboratorio di Sintesi, Cdl. Design. A.A. 22|23
Docente: Lorenzo Imbesi
Tutors: Luca D'Elia, Lina Monaco, Sara Muscolo, Teodora Ivkov, Francesco Scalera

SAPIENZA
Università di Roma

MakiN'
ROME

Poster of the project made by the Design team

customize and finish the prototype on their own, which became the final product right away. The practical aspect of implementation faced and overcame several challenges by focusing the designer's and involved parties' efforts on optimizing the material and production times. Practically, the board size was chosen based on the easily available sizes in dedicated sales centers. For this reason, one of the indirect effects of the project was the consideration of labor economy and the final cost of production, which were kept extremely low and accessible. Above the green vertical wall, these modules were divided by theme (e.g., the first one created integrated modules for neighborhood care and public communication like brochure holder and posters). The work team also had the opportunity to experience, during one of the material acquisitions, the limitations of materials suitable for CO_2 laser cutting. This led to carefully considering, in view of the client's acquisition of *My Garba* materials, the future creation of a series of dedicated documents. The first of these documents is a clear guide to materials and allowed treatments, to have a clear reference regarding any manufacturing and usage needs. The second guide referred to the plants the user could possibly choose from, and their needs in terms of sunlight exposition, water consumption and so on. The third and final 'instruction booklet' is the assembly manual, which also contains all the useful possible configurations. A significant development that occurred was the expression of interest from the Garbatella Entrepreneurship Association, indicating a strong desire to establish tailored and individualized offerings for its local members as a tangible demonstration of its proactive and engaged business support network.

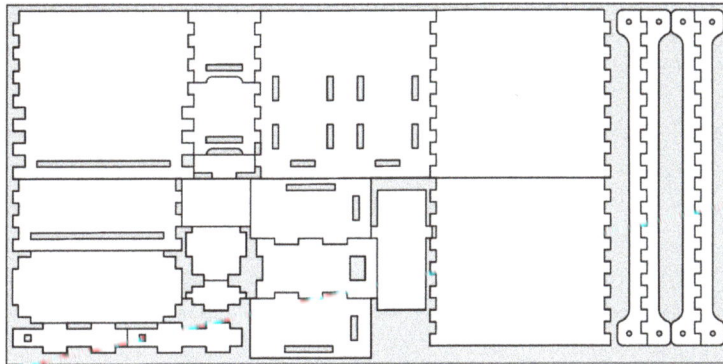

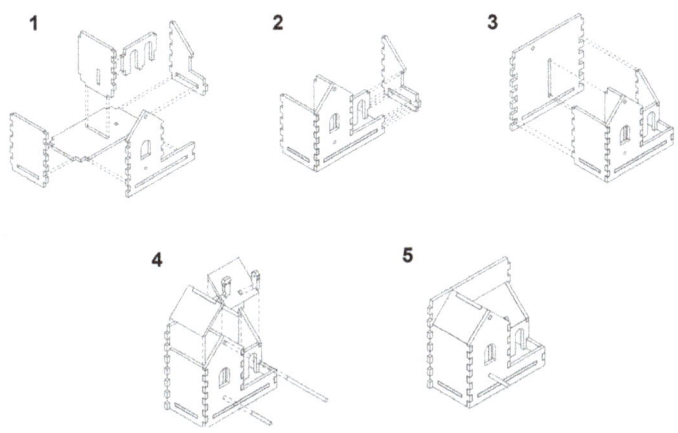

(From above) Part of the plant instruction flyer; scheme of the cutting workspace and pieces disposition; birdhouse assembling instructions.

Isola Verde

Isola Verde is a workshop designed to educate children about the creativity that can come from reusing waste materials that are produced in large quantities every day. During this activity, they will become the protagonists of the neighborhood, going around collecting coffee grounds and paper. The first phase of the workshop involves creating paper pots using molds, making the process simpler for the child. Once the pots are created, in the second phase, they can use coffee grounds instead of soil to grow sprouts inside. At the end of this phase, they can take home their plants with a tray, contained within the kit that is distributed and produced by the makerspace Famo Cose, using coffee grounds and resin.

Design team: Iannelli D., Ledda A., Velluti E.
Lab referent: Magarò L.

The project is entirely developed and conducted within the Famo Cose workshop but opens to a network of local partners and producers with whom it makes contact for the recovery of raw materials and the sharing of laboratory activities, as well as its results, which become a means of communication and mutual advertising among the residents of the Casilino neighborhood. In the first phase of analysis the working group delved into the Famo Cose's tools and equipment, noticing here as well a strong inclination towards reuse and preservation of waste materials from subtractive processes. The working group was able to identify a common (and perhaps unconscious in some cases) dynamic of self-sustenance and a sense of belonging to the Casilino and Pigneto neighborhood. This sense of belonging, common to the majority of the neighborhood's residents, also pours into actions of urban

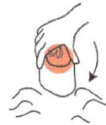

ISOLA VERDE   Pianta uno scarto

I bambini diventano artisti di strada, decorando aiuole e spazi pubblici del quartiere con le loro piantine nate dagli scarti del quartiere stesso (fondi di caffè e carta). I bambini giocano con i vasetti, che, avendo forme diverse e intercambiabili, possono essere posizionati in modo differente e creare molteplici conformazioni. Gli esercenti del quartiere beneficiano della loro partecipazione vedendo gli spazi antistanti ai loro locali, non più abbandonati a loro stessi, ma bensì trasformati in piccole isole verdi. Grazie a questa attività i bambini imparano l'importanza del riciclo e del riuso di materiali di scarto e avranno una maggiore consapevolezza del loro impatto sul quartiere, sviluppando inconsciamente una sensibilità alla cura degli spazi pubblici.
Il workshop non si limita alla dimensione del quartiere ma si allarga anche a quella domestica. Alla fine di questa attività ogni bambino tornerà a casa con un proprio kit (stampi e vassoio) con il quale potrà creare la sua piccola isola verde.

Studenti: Donato Iannelli, Alessandra Ledda, Elisa Velluti
Laboratorio di Sintesi, CdL Design, A.A. 22|23
Lab: Famo Cose - Luca Megarò
Docente: Lorenzo Imbesi
Tutors: Luca D'Elia, Lina Monaco, Sara Muscolo, Teodora Ivkov, Francesco Scalera

SAPIENZA
Università di Roma

MakiN'
ROME

Poster of the project made by the Design team

furnishings personalization that are decorated with murals, graffiti, stickers, which are 'notoriously' recognized as true works of street art (also attracting the attention of known national and international street artists). The working group therefore focused its work on developing a project that allows the development of tools for self-sufficiency. The project is finalized as a long exploratory workshop divided into three phases: the workshop begins in the Famo Cose laboratory for a quick introduction, then immediately moves to the streets of the Pigneto neighborhood. In this phase, the group of participants (for this specific experiment, made up of children and their companions/parents) recovered wastepaper from some neighborhood businesses before it was thrown away, and then brought it to the laboratory to be transformed into papier-mâché to make vases with designated shapes. The vase molds were given different geometric shapes, allowing the young participants to have different shapes and sizes of vases. This aspect will be particularly useful in the third phase, where the individual vases will compose a pattern designed by the participants themselves. The second phase involves the collection of coffee grounds, recovered from local bars and restaurants. The collected material is then divided into two parts: one part is used as soil to grow seeds, and the other part is used for a transformation process that compacts the dust and papier-mâché mixture into a mold to generate a tray that the participants can use as a "underpot" to host the papier-mache works. On the last day of the workshop, the participants can decide to bring the vases and the plants back to the Famo Cose. From there, they are guided outside the laboratory to the local green patches where the young participants are invited to plant their vase following a pattern, they have established by themselves, composing (like a puzzle) the individual vases they have made.

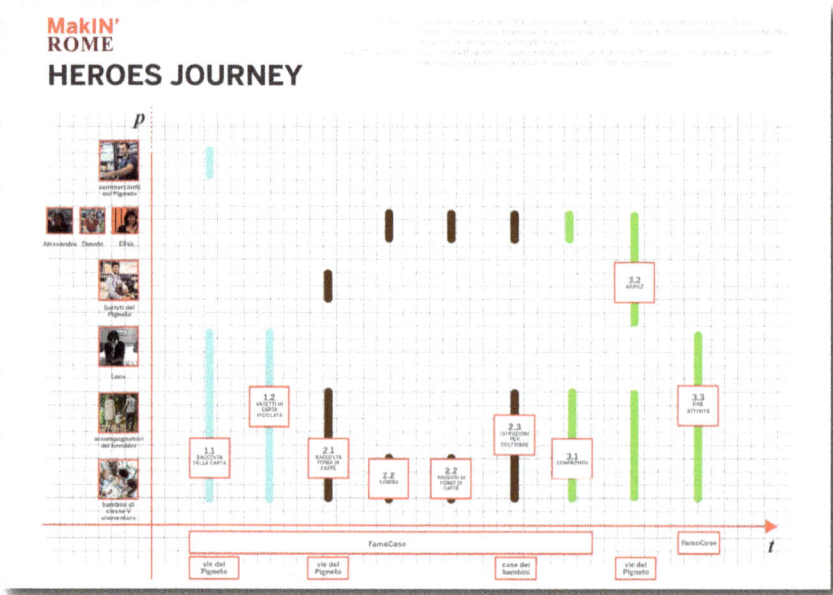

Photos shots of project during the presentation day. Photo courtesy of Teodora Ivkov.

Slab

Slab is a modular, scalable, and sustainable board system inspired by the Montessori method. Its strength lies in the experiences it offers, allowing parents and children to rediscover the traditional crafts of the neighborhood and the increasingly popular digital manufacturing machines. Through laser cutting technology and nesting processing, the product is made from simple plywood boards, minimizing waste and processing.

Design team: Mora P., Ricci E., Zannetti E.
Lab referent: Splendori A., Loparco, F.

The fundamental elements in the Slab boards are the geometric blocks, which allow children to stimulate their creativity with different compositions and serve as supports for reusing objects considered waste but sensory stimulating, according to the principle of upcycling. The blocks are also available in various kit types suggested for different ages, from one to three years, to accompany children as they grow and evolve their games on the board based on their needs.

The external analysis of the laboratory highlighted both known and unexpected issues, but the focus was on uncovering values that would cater to local needs. The research showed a thriving community consisting of young families and a significant presence of Montessorian[1] schools in the area. The laboratory's commitment to sustainable practices, as well as its focus on community building and empowerment, was evident and held significant potential for making a positive impact on the local community. The working group believed that these values were critical in meeting the needs of the neighborhood and further establishing the laboratory as a cornerstone of the local community. For the purpose of the project, it has been planned to co-build a network of partners composed of local carpentry workshops identified during the first research phase, which are trained regarding the technologies and potential of digital processes and introduced to the SLAB project. The customer journey then starts by purchasing one of the previously created construction files from the work group. After selecting their preferred shape, the website returns a map to identify the partner carpentry that can provide suitable material for the work.

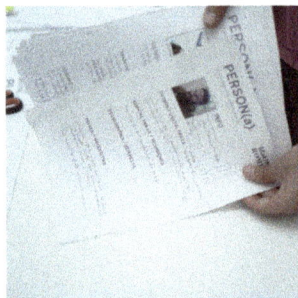

[1] Montessori's educational model is based on human development which relies on two principles: that psychological self-construction in children, which develops in adulthood, occurs through environmental interactions and that child (especially under the age of six) have an innate path of psychological development.

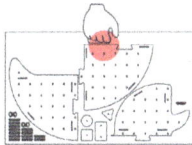

Slab

Slab è un sistema di tavole modulari, scalabile e sostenibile di ispirazione montessoriana. Il suo punto di forza sono le esperienze che offrono, permettendo a genitori e bambini di riscoprire le realtà artigianali del quartiere e le sempre più diffuse macchine di fabbricazione digitale. Tramite la tecnologia del taglio laser e la tecnica di lavorazione nesting il prodotto è ricavato da semplici tavole di compensato riducendo al minimo le lavorazioni e gli scarti. Fondamentali nelle tavole Slab sono i tasselli geometrici, che permettono ai bambini di stimolare la creatività con composizioni sempre diverse, oltre fungere da supporti per il riutilizzo di oggetti considerati di scarto ma sensorialmente stimolanti, secondo il principio dell' upcycling. I tasselli sono disponibili anche in kit di vari tipi suggeriti per diverse età, da uno a tre anni, per accompagnare i bambini durante la loro crescita evolvendo i giochi sulla tavola in base alle loro necessità

Studenti: Paolo Mora, Eleonora Ricci, Edoardo Zannetti
Laboratorio di Sintesi, CdL Design, A.A. 22|23
Docente: Lorenzo Imbesi
Tutors: Luca D'Elia, Lina Monaco, Sara Muscolo, Teodora Ivkov, Francesco Scalera

SAPIENZA
UNIVERSITÀ DI ROMA

MakiN'
ROME

Poster of the project made by the Design team

The carpentry workshop (empowered by the knowledge provided by OZ laboratory workshops), produces the shapes on demand and notifies the customer once they are ready.

Meanwhile, during the first phase described above, the parent is invited to collect a series of broken or unused household items, which will later be brought to a dedicated workshop where they will be evaluated and inserted into the previously created kit. The parent is then invited to participate in a first workshop where they are introduced to the basics of digital fabrication using laser cutting and CNC, followed by a quick 2D modeling module on the computer where the shapes that will generate the "puzzle" will be modeled. Once worked, the modules are then picked up by the customer who can start the workshop phase involving both adults and children to create customized pieces.

These pieces, as previously mentioned, will be decorated with common objects, in discussion with the child, and will allow the child to safely interact with and explore its tactile, visual, and auditory characteristics, as well as personalize their play experience. With its instructions directly engraved on the boards, the educational value of Maker practices in this project has been particularly highlighted, since knowledge transfer looks at both the adult and the new generation.

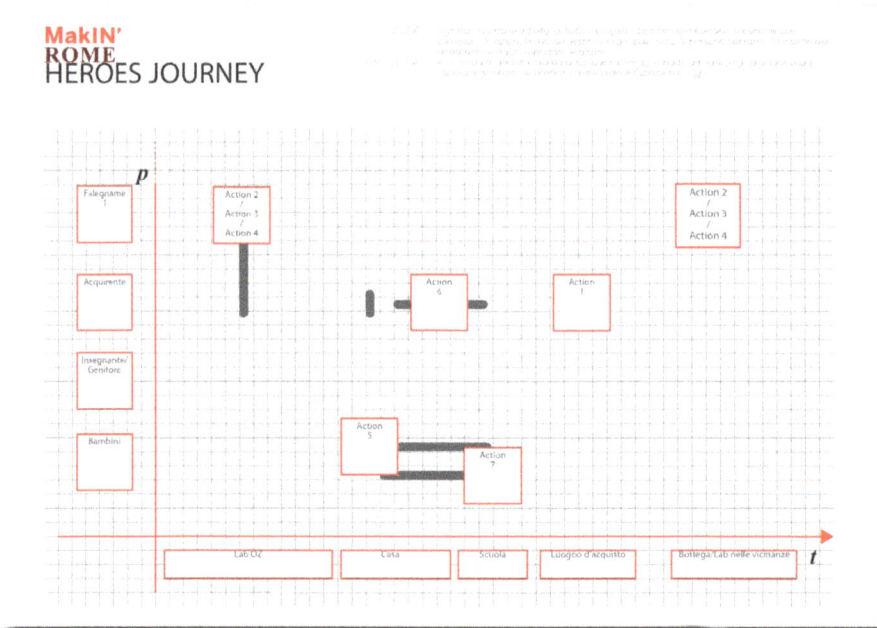

MakIN'
ROME
HEROES JOURNEY

Photos shots of project during the presentation day. Photo courtesy of Teodora Ivkov.

FitBox

Design team: Barberis L., Cibotaru C. G., Guarnieri E.
Lab referent: Splendori A., Loparco, F.

FitBox is an urban fitness product co-designed with local sports communities. It operates at multiple levels of environmental and social values, made exclusively with natural and recyclable materials, and by attracting the sports communities who lives the surroundings of the parks. FitBox is designed to support and create communities: its 'monolithic' presence in the Ionio neighborhood park positions it as a totem, telling the story of the community that created it, inviting others to join in sports activities. The product is designed to be recognized as a contextually customizable advertisement in other green areas and to be used both inside and outside. It has six customizable sides with bodyweight exercises to be performed independently or with others. When closed, it becomes a training pedestal, useful for stretching, stepping, and other exercises illustrated on different sides of the cube. FitBox is a project born from the collaboration of OZ - Officine Zero, the sports community of the Ionio neighborhood of Rome managed by the personal trainer. Flavio Ales[1] and the Fercam Echo Labs association[2].

The analysis phase immediately identified, as with the previous working group, the strong presence of skills and tools that could combine carpentry with circularity and recycling themes. Despite this first common conclusion, the working group in this case found of greater interest the presence outside the workshop of a dynamic and dense urban situation, which sees different people in the surrounding green areas living in the green spaces and populating local activities. It was therefore

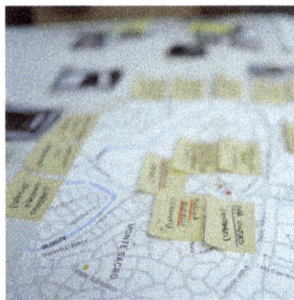

Macro shot of the mapping scheme mad by the Design Team. Photo courtesy of Teodora Ivkov.

preferred to investigate the city dimension more thoroughly in order to highlight the resources expressed by the presence of active and proactive communities within the urban space, and to question the criticisms of the neighborhood that limit and risk undermining the quality of life. The project thus identified a series of easily obtainable materials (in this case, wooden pallets from the Fercam association) for the construction of panels designed specifically for the construction of a multi-functional base in response to the exercises indicated by the personal trainer.

[1] www.facebook.com/pages/Fit%20Club%20Salario/101059689548689/
[2] www.echolabs.fercam.com/it

Fit Box Un progetto pensato dagli sportivi, per gli sportivi.

Apri, scopri, crea! Fit Box è un progetto d'intervento urbanistico tattico, nato nel quartiere Jonio dalla collaborazione di Design La Sapienza e Officine Zero. Lo scopo è quello di incentivare la creazione, l'ampliamento e il mantenimento di contesti sociali e la loro identificazione all'interno dei parchi pubblici delle città. Fit Box è una scatola pliometrica eco-sostenibile, perche realizzata con pallet recuperati. Si può utilizzare da chiusa, come box pliometrica e supporto per lo stretching, ma anche da aperta in quanto presenta esercizi a corpo libero incisi sulle sue facce interne. Gli esercizi, vengono scelti da una comunità di sportivi locale, durante un workshop di tre giorni, nei laboratori di Officine Zero. Fit Box può essere riparata, mantenuta e aggiornata dai gruppi stessi, tramite ulteriori workshop; una volta inserita nel parco, svela ai cittadini curiosi quali attività vengono svolte dalle comunità di sportivi, favorendo nuove connessioni sociali.

Studenti: Cosmin - Gabriel Clubotaru, Elena Gaurnieri, Lorenzo Barberis.
Laboratorio di Sintesi, CdL Design, A.A. 22|23
Docente: Lorenzo Imbesi
Tutors: Luca D'Elia, Lina Monaco, Sara Muscolo, Teodora Ivkov, Francesco Scalera

Poster of the project made by the Design team

Through a reiterative refining process of the prototypes, the working group proceeded to a decisive simplification of the product, also finding in the laboratory activities conducted with the involved *PERSON(a)s* a need to leave as much customization of the product open. This was designed to be made entirely of recycled wood, mainly extracted from discarded decking boards. Through a series of laboratory activities conducted with each member of the different involved associations, the effort conducted by each figure contributes to the implementation of the product that boasts the specific contribution of all.

The first step is then the recovery of the wood from which to make the building elements guided by the joint expertise of Fercam and OZ, who select discarded pallets for their easy availability and repeatability of the process. These are then worked on by OZ in order to obtain panels useful for manual work and in CNC for which the fittings and joints necessary for box construction are made. Once the base model is obtained, it is then post-processed during a workshop organized with the local sports community that selects the exercises, the physical and graphical elements (e.g., handles, hooks, cavities, etc) necessary for their execution. At the end of this first phase, the workshop proceeds with customization through laser engraving and freehand writing to "communicate" the community.

Subsequently, after its creation, a few times passes, and the product's state and social impact are checked through interviews. It is hypothesized that the box connects solitary athletes with training communities and other sports communities are encouraged to make their own box. Another aspect taken into consideration is the care of the object, which is hypothesized to be greater given the bond with the community and the skills acquired in the workshop by the participants.

Photos shots of project during the presentation day. Photo courtesy of Teodora Ivkov.

Frames EXP

Frames EXP is (in fact) an experience that combines craftsmanship and design. A service that allows users (regardless of their background) to design and create their own frame. A workshop that focuses on creating unique, highly customizable pieces through a defined process, which increases awareness of the value of the object itself due to craftsmanship, something that is being lost in the era of mass production. The project was conducted thanks to the shared availability of the Fab Lab workshop at Spazio Attivo Roma Casilina and the local artisan workshop La Bottega Delle Cornici of Modesto Darini[1].

Design team: Randi L., Mendoza K. G., Felipe R.
Lab reforent: Mariani D., Zampieri A.

Two fundamental aspects emerge from these preliminary interviews: the first is that, despite the high production capacity of the Fab Lab, which proves capable of meeting the numerous requests not only for prototyping but also for production, it does not have an adequate space for heavy and 'dusty' work such as milling or a separate space for painting, forcing it to outsource; the second aspect is instead related to the principles of the Active Spaces network of which it is a part, which frames the physical space of the Fab Lab as a business aggregator and accelerator and for which a constant contribution is required. During the research phase outside the laboratory, the working group was able to identify laboratories of different natures, from artisan workshops to modern workshop spaces.

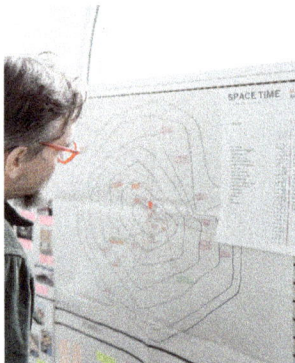

Map of the 15-minutes city area investigated by the Design Team. Photo courtesy of Teodora Ivkov.

Despite the presence of productive realities, more targeted interviews with the managers and responsible parties of these businesses showed a slow and difficult process of networking, which leads the realities almost to isolate themselves or to rely exclusively on a narrower circle of partners. While this aspect can be a guarantee of stable co-existence, the precarious general economic situation (declared by the same practitioners) seriously risks the continuity of many of the businesses that unfortunately struggle to support each other and exchange know-how to open up to new markets or simply find more economically advantageous solutions. The working group established during the interviews an extended dialogue with a

[1] www.cornicistampesangiovanni.it/laboratorio-cornici-roma.html

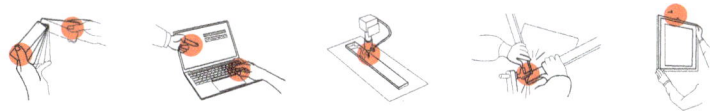

Frames EXP Design your frame.

Frames EXP è un'esperienza che unisce artigianalità e design. Un servizio che permette agli utenti di progettare e dare vita alla propria cornice, giocando con la fantasia e modificando pattern vettoriali e fotografie astratte, incidendole sulla superficie del legno. Il laboratorio è pensato per tutti, dall'arredatore che richiede un design specifico al cliente creativo che ha voglia di mettersi in gioco. Punta a creare consapevolezza sui processi di produzione che portano i prodotti nelle nostre case, e mette l'accento su di un nuovo modo di fare industria attraverso un workshop semplice e guidato. L'iter è estremamente variabile, e lo sviluppo creativo è affidato all'utente stesso. Durante tutto il processo (dall'ideazione alla produzione finale) l'utente è seguito dalle mani esperte di un corniciaio artigiano e da un operatore di macchina laser e docente Illustrator.

Studenti: Rafaela Filipe, Karl Gaddiel Mendoza, Leonardo Randi
Laboratorio di Sintesi, CdL Design, A.A. 22|23
Docente: Lorenzo Imbesi
Tutors: Luca D'Elia, Lina Monaco, Sara Muscolo, Teodora Ivkov, Francesco Scalera

SAPIENZA
Università di Roma

MakIN'
ROME

Poster of the project made by the Design team

particular artisanal reality, La Bottega Delle Cornici, whose owner and artisan, Modesto Darini, was extremely available and interested in a process of updating and experimenting with new technologies and solutions. The following weeks after the analysis phase were dedicated to engagement and direct experimentation that involved the artisan Darini and the work group in a virtuous example of mutual contamination and exchange of expertise. The design team defined the project by structuring it as a workshop designed to involve different consumer groups, from the interior designer, who requires a specific design, to the creative customer, who wants to get involved in the process of creating a truly personalized object. It aims to create awareness of production processes and emphasize the new way of doing industry, through a simple and guided design laboratory. The design process is extremely variable, and creative development is left to the user himself. During the entire process (from ideation to final production), the user is assisted by the skilled hands of a frame maker and the machine operator and graphic teacher. Users can therefore choose to participate in the workshop in two ways: by following the "Full Workshop," a four-hour training activity in a single day, where users are introduced to the world of vector illustration through an introductory course followed by a tutorial on using the laser cutting machine, to learn the basics of use; or by participating in the "Light Workshop," aimed at customer autonomy, where a laboratory expert guides participants through a two-hour tutorial on using the laser cutting machine, illustrating calibration procedures and the basics of management software.

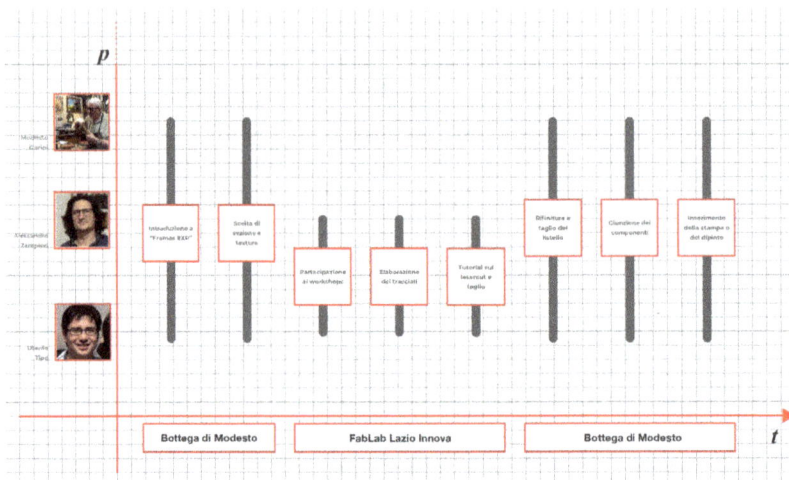

Photos shots of project during the presentation day. Photo courtesy of Teodora Ivkov.

Design team: Faella A., Gassani G., Mauro M.
Lab referent: Niro V.

Playgroundify

Playgroundify is a design kit for playground design. With this kit, the user will be able to design and configure their own green area, adding games, furnishings, and creating paths, stamps, and patterns on the flooring. This project, aimed at adults and children, allows the approach to the world of public space design, contributing to the investigations for the redesign of play areas. The project empowers the citizen who becomes a participatory designer of the urban space by providing enabling tools that are also highly guided to increase accessibility. *Playgroundify* was made inside the 3DZ Rome laboratory, tested with the citizens of the Balduina neighborhood in Rome, supported by the neighborhood association network of Balduina's[1] and sponsored by the business incubator Seedble[2].

The design team found the lateral activity of the laboratory, which designs, produces, and sells custom figures through its brand line HDModels[3] particularly interesting, as well as the presence of various neighborhood initiatives in the surroundings that focus on different levels of local development (from natural spaces to local business support). These aspects paint a clear picture of a purely vibrant and growing locality aimed at promoting and advocating for sustainable and responsible interaction between citizens and local resources (natural, energy, and infrastructural).

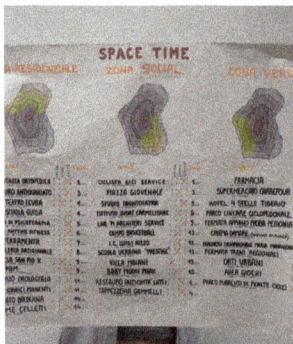

Map of the 15-minutes city area investigated by the Design Team divided as per three-place category.
Photo courtesy of Teodora Ivkov.

Thanks to the acknowledgment of those realities, it has been hypothesized that the result of the Tinkering experiment itself could be the project, consisting of a series of interventions that examine the potential involvement of younger individuals in crafting activities that could lead to a deeper understanding of the impact of public spaces on citizens and, conversely, the potential impact that citizens could have on these places. This latter part was then tested and validated in the third review.

The final project was carried out at the event held on December 18th, 2022, during the neighborhood Christmas fair. The experience was carried out using a special kit of tools consisting of a board with a thin ferromagnetic metal core on which a sheet

[1] www.balduina.org/
[2] https://seedble.com/
[3] https://hdmodels.it/

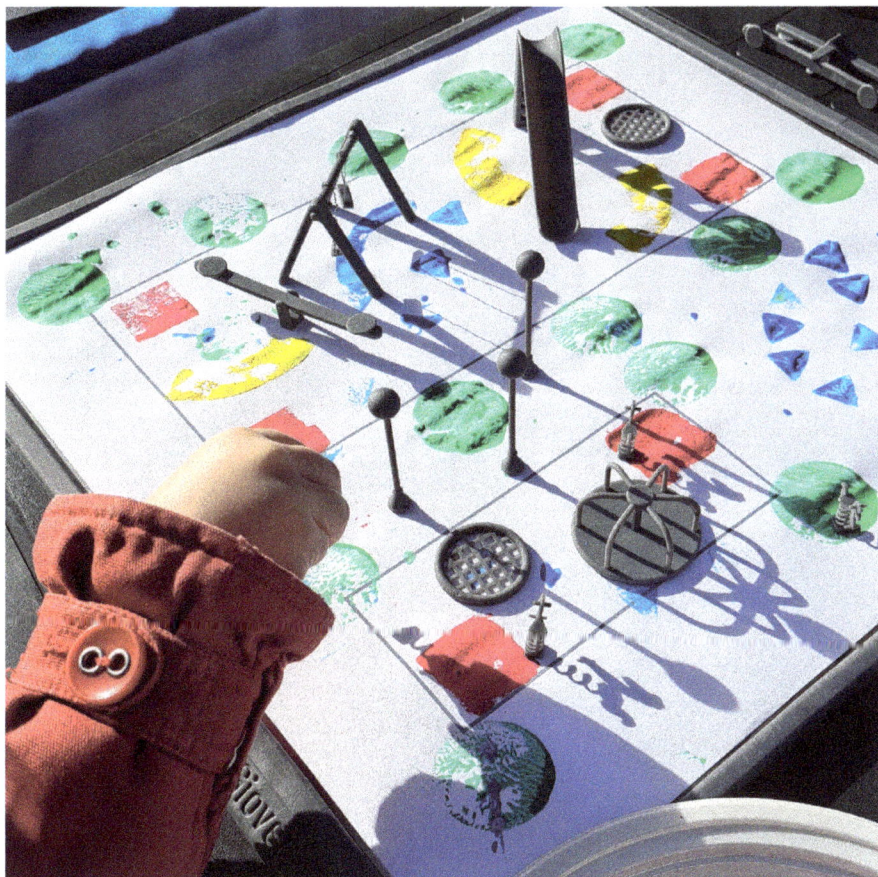

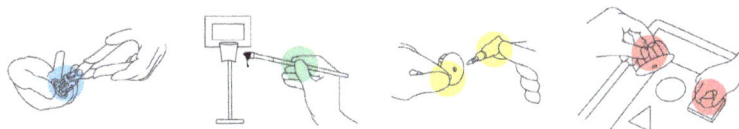

Playgroundify Kit di Design per lo Spazio Pubblico

Playgroundify è un kit di design per la progettazione di parchi giochi. Attraverso questo kit l'utente sarà in grado di progettare il parco giochi dei suoi sogni, inserendo giochi, elementi di arredo e realizzando, attraverso timbri, percorsi e pattern sulla pavimentazione. Questo progetto, destinato ad adulti e bambini, consente l'approccio al mondo del design per lo spazio pubblico, dando un contributo alle indagini per la riprogettazione delle aree gioco. Playgroundify, realizzato con l'aiuto di 3DZ, è stato testato dai cittadini del quartiere romano Balduina, che avranno la possibilità di partecipare a workshop per la realizzazione del kit. Partendo dalla rimozione dei supporti di stampa fino all'assemblaggio dei vari pezzi, l'obiettivo è quello di avvicinare i cittadini al mondo dei Makers.

Studenti: Andrea Faella, Giacomo Gassani, Martina Mauro
Lab: 3DZ - Vincenzo De Niro
Laboratorio di Sintesi, CdL Design, A.A. 22|23
Docente: Lorenzo Imbesi
Tutors: Luca D'Elia, Lina Monaco, Sara Muscolo, Teodora Ivkov, Francesco Scalera

SAPIENZA
UNIVERSITÀ DI ROMA

MakiN'
ROME

Poster of the project made by the Design team

was placed for each participant, depicting a map of the local neighborhood park divided into walkable areas, sports and play areas for children (these latter being predominantly characterized by an anti-impact covering). Each participant was then equipped with two sets: a set of stamps – each depicting a particular pattern or symbol (i.e. a leaf, a circle, a triangle, a square) accompanied by a tempera color palette; one of miniatures of urban furnishings (benches, street lights, fountains), games (swings, spring seats, slides) and sports (basketball hoops, soccer goals) each with a small magnet to adhere to the ferromagnetic base. During the event, the working group asked young participants and their parents to configure and customize their park idea.

An interesting interaction that took place during the workshop (confirming the hypotheses made during the experimentation phase) was when the parents at the end of the workshop insisted on affixing small written indications using post-its, to indicate more specific possible improvements and suggest different types of implementations. On this occasion, the group intercepted several families with children aged five to ten who were able to interact with the product and provide useful project insights to the neighborhood association.

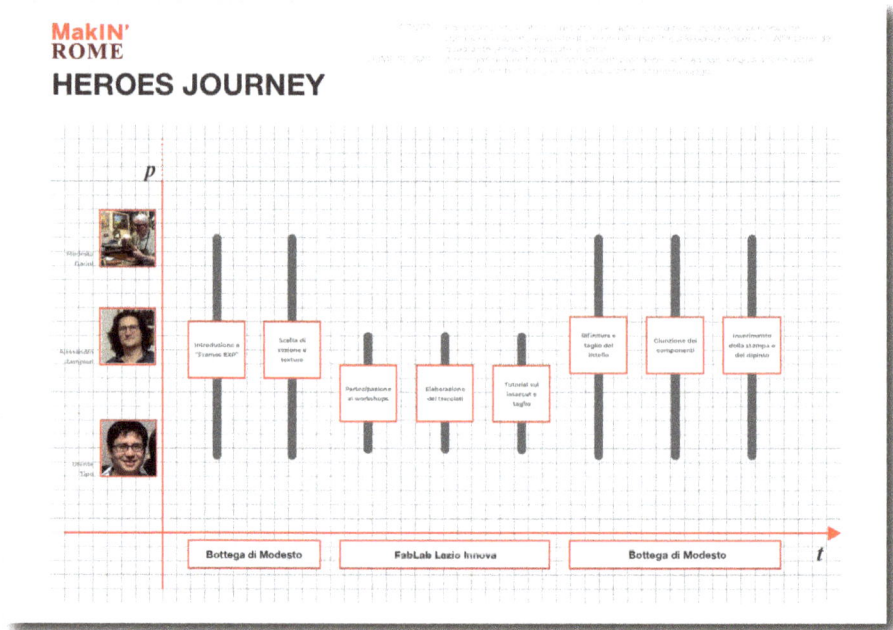

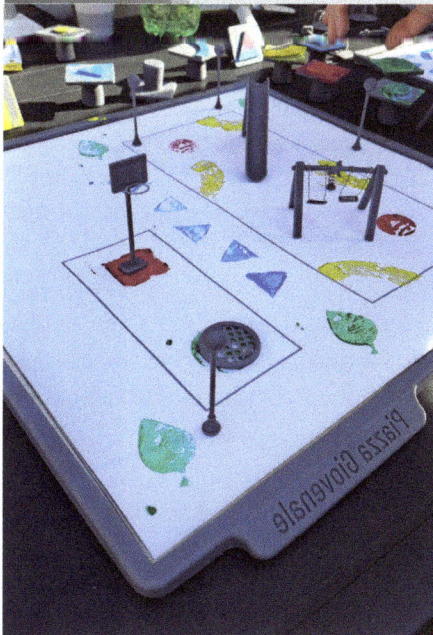

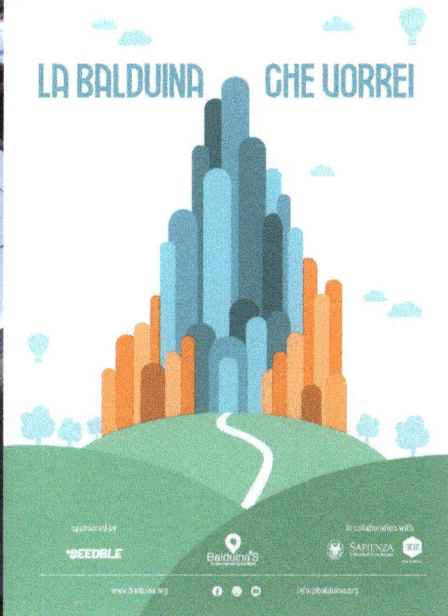

(From above) Photo of project during the presentation day (photo courtesy of Teodora Ivkov); photo of project during the workshop held by the Design team (photo courtesy of the Design team); flyer graphic

Design team: Marani G., Miglietta A.
Lab referent: Tassinari S.

Gabyrinth

Garbyrinth is a game representative of the Garbatella neighborhood. It can be played by up to four people, positioned along the sides of the game, each of whom will be assigned a different color (orange, blue, red, green). To score a point, you must drop the ball into the hole belonging to your team's color, and the winner will be the one who reaches the maximum score decided at the beginning of the game first. The game showcases some of the characteristic references of the neighborhood: the Cavallo Pazzo park, where the game is located, the metro station, the Carlotta fountain, the Settimia Spizzichino bridge, the market, the Palladium theatre, the mural created for the centenary of Garbatella, and the FabFactory where it was built.

The design team discovered that there was a strong attachment to the territory and a tenacious social fabric in the community, but many residents felt limited in their ability to participate in outdoor activities due to a lack of places for open-air activities and a general degradation of public spaces. The findings of the first phase led the project team to make a significant investment in a long-term project aimed at promoting greater community engagement and environmental awareness. The team proposed the development of a project that would possibly encourage residents to participate in outdoor activities and discover the Garbatella neighborhood. The first concept was created to simulate a series of 'games' with some neighborhood children involved in a series of short workshops aimed at building their own set of public games that revolved around the concept of 'discovery'. The starting point was therefore to work on the construction of "installations/dashboards" that would allow the completion of a path to discover the park.

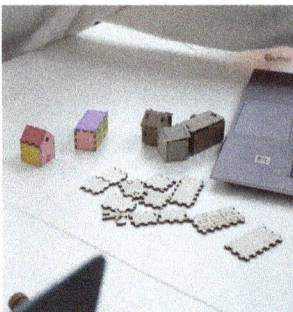

Some prototype pieces of the building blocks.
Photo courtesy of Teodora Ivkov.

The project was then defined as a proposal consisting of two training workshops specifically designed for groups of six children between the ages of five to ten (whose participation is accompanied by parents and/or guardians):

'*Costruisci il tuo quartiere*' ('Build your neighborhood') is the first training workshop in which digital wood cutting laser processing is introduced. The children and accompanying adults will then be introduced to a kit of flat wooden blocks built through a series of laser cut wooden plane pieces of about 4x3 cm.

Garbyrinth

Garbyrinth è un gioco rappresentativo del quartiere Garbatella. Si può giocare fino a un massimo di 4 persone, posizionate lungo i lati del gioco, a ciascuna delle quali verrà assegnato un colore diverso (arancione, blu, rosso, verde). Per segnare un punto si dovrà far cadere la pallina nel foro appartenente al colore della propria squadra, vincerà chi raggiungerà per primo il punteggio massimo deciso all'inizio della partita.
Il gioco espone alcuni dei riferimenti caratteristici del quartiere: il parco Cavallo Pazzo, in cui il gioco è situato, la fermata della metro, la fontana Carlotta, il ponte Settimia Spizzichino, il mercato, il teatro Palladium, il murales realizzato per il centenario di Garbatella ed il FabFactory in cui è stato costruito.

Studenti: Giorgia Marani, Alessia Miglietta
Lab: FabFactory - Silvio Tassinari
Laboratorio di Sintesi, CdL Design, A.A. 22|23
Docente: Lorenzo Imbesi
Tutors: Luca D'Elia, Lina Monaco, Sara Muscolo, Teodora Ivkov, Francesco Scalera

SAPIENZA
Università di Roma

MakIN'
ROME

Poster of the project made by the Design team

With this kit, the participants are guided in the construction of building models that, thanks to the modularity of the simple blocks, can have different shapes and sizes (making sure they are suitable for the second workshop). After assembly and painting, the children will position their work inside the Garbyrinth map. The workshop then ends with the construction of the labyrinth that will be the basis of the game that will be set up by the laboratory separately.

'*Impara anche tu a modellare*' ('Learn to model') is the second training workshop focused on 3D printing. Following a first rapid introduction by the laboratory managers on filament printing and modeling in Tinkercad (for which pre-set programs are established), the children and accompanying adults model a geometry that will become the personalized handle of the game and that the child can decide to take with them to the park when they want to play. Once the activity is completed, the models are printed and distributed to the children.

The ultimate result of these activities will be the installation of a series of personal games in which children can find their own buildings positioned on the map, depicting the neighborhood of Garbatella with some of its most historic buildings, but in which the child can glimpse their personal contribution. On the other hand, the personalized and removable handle will make the child feel more 'owner' of that part of the park and city, instilling a new sense of belonging to public space.

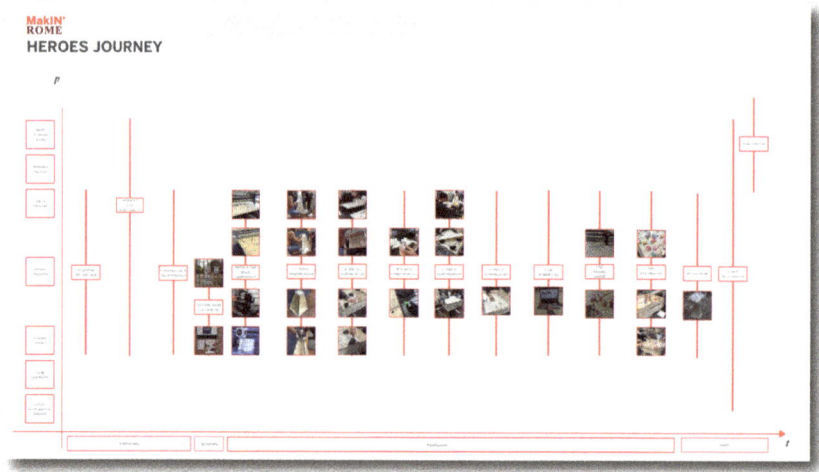

(From the top and lower-left) photo of product exposed during the presentation day. Photo courtesy of Teodora Ivkov; Flyer graphic made by the Design Team

Tavoludico

Design team: Perugini A., Quartucci M., Sale G.
Lab referent: Mariani D., Zampieri A.

Tavoludico is a pub table designed to hold board games and social games inside contained in its four doors that also form the tabletop itself. The product's aesthetic is meant to be consistent with its practical application of being a table and a container, appearing playful and cheerful but still maintaining appropriate formal sophistication. Tavoludico is designed to connect three realities in the Pigneto neighborhood in Rome to encourage the creation of a new production network. In this project, the skills of the Fab Lab Spazio Attivo Roma Casilina, Spring Lab by Paola Primavera[1], a craft laboratory with a strong focus on upcycling, and Mr. Ibis Ludopub[2], which kindly offered to test the project by providing a solid case study and further contributing through development suggestions, converge.

The workshop, designed to generate a network of various realities, is identified in a "style exercise" that sees participants competing to develop skills, know-how, technologies, and guidelines for the creation of a highly personalized and customizable product. The process is structured into eight phases that start with the engagement of participants intercepted within the spaces of the ludopub, who will then sign up for the workshop. The ludopub, aware of the number of participants, makes available its wooden wine boxes that the venue often receives from suppliers and equally often must throw away despite the valuable material. Participants are then invited to the nearby Casilina Fab Lab, where they will be greeted by Alessandro,

Workshop carried on with the Design Team and Paola Primavera inside the Casilina Fab Lab.

the manager, and reference person for the working group for this project, and Paola, a designer from Springlab.

The first phase of the workshop will focus on the craft and artistic aspect where Paola will show and guide participants in cleaning, restoring, and decorating through resin casts of the boxes. The second part of the workshop deals with digital processing, where Alessandro introduces a few simple commands from the modeling program for the generation of basic geometries that will generate the distinctive leg of the table (the trademark of the Springlab).

[1] https://springlab.art/
[2] https://www.misteribis.it/

TAVOLUDICO costruisci con noi il tuo Tavoludico personalizzato

Tavoludico

Poster of the project made by the Design team

The first day of the workshop ends by leaving the resin elements to dry and the prints to be realized (as a process that requires a few hours). It will then be the ludo-pub to retrieve the tables and make them available inside its venue for an inaugural day with the workshop participants (and of course the regular clientele).

The project therefore allows participants to "settle" within the meeting place and become a small part of it, thus encouraging a sense of belonging to that space and sensitivity to the concept of common good in this small laboratory space.

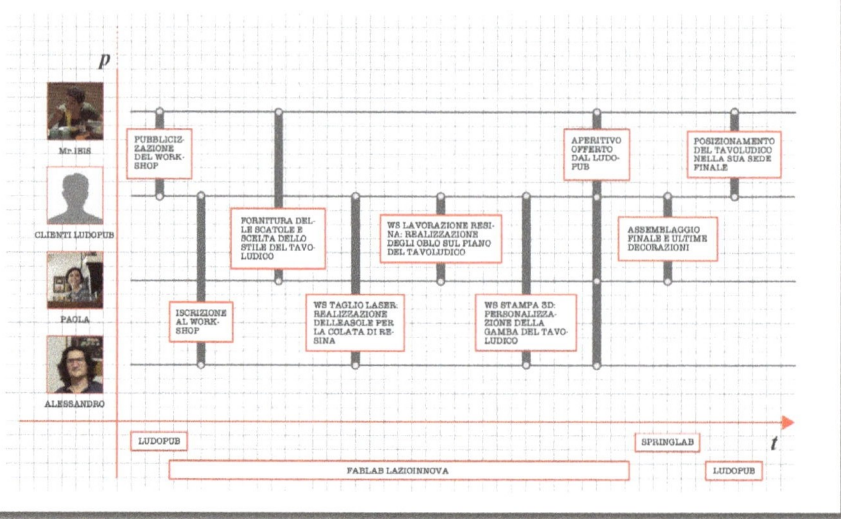

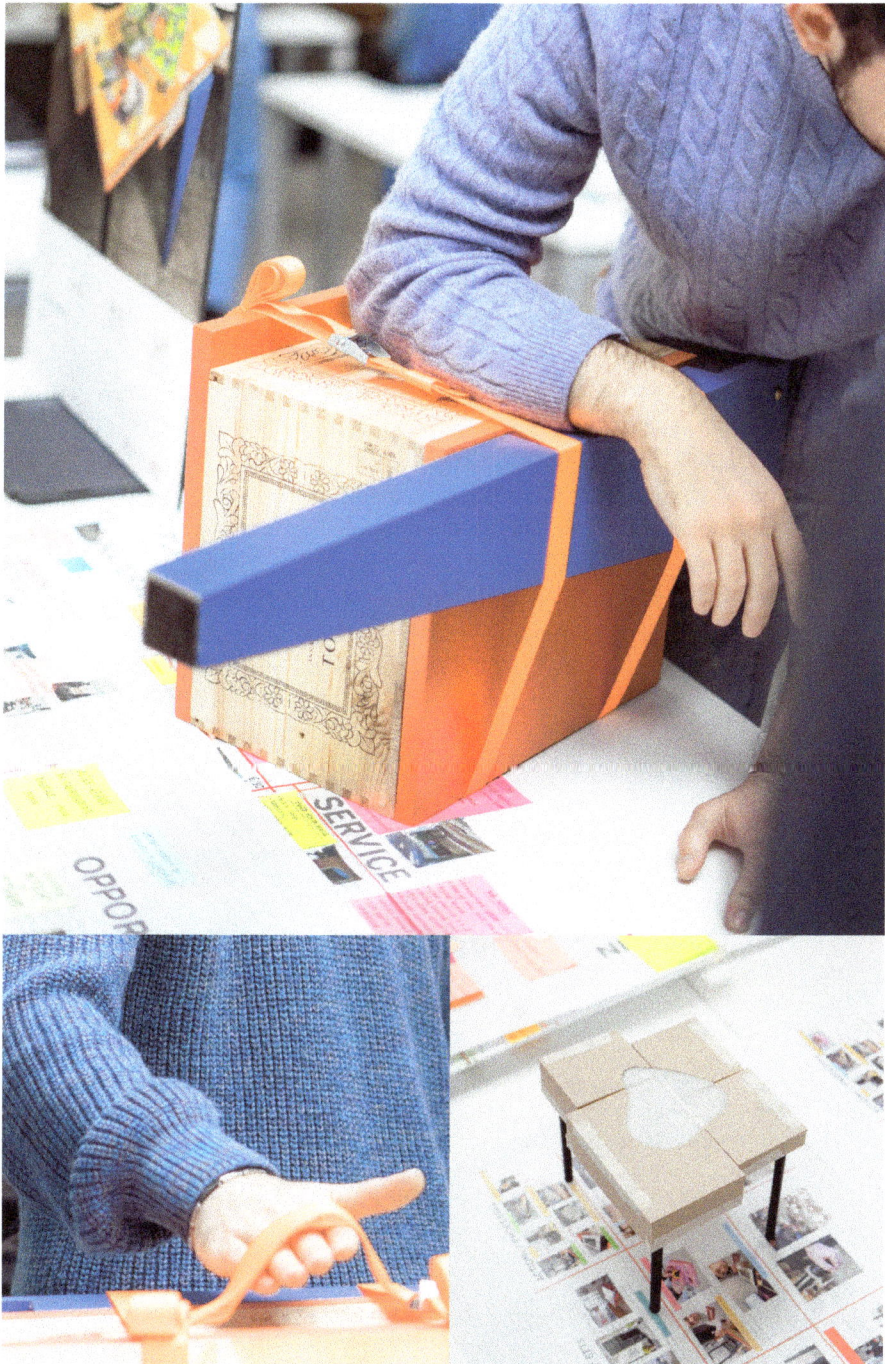

Photos shots of project taken during the presentation day. Photo courtesy of Teodora Ivkov.

8.7 What is left?

As part of the validation of the effectiveness of the tool just presented, at the end of the laboratory process, the Research Department submitted a questionnaire to the designers to evaluate the impact that the set of tools had on their design and relative practicality of use. To do this, a Likert method was adopted (Joshi et al., 2015) which integrated, among the various questions relating to the precise impacts of the project and the relational experience with the individual laboratories involved, a specific section dedicated to the System Usability Scale (SUS). The use of SUS has become prevalent in various industries (Brooke, 2013) as a practical and reliable tool for measuring perceived ease of use, and it can be used across a broad range of digital products and services to help UX practitioners determine if there is an overall problem with a design solution. Unlike something like a usability report, SUS is not diagnostic and is used to provide an overall usability assessment measurement[1]. SUS is favored for its ease of administration and reliability on small sample sizes, along with its ability to differentiate between usable and unusable systems[2]. However, it is important to keep in mind that interpreting the scores can be complex, and the scoring system should not be interpreted as percentages. Normalizing the scores to produce a percentile ranking is the best way to interpret results. The SUS questionnaire consists of ten items that participants score on a scale of 1 to 5. The items are:

1. *I think that I would like to use this system frequently.*

2. *I found the system unnecessarily complex.*

3. *I thought the system was easy to use.*

4. *I think that I would need the support of a technical person to be able to use this system.*

5. *I found the various functions in this system were well integrated.*

6. *I thought there was too much inconsistency in this system.*

7. *I would imagine that most people would learn to use this system very quickly.*

8. *I found the system very cumbersome to use.*

9. *I felt very confident using the system.*

10. *I needed to learn a lot of things before I could get going with this system.*

[1] As defined by ISO 9241-11
[2] SUS was developed as part of the usability engineering program in integrated office systems development at Digital Equipment Co Ltd., Reading, United Kingdom

The SUS is therefore a Likert scale, but the construction of a Likert scale is not as straightforward as simply using forced-choice questions on a point scale. To construct a Likert scale, extreme examples are identified to capture attitudes, and a sample of respondents rates a pool of potential questionnaire items based on these examples.

The items with the most extreme responses are selected for the Likert scale, with half of them being positively worded and the other half being negatively worded to prevent response biases. The SUS provides a single score that reflects the overall usability of the system being evaluated. It's important to note that the scores for individual items do not have any meaning on their own. Based on Brooke (1995) work, to calculate the SUS score, it is required to add up the score contributions from each item, which can range from 0 to 4.

The score contribution for items in odd questions (OqS) 1, 3, 5, 7 and 9 is equal to the scale position minus 1, while for items in even position (EqS) 2, 4, 6, 8 and 10, it is equal to 5 minus the scale position. Once the sum of the scores is revealed, it has to be multiplied by 2.5 to obtain the final SUS score, which ranges from 0 to 10. Therefore:

$$OqS = (Q1-1)+(Q3-1)+(Q5-1)+(Q7-1)+(Q9-1) = SUM(Qn) - 5$$

$$EqS = (5-Q2)+(5-Q4)+(5-Q6)+(5-Q8)+(5-Q10) = 25 - SUM(Qn)$$

$$SUS\ Score = (OQ+EQ) \times 2.5$$

To give an example of scoring:

$$OqS = (4+5+3+4+3) = 19 - 5 = 14$$

$$EqS = (2+1+3+1+1) = 25 - 8 = 17$$

SUS Score would be: $(14+17) \times 2.5 = 77.5$

The survey in question was structured with 16 multiple-choice questions (introduced by a first request for authorization for data processing and concluded with a final open ended question that allowed responders to add a personal comment on the experience as a whole).

As previously mentioned, all questions followed a Likert structure with values ranging from 1 to 5 and were structured into four sessions referring to: the experience of individual designers before the Lab (Before the Lab); the experience with the adopted tools (On Adopted Tools); a self-evaluation of the project impacts (On Your Project); the impact that this experience had on their future perspectives (At the End of the Lab).

Regarding the tool, the initial screening of the adopted tools revealed a strong inclination of Design to positively evaluate the impact and interaction with people, reporting a 'degree of satisfaction' index (to be understood as a rediscovered usefulness in the systematization of information) more focused on the *PERSON(a)* cards related to people. The spatial dimension was less interesting, instead focusing more on the laboratory space as a container for "dusty" activities, technologies, and technical skills useful for product realization. Over 50% of respondents expressed the need to always have a synthesis tool readily available, particularly when dealing with complex information flows generated during the initial analysis phase. The SWOT analysis, though new to all working groups, proved successful in identifying focal points that formed the basis of the subsequent work. Notably, 30% of the laboratories frequently participated in activities conducted by designers, and only 20% reported a constant and continuous working relationship.

The Research considers this factor not as a lack of attention on the part of the laboratories but as a disillusioned expectation on the part of students who had hoped for a more constant and participatory approach or closer contact with the machinery. Before introducing the System Usability Scale (SUS) analysis, which provides the most tangible and exploitable data for future laboratory implementations and replications, it is worth noting from the responses on possible tool implementations that new generations of designers naturally prefer digital solutions over analog ones. This approach seems to be aimed more at the immanence of information than at the ease with which it is recorded. To clarify, while the majority (90%) of respondents suggested a digital interface, compared to 66% who considered a public repository necessary, a more detailed analysis of the survey revealed that approximately 46% of respondents associated digitization with tool sharing. The last question, which predominantly requested a repository aimed at comparisons with external agents, leads to a re/evaluation of the trend of the first question that suggests digitization of the tool. This is because it highlights the value of a traditional and physical approach, rather than simply the ease of recording information. SUS scores fall into an "Acceptability Range" in which there could be identified three sectors identified by Bangor et al., (2009) as:

- *Not acceptable*, in a score range that goes from 0 to 50 – in which it is possible to find results that could be addressed as Worst imaginable (score point 25) and Poor scenario (around a score of 38);

- *Marginal*, in a score range that goes from 50 up to 70 – in which it could be possible to find Low Marginal results (up to 65 and in which it would be possible to identify those OK results around a score of 53) and High Marginal results (up to 70);

I think the tools were too inconsistent with the goals of Design

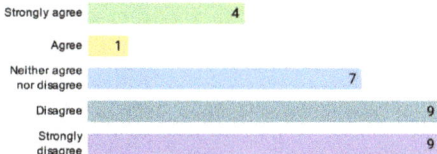

Strongly agree	4
Agree	1
Neither agree nor disagree	7
Disagree	9
Strongly disagree	9

I found the use of the tools quite intuitive

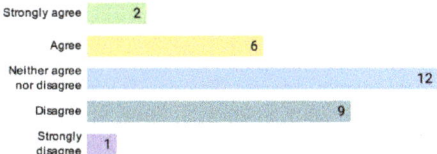

Strongly agree	2
Agree	6
Neither agree nor disagree	12
Disagree	9
Strongly disagree	1

I found technical support is needed for using the tools

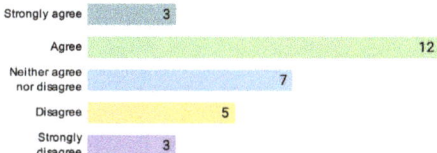

Strongly agree	3
Agree	12
Neither agree nor disagree	7
Disagree	5
Strongly disagree	3

I found other people can easily learn to use the tools

Strongly agree	5
Agree	8
Neither agree nor disagree	10
Disagree	5
Strongly disagree	2

I found the tools very cumbersome to use

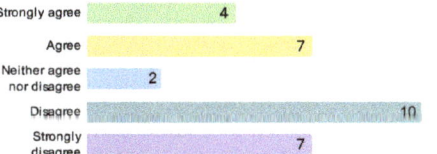

Strongly agree	4
Agree	7
Neither agree nor disagree	2
Disagree	10
Strongly disagree	7

I found the tools unnecessarily complicated

Strongly agree	4
Agree	5
Neither agree nor disagree	13
Disagree	5
Strongly disagree	3

I think I need to understand many things before considering use these tools again

Strongly agree	2
Agree	9
Neither agree nor disagree	8
Disagree	7
Strongly disagree	4

I felt very confident in using the tools

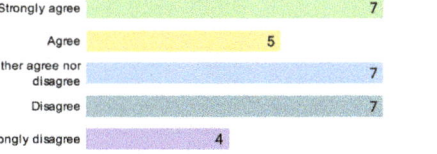

Strongly agree	7
Agree	5
Neither agree nor disagree	7
Disagree	7
Strongly disagree	4

I found that I would like to use this tools frequently

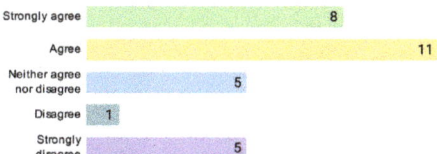

Strongly agree	8
Agree	11
Neither agree nor disagree	5
Disagree	1
Strongly disagree	5

I understood how the different functions of the tools integrate with each other

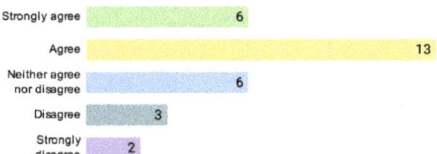

Strongly agree	6
Agree	13
Neither agree nor disagree	6
Disagree	3
Strongly disagree	2

- *Acceptable* results are gained in a score range that goes from 70 to 100 in which it could be possible to find a Good score of about 74, an Excellent score of 85, and the Best imaginable score of 100.

From the collected responses, six graphs were created to show the level of agreement and disagreement for each item of the System Usability Scale (SUS). Data analysis revealed that positive responses were higher in odd-numbered questions (OQ), while negative responses were higher in even-numbered questions (EQ).

These results suggest that there are no significant usability problems with the SUS. However, the overall score obtained is rather low, at 55.5, indicating that there is still ample room for improvement that should be explored in more depth. It is important to note that the usability of a tool can be influenced by understanding its purpose. This is particularly true for cognitive and knowledge-based tools such as the SUS, which can be frustrating if not fully understood.

The results of the data analysis show that the SUS has a slightly more than OK level of usability, therefore having still areas that can be improved. To achieve optimal results, it is necessary to do an in-depth analysis, understanding its purpose and improve the aspects that have influenced the overall score. These aspects could provide useful insights also for further researches that will tackle similar issues: moreover (in the conclusions) few tips will be given in order to give an overall foresight to glimpse futureable use of the toolkit.

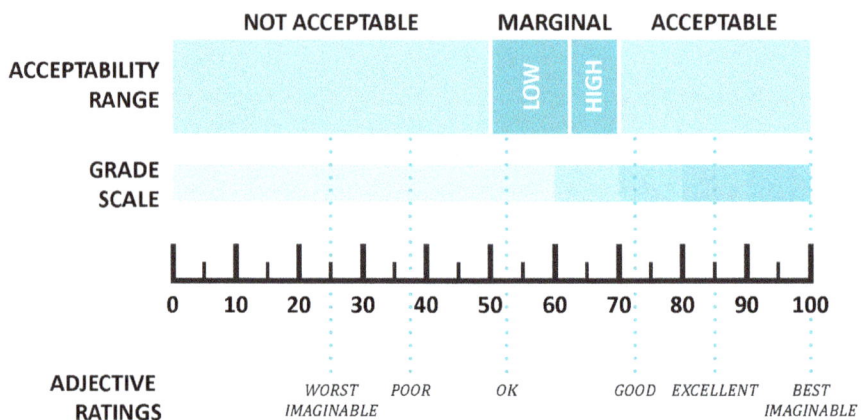

Graphic reconstruction of the SUS Acceptability scale.

LEGEND

	Value
(red)	4
(tan)	3
(yellow)	2
(light blue)	1
(grey-blue)	0

	Q1	Q2	Q3	Q4	Q5	Q6	Q7	Q8	Q9	Q10	OQ	EQ	SCORES
R1											7	13	50
R2											8	14	55
R3											6	13	47.5
R4											7	15	55
R5											10	15	62.5
R6											9	23	80
R7											11	15	65
R8											4	12	40
R9											4	15	47,5
R10											7	12	47.5
R11											9	15	60
R12											0	11	27.5
R13											-1	12	27.5
R14											6	13	47.5
R15											0	13	32.5
R16											7	19	65
R17											3	8	27.5
R18											13	24	92.5
R19											13	22	87.5
R20											4	15	47.5
R21											15	16	77.5
R22											-5	21	40
R23											9	16	62.5
R24											6	15	52.5
R25											8	18	65
R26											3	17	50
R27											7	16	57.5
R28											5	18	57.5
R29											8	14	55
R30											13	20	82.5

AVERAGE SCORE	55.5

SUS reply table

CONCLUSIONS

It should be acknowledged that the tool itself enables a fluid work path, but it is easily subject to graphic review and content adaptations by the designers who augmented information with custom elements (such as using layers of thin semi-transparent paper to visualize dynamics by breaking it down for each person and process, or by adding other papers concerning more detailed maps). The new lines of action that emerged and would possibly emerge in future simulation and undertaken in the experimental phases could therefore stimulate a review of the steps to let the tool evolve along the process. Indeed, in order to obtain results as much reliable as possible, it is advisable to ultimately carry out a review of the contents at the end of the compilation to verify the consistency of all the fields and fill any deficiencies: this could lead to a possible denial of the project hypotheses and of the figures involved by finalizing the skills and improving the design capabilities of a company, with a relatively minimal risk. Each phase of the tool should be followed immediately by a pre-defined roadmap, articulating timelines and reviews of the work; considering the didactic experiences carried out, it is advisable to dedicate at least ten days to the first ethnographic phase, however avoiding diluting the analysis too much over time (no more than two weeks) since more 'rare' results make it more difficult to find the same elements in the following phases. The experimentation phases may vary according to the nature of the project and the areas identified but should not go beyond the working week (considering that the workshop activities do not last more than one day). In this case, the educational path has been undertaken, and the projects were developed in a total of four months of work (three main ones dedicated to the projects development, and one last month to resume all of them).

Going beyond the application in the academic field, next paragraphs introduce in detail how within this path we have been able to promptly respond to the some significant questions stated at the very beginning of this journey and the objectives achieved in relation to this tool set and ultimately would make possible the evolutions that can be adopted to improve the tool identifying optimized applications (such as with a more business-oriented approach).

Mapping, profiling, defining Roman Makers

The mapping process, which began in 2020, has undergone several updates, with the latest one in June 2022 revealing no substantial changes. In fact, the few new entities detected were already present in the first mapping but were initially discarded due to incomplete data.

Additionally, no significant absences were recorded among the registered entities. The forty-nine entities were distributed freely throughout the region, with a higher concentration of forty-two active labs in the metropolitan area of Rome. The specific objective of the mapping process was successfully achieved, resulting in the creation of a preliminary database that can be further developed, such as the establishment of an observatory focused on digital manufacturing and urban development. This observatory would directly address design, production, and distribution practices within individual neighborhoods and the 15-minute city concept.

The Research analyzed Maker culture practices, providing a clearer vision that could potentially aid the resilient response of the Lazio region. Starting from post-crisis scenarios, the study capitalized on the social response of makers and entrepreneurs to the previous health emergency experience. They unanimously promote new models of citizenship. This investigation, based on the census of maker entities, focusing on the distribution and quality of the maker network, and the evolution of the Maker community, revealed a set of missed opportunities and needs. These have become milestones in defining the final tool's model. The analysis of Experts profiles demonstrates that, despite a solid laboratory infrastructure, there is an unstable definition of the digital fabricator's role.

From the aforementioned considerations, three essential factors emerged from the considerations that must be considered at the foundation of citizen empowerment as makers, designers, and self-entrepreneurs:

1) Maker practice, which includes digital manufacturing technologies and Open-Source sharing practices;

2) hyper-local[1] proximity, a condition imposed during the pandemic and defined as a mediation process;

3) vertical proximity among multiple stakeholders and public administration, defined as the real empowerment of citizens in the participatory process.

Imagining a replicable general model of citizenship interaction between the Public Administration and the territory, involving citizens, makers, and experts in proposing, developing, and implementing projects, it requires defining a customizable constraint system capable of dynamically responding to hyper-localism and supporting grassroots initiatives. Operating in a distributed and still-open research field, however, entails the social responsibility of empowerment that has long declared its potential and continues to open to new ways of bringing together spontaneous and autonomous communities.

[1] The prefix hyper- brings specific meaning that should be acknowledged: from the dictionary hyper stands for "over", or "on top of" something, but still remaining within the context. For instance, other similar and more common terms such as super- (super-local) would be inappropriate since the prefix stands for something that "goes beyond" therefore out of given ground. The Research reflects that some of the mistakes made around locality are resulted from a misuse of some terms.

Design approaches and Maker technologies

Digital manufacturing has direct implications on culture and subculture evolution and production systems. Technological improvements, market development, and business model evolution towards enabling technologies implies a bases of Design approach which endorses critical thinking towards a system that develops responsible and empowering policies. While the use of sustainable materials, bioplastics, circular economy strategies challenge the everyday product production, distribution, and consumption up to the waste management, digital manufacturing provides answers to this challenge through the production of edible compounds, valid alternatives from food waste, thereby revolutionizing the technology sector itself. Despite that, if not properly designed to fit the everyday behavior, to push towards new responsible routines, those harming elements of the previous system will be an obstacle to the otherwise effective push allowed by these technological innovations. Design has been demonstrated to be more than just a disciplinary approach that facilitates an iterative process; its cognitive dimension has also provided a deeper comprehension of the dynamics and vocabulary necessary to empower citizens to engage with technology and become more sensitive.

As mentioned above, without Design, technology risks to remain a niche content; on one hand, these technologies can improve the quality of life and social participation for people with disabilities or the elderly, but on the other hand, they can increase dependence on machines and loss of autonomy. Moreover, the complexity of these technologies requires greater digital literacy to be able to use them effectively and safely. Therefore, it is important for citizens to be involved in the design and development process of enabling technologies to ensure that they meet the real needs of users and that the necessary resources are provided for their correct and conscious use. Design considers the design process to be more relevant in the face of the possibility of innovating through technology. While production processes are important, it is the design process that determines the functionality and usability of a product or technology. The design process considers the needs of the user, the constraints of the technology, and the overall goal of the product or technology. By prioritizing the design process, designers can ensure that the technology is not only innovative but also meets the needs and expectations of its intended users.

Design methods and Maker practices in Rome

Among those forty-nine realities identified in the Lazio Region, it has been possible to describe three main identities of the digital fabrication laboratory: a public one (PubO), open to everyone; a public one, but open only to specific citizens (e.g., students) or selected subjects (PubR); a private one (PrivO) which defined independently its clientele.

In this scenario, always referring to the regional context, while some approach to capitalize on digital fabrication are established, the feasibility of compensating those Makers through Open concepts is still hypothetical. Regulatory requirements for project blueprints are still unclear, which poses a challenge for the widespread implementation of Open Design. The real challenge lies in developing an economic model that lets technology generate shared value accessible to everyone. Findings shows how the post-pandemic shift led the PubO to get more interested in private and massive production field (leaving as a side effect the citizen empowering), while the frenzy and constant fear of local entrepreneurship have led private laboratories to take a greater interest in the public sphere and direct social innovation with citizens, seeking more free fields of application and consensus that fuel their entrepreneurial growth.

One of the most significant ways in which regional networks are using these technologies is by developing new applications that can be used in a variety of fields. In addition to this, some of the key projects being developed by Maker networks include Open-source prosthetics, biomaterial development and bio-based product with special organic features, educational toys and games that teach children about STEAM concepts, sustainable energy solutions for generating and storing renewable energy. It is possible to state that there are numerous networks with the Lazio Region, some of them are made by established authorities and public (already networked) realities which are always open for new opportunities and to share opportunities. This sharing, anyway, does not pass through project sharing, but instead of a continuous flow of works and consulting.

Maker culture and related economy is gaining relevance at the European level, but its impact on local policies is more noticeable in smaller territorial areas, especially at the urban or metropolitan level. In this regards, local governments play a critical role in promoting the new maker economy by intervening with policies and programs aimed at strengthening existing communities or establishing new ones. While focusing on identifying the most complete or divergent profiles in the mapping process, investigating their complexity and inclusion within an ecosystem from economic, ecological, and social perspectives, the Research confirmed as knowledge is produced in a distributed system which shares open information and data; within our local contexts they are more likely to become a "Distributed Networks Generators", which may ultimately be connected with other similar networks, promoting its sustainability on different level. Nonetheless, there are controversies around the competence and the quality of the outcomes and their relationship to basic values traditionally associated with sharing economies concepts. Findings provided a neutral and inclusive descriptive framework which lays the ground for discussing normative aspects separately and with explicit reference to normative frameworks such as sustainable development.

From an hyper-localistic view, design could operate even at urban planning and policy making level by providing punctual tools and methodologies to visualize and communicate complex data and information. With the rise of big data and the increasing availability of digital tools, urban planners and policymakers can use design to create compelling visualizations that can help them make informed decisions about the design of cities and the allocation of resources.

It is already acknowledged the increasingly important of Design role in urban planning and policy making regarding modern conditions and digital transformation. Within this context, Design can play a significant role in shaping cities that are livable, sustainable, and responsive to the needs of their inhabitants. In this sense, Design consider and generate inclusive and participatory urban planning processes, by engaging with communities and using design thinking methodologies, planners and policymakers can ensure that the needs and perspectives of all stakeholders are considered in the development of urban policies and plans. In practical and more immediate terms, by integrating sustainable design principles into urban planning and production, Design can help in reducing reduce their environmental impact and improve their ability to adapt to changing conditions. By encompassing, visualizing and engaging communities, Design can contribute to urban development and citizen empowerment by maintaining those indispensable principles of sustainability, and resilience. As cities continue to grow and evolve in the digital age, the role of Design in shaping their futures will become increasingly critical.

Designers, Makers, manufacturers

Regarding the practice of Tinkering applied to the discipline of Design, it is noted that the designer (and in this specific case, we are talking strictly about the Roman Designer) struggles to design the process without knowing the final product (even if he himself is impressed by its effectiveness). This aspect falls on the pedagogical methods of Design applied to Experts: after passing the Grundkurs[1], in this sense, tinkering practices seem to conflict with the latest approaches to design, which first want to know "where to go." This aspect is closely linked to the acceptance of error which, in addition to not being foreseen as such, is still misunderstood as an inevitable failure: which would require an even more detailed analysis of the education system starting from primary schools where (especially in Italy) the creative approach and artistic laboratories have been lost. Although in contrast to this deficiency, specific Montessori and Steiner-style institutes have been established, a large portion of the population that navigates in a world constantly searching for immediate certainties and fear of error is being left out.

---

[1] Regarding the classical tools of the Bauhaus, in addition to the basic courses (grundkurs in German), there were numerous experimental workshops that focused heavily on prototyping or experimentation with materials.

On the one hand, it could be said that this attitude leads to always having only usable results that can be spent directly in a scale economy, capable of creating and effectively managing workflows, generating networks, and efficiently managing internal resources in an increasingly conscious and sustainable way. On the other hand, the self-sufficiency of the Roman production system has not yet been reached, which, in confronting Design, focuses too much on the final product, in an excessively pragmatic way, to adequately consider the process that would lead to a purpose economy (perhaps more effective in the Roman local context). Therefore, future research believes it is necessary to question the knowledge tools of Design and evaluate experimentation in other contexts to assess their replicability and compare results (potentially validating them always with the survey used for this experimentation).

During the interviews, participants were asked about the presence of designers in the laboratories, specifically investigating their potential as "digital manufacturers": this term encompasses various aspects attributed to designers over time, such as "Maker," "digital artisan," and finally "manufacturer." While the role of the digital manufacturer is established within the laboratory spaces, it presents different facets depending on their nature. Concerns have been raised about the possible directions this figure may take at a public or official level. Interestingly, there are two opposing views on this matter. In public laboratories, digital manufacturers and manufacturing tools should be seen as an added value to pre-existing skills, which can potentially contaminate the field of digital manufacturing. Conversely, entrepreneurs and private individuals are demanding that this role be recognized at the state level. They believe that their efforts in bringing technology, expertise, techniques, and products related to this production system should be included in a recognized category of outcomes of innovation. It is noteworthy that this split in thinking has paralleled the shift in direction that laboratories have undergone towards the educational and training system. The convergence of these divergent thoughts towards the generation and distribution of knowledge could lead to new forms of consideration for the role of the manufacturer in the public context. Alternatively, as often happens, one of the two viewpoints may ultimately prevail.

"Design is a mess. And that's the framework." (Kolko, 2020)

On MakIN'Rome tool and further developments

The project has explored the benefits of focusing on the temporary aspects of autonomous spaces, temporary communities, and community-based projects. These three aspects becomes the pillar which Design should focus on. Autonomous spaces provide a place to aggregate a diverse range of citizens in a transversal way that enables beneficial contamination. These spaces are vibrant and foster a sense of community, allowing people to come together and share their skills and knowledge.

Temporary communities are the physical equivalent of online communities such as the Makers, which are present on various online repositories and social platforms. These communities form within autonomous spaces, and they provide a platform for like-minded individuals to collaborate and work towards a common goal. Finally, community-based projects are designed and implemented by members of a particular community to address local issues or concerns. These projects are often collaborative and participatory, involving community members in decision-making and implementation.

The goal of community-based projects is to empower communities to create positive change and improve their quality of life. The Research project aimed to provide a solid basis for future research work aimed at local development and civic empowerment. It has identified an initial pool of information that is often over looked or analyzed in a sporadic and inconsistent manner. By providing a systematic approach to analyzing this information, the Research project has identified the strengths and weaknesses of a given area defined by the isochrone of the 15-minutes city. This information is essential for policymakers and community organizers to develop effective strategies for improving the quality of life in their communities. The Research project highlights the importance of involving practitioners in a more meaningful way, which can lead to more effective community-based projects and, moreover, have highlighted the importance of focusing on the temporary aspects of autonomous spaces, temporary communities, and community-based projects as crucial for promoting community engagement, collaboration, and empowerment.

Based on the data collected and analyzed using the System Usability Scale (SUS), it can be concluded that the tool has a moderately acceptable level of usability. The graphs created from the responses indicated that there were no significant usability problems with the SUS. However, the overall score obtained was rather low, at 55.5, which suggests that there is still room for improvement. It is important to note that the usability of a tool can be influenced by understanding its purpose. This is particularly relevant for cognitive and knowledge-based tools such as the SUS, which can be frustrating if not fully understood. Therefore, it is recommended that further development should focus on improving the aspects that have influenced the overall score. Overall, improving the usability of the SUS tool will require a comprehensive understanding of its purpose, user testing, and continuously improvement of its design.

From a Design perspective, specific topics should be taken under consideration for further development of the aforementioned tool and the implication of Design involvement in Community-based project proposal. From the experience made with Roman design practitioners, different improving topics have emerged such as the user testing reiteration, data distribution, improved instructional material and feedback loop design.

A second level of 'design-led' investigation leads to a more sensitive identification of critical issues and application of resources, but only after a first phase that necessarily involves a more 'obvious' experimentation, confirming the value of rough prototypes. The SUS has highlighted several critical issues related to the tool, which will be the subject of future investigation and implementation. Compared to the laboratory experience conducted with the laboratories in the city of Rome, it may be useful to capitalize on the considerations presented in this book as a starting point for that researches that investigate educational technologies (Chimalakonda and Nori, 2020; Gruzdeva et al., 2020; Vlachogianni and Tselios, 2022) and STEAM pedagogical systems (Bautista, 2021; Henriksen et al., 2019; Spyropoulou et al., 2022). The development of the conceptual design methods and tools presented have the potential to make a significant impact on the Design process and education. By providing designers with a framework for conceptualizing and developing projects that find direct correlation with real and practical needs or potentials, the results of this journey can help to ensure that designers are more coherent and consistent, while also reducing the risk of errors and omissions.

However, to fully realize the benefits of this approach, it is necessary to conduct further research and dissemination efforts. It is important to verify the efficacy of the new knowledge generated through this approach in 'other' real-world. This will help finding insights to upgrade the original base while ensuring benefits for the designers, for the Makers and citizens (intended as communities) from the insights and innovations generated through this work. It is important to disseminate the research findings to a broad audience, including not only the academic community but also the aforementioned stakeholders to enhance the overall quality of Design practices and promote greater collaboration and Innovation in the Maker field.

Moreover, and finally, it is not possible to not consider Munari's words, remembering us that nothing is never obvious until it comes in front of us, and if we do not share these practices, or if we do not confront each other, those simple gestures will be so "obvious" the would become mistakenly irrelevant. As Munari said:

> *"When someone says: 'I could have done that too,' it means that they can redo it, otherwise they would have already done it before." (Munari, 1992)*

So Long...

"[...] Like in the stone that Euripides called "Magnet" [...] Also, this stone, in fact, not only attracts iron rings, but also infuses a force into the rings themselves, so that they can, in turn, produce the same effect as the stone and attract other rings. And in this way, sometimes, a long chain of rings is formed that take from each other. And all of them depend on the strength of that stone!" (Platone, Ione, 533d, p. 1027)[1]

The increasing growth of knowledge and related competence in the Design field is seeing the figure of the designer almost split into entities that are increasingly highly specialized in micro-disciplines (as happens in everything else) where we no longer talk about 'discovery', but 'rediscovery'. The designer moved from the material to the immaterial, developing complex tools of thought and cognition (sometimes overly so) to be able to take the existing and reprogram it. No longer inventors, but innovators, only a few of those designer 'magicians' remain of whom Santachiara speaks. The designer, in fact, has always been considered a more liquid figure, a profession that has been able to move and evolve over time, in society and in the dynamics of everyday life. Design itself is the evolutionary result of disciplines that have split and reunited over time, assimilating, and treasuring an essential part of the latter at each evolutionary 'leap', but above all leaving an indelible and unmistakable mark of their passage in the dynamics of companies, production, economies, and social dynamics. Since its emancipation as an autonomous discipline, it has cultivated its own culture of design and designing, becoming increasingly interdisciplinary, multidisciplinary, and transdisciplinary. The designer has evolved to a level of complexity such that they always find a completely personal way to define themselves. Designers are the expression of their own practice, of their own research into Design itself. Influenced as much by the past as by aspirations for the future world. And today we find these cognitive tools in those everyday object that we build when we are sold "deconstructed", that we hack when they break or repair with DIY practices, that we personalize with rapid modelling programs and indoor CNC machines. We are designers even when we don't know it, sometimes diluted in routine, but we do not go unnoticed. On the contrary, as well as we cannot talk of a designer behind the product anymore, the designer is the product. And if it is true that we can all design, and, as Paul Rand said, "everything is Design", as for Plato's 'stone', designers should always attract those rings of this mesh that is the city, the society, and (why not?) the world. Wherever we are, wherever we go, we leave a 'magnetic' mark that echoes and attracts those new 'rings' to itself and get stronger. So, whatever Design is, let's spread it!

---

1 Retrieved from "Platone. Tutti gli scritti", edited by G. Reale, Milano, Bompiani 2000.

REFERENCES

Abalo, J., Varela, J., & Manzano, V. (2007). Importance values for Importance–Performance Analysis: A formula for spreading out values derived from preference rankings. *Journal of Business Research*, 60(2), 115–121. https://doi.org/10.1016/j.jbusres.2006.10.009

Aguilera, D., & Ortiz-Revilla, J. (2021). STEM vs. STEAM Education and Student Creativity: A Systematic Literature Review. *Education Sciences*, 11(7), Art. 7. https://doi.org/10.3390/educsci11070331

Albers, J., & Weber, N. F. (2013). *Interaction of Color: 50th Anniversary Edition* (50th Anniversary edition). Yale University Press.

Alexander, C. (2002). *The Nature of Order: An Essay on the Art of Building and the Nature of the Universe*, Book 1 - The Phenomenon of Life.

Allam, Z. (2020). *Cities and the Digital Revolution Aligning technology and humanity*. Palgrave Macmillan. https://doi.org/10.1007/978-3-030-29800-5

Anderson, C. (2006). *The Long Tail: Why the Future of Business is Selling Less of More* (First Edition First Printing). Hachette Books.

Anderson, C. (2014). *Makers: The New Industrial Revolution*. Currency.

Angelisi, S. (2016). *Il consumo critico: Spazio interstiziale tra emozione e ragione* [Thesis]. https://doi.org/10.13126/UNICAL.IT/DOTTORATI/899

Angolino, A., Balda, F., Emiliani, D., Romano, G., Oliviero, F., Sampoli, L., & Schivardi, F. (2022). *Rapporto Cerved PMI 2022*. Cerved Research.

Angolino, A., Balda, F., Emiliani, D., Romano, G., Sampoli, L., & Schivardi, F. (2019). *Rapporto Cerved PMI 2019*. Cerved Research.

Anitori, R. (2012). V*ite insieme. Dalle comuni agli ecovillaggi*. DeriveApprodi.

Antonelli, P. (2011, novembre 4). States of Design 03: Thinkering—Domus. *DOMUS*. Retrieved on November 4th, 2019 from https://www.domusweb.it/it/design/2011/07/04/states-of-design-03-thinkering.html.

Artigiani, R. (1988). Scientific revolution and the evolution of consciousness. *World Futures*, 25(3–4), 237–281. https://doi.org/10.1080/02604027.1988.9972088

Austin, J., & Delaney, P. (1998). Protocol Analysis as a Tool for Behavior Analysis. *The Analysis of verbal behavior*, 15, 41–56. https://doi.org/10.1007/BF03392922

Bailey, M., Spencer, N., Carrion-Weiss, J., Arakelyan, A., & Carter, A. (2022). Design-led Innovation Readiness: Priming micro SMEs for strategic innovation.

Design Management Journal, 17(1), 5–17. https://doi.org/10.1111/dmj.12074

Bakırlıoğlu, Y., & Kohtala, C. (2019). Framing Open Design through Theoretical Concepts and Practical Applications: A Systematic Literature Review. *Human–Computer Interaction*, 0(0), 1–45. https://doi.org/10.1080/07370024.2019.1574225

Bangor, A., Kortum, P., & Miller, J. (2009). Determining What Individual SUS Scores Mean: Adding an Adjective Rating Scale. *Journal of Usability Studies*, 4(3), 114–123.

Bassi, A. (2013). *Design. Progettare gli oggetti quotidiani*. Il Mulino.

Batat, W. (2019). *Consumer Behavior, Customer Experience and The 7Es*. Routledge. https://doi.org/10.4324/9781315232201

Batat, W. (2021). How augmented reality (AR) is transforming the restaurant sector: Investigating the impact of "Le Petit Chef" on customers' dining experiences. *Technological Forecasting and Social Change*, 172, 121013. https://doi.org/10.1016/j.techfore.2021.121013

Baudisch, P., & Mueller, S. (2016). Personal Fabrication: State of the Art and Future Research. *Proceedings of the 2016 CHI Conference Extended Abstracts on Human Factors in Computing Systems*, 936–939. https://doi.org/10.1145/2851581.2856664

Bauman, Z. (2000). *Liquid Modernity* (1st Edition). Polity Pr.

Bauman, Z. (2003). *City of fears, city of hopes*. Goldsmiths' College, Centre for Urban and Community Research.

Benasayag, M., & Meyran, R. (2020). *La tirannia dell'algoritmo* (E. Missana, Trad.). Vita e Pensiero.

Benkler, Y. (2006). *The Wealth of Networks: How Social Production Transforms Markets and Freedom*. Yale University Press.

Bersano, G. (2019). *Post-design*. Meltemi.

Beveridge, R., & Koch, P. (2016). The post-political trap? Reflections on politics, agency and the city. *Urban Studies*, 54. https://doi.org/10.1177/0042098016671477

Bey, H. (1991). T.A.Z.: The Temporary Autonomous Zone, Ontological Anarchy, Poetic Terrorism.

Bonomi, A. (2021). *Oltre le mura dell'impresa. Vivere, abitare, lavorare nelle piattaforme territoriali*. DeriveApprodi.

Borgelt, K., & Falk, I. (2007). The leadership/management conundrum: Innovation or risk management?. *Leadership & Organization Development Journal*, 28(2), 122–136. https://doi.org/10.1108/01437730710726822

Bourgon, J. (2011). *A New Synthesis of Public Administration: Serving in the 21st Century*. McGill-Queen's University Press. https://www.jstor.org/stable/j.ctt7zp3k

Bratton, B. H. (2016). *The Stack: On Software and Sovereignty* (1ˢᵗ edition). The MIT Press.

Breiner, J. M., Harkness, S. S., Johnson, C. C., & Koehler, C. M. (2012). What Is STEM? A Discussion About Conceptions of STEM in Education and Partnerships. *School Science and Mathematics*, 112(1), 3–11. https://doi.org/10.1111/j.1949-8594.2011.00109.x

Brink, G. (2015). Iterate, Iterate, Iterate. By iterating, we validate our ideas along the way beacause we're hearing from the people we're actually designing for. In *Filed Guide to Human-Centered Design* (p. 25). IDEO.

Brooke, J. (1995). SUS: A quick and dirty usability scale. *Usability Eval.* Ind., 189.

Brooke, J. (2013). SUS: A Retrospective. *Journal of Usability Studies*, 8(2), 29–40.

Browder, R. E., Aldrich, H. E., & Bradley, S. W. (2019). The emergence of the maker movement: Implications for entrepreneurship research. *Journal of Business Venturing*, 34(3), 459–476. https://doi.org/10.1016/j.jbusvent.2019.01.005

Brown, J. R., Morris, E. A., & Taylor, B. D. (2009). Planning for Cars in Cities: Planners, Engineers, and Freeways in the 20th Century. *Journal of the American Planning Association*, 75(2), 161–177. https://doi.org/10.1080/01944360802640016

Brown, T. (2009). *Change by Design: How Design Thinking Transforms Organizations and Inspires Innovation* (1st Edition). HarperCollins e-books.

Brynjolfsson, E., & McAfee, A. (2015). *La nuova rivoluzione delle macchine. Lavoro e prosperità nell'era della tecnologia trionfante* (G. Carlotti, Trad.). Feltrinelli.

Buchanan, R. (2009). Thinking about Design: An Historical Perspective. In A. Meijers (Ed.), *Philosophy of Technology and Engineering Sciences* (pp. 409–453). North-Holland. https://doi.org/10.1016/B978-0-444-51667-1.50020-3

Buono, M. (2018). Design as inventor. *DIID, Disegno Industriale Industrial Design*, 65(18).

Büttner, B., Seisenberger, S., Baquero Larriva, M. T., Rivas De Gante, A. G., Haxhija, S., Ramirez, A., & McCormick, B. (2022). ±15-Minute City: Human-Centred Planning in Action (p. 66). *EIT Urban Mobility*. https://www.eiturbanmobility.eu/%C2%B115-minute-city-human-centred-planning-in-action/

Bybee, R. W. (2013). *The Case for STEM Education: Challenges and Opportunities*. NSTA Press.

Capasso Da Silva, D., King, D. A., & Lemar, S. (2020). Accessibility in Practice:

20-Minute City as a Sustainability Planning Goal. *Sustainability*, 12(1), Art. 1. https://doi.org/10.3390/su12010129

Capdevila, I. (2014). Different Entrepreneurial Approaches in Localized Spaces of Collaborative Innovation (SSRN Scholarly Paper ID 2533448). *Social Science Research Network*. https://doi.org/10.2139/ssrn.2533448

Capdevila, I. (2015). How Can City Labs Enhance the Citizens' Motivation in Different Types of Innovation Activities? In L. M. Aiello & D. McFarland (Ed.), *Social Informatics* (pp. 64–71). Springer International Publishing. https://doi.org/10.1007/978-3-319-15168-7_9

Caprile, M., Palmén, R., Sanz, P., & Dente, G. (2015). Encouraging STEM studies. *Labour Market Situation and Comparison of Practices Targeted at Young People in Different Member States*. European Parliament.

Caso, O. (2019). Public libraries and "Making." Experiences in the Netherlands. European Journal of Creative Practices in *Cities and Landscapes*, 2(2), Art. 2. https://doi.org/10.6092/issn.2612-0496/9547

Castells, M. (1996). *The rise of the network society*. Blackwell Publishers. http://disruptiv.biz/home/networked-disruption-the-book/

Castells, M. (2009). *The Rise of the Network Society: The Information Age: Economy, Society, and Culture* (2a ed., Vol. 1). Blackwell Pub.

Cecchini, C. (2012). *Le parole del design. 150 lemmi liberamente scelti*. List

Celaschi, F., Di Lucchio, L., & Imbesi, L. (2017). Design e Phygital production: Progettare nell'era dell'industria 4.0. In *Design & industry 4.0 revolution* (Vol. 4, pp. 6–13). Acocellla Alfonso.

Cellamare, C. (2014). *Roma città autoprodotta. Ricerca urbana e linguaggi artistici (S.MU.R. Self Made Urbanism Rome)*. Manifestolibri.

Cellamare, C. (2018). Cities and Self-organization. Tracce Urbane. *Rivista Italiana Transdisciplinare Di Studi Urbani*, 3, Art. 3. https://doi.org/10.13133/2532-6562_2.3.14298

Censis. (2015). *Quarantanovesimo Rapporto sulla situazione sociale del Paese 2015*. FrancoAngeli.

Cervero, R., & Kockelman, K. (1997). Travel demand and the 3Ds: Density, diversity, and design. *Transportation Research Part D: Transport and Environment*, 2(3), 199–219. https://doi.org/10.1016/S1361-9209(97)00009-6

Chermayeff, I., Federal Council on the Arts and the Humanities, National Endowment for the Arts, & Federal Design Assembly (1st : 1973 : Washington, D. C.). (1973). *The Design necessity: A casebook of federally initiated projects in visual communications, interiors and industrial design, architecture, landscaped environment.* Cambridge, Mass: MIT Press. http://archive.org/details/designnecessity00cher

Chesbrough, H. (2007). Business model innovation: It's not just about technology anymore. *Strategy & Leadership*, 35(6), 12–17. https://doi.org/10.1108/10878570710833714

Chesbrough, H. (2010). *Business Model Innovation: Opportunities and Barriers. Long Range Planning*, 43(2), 354–363. https://doi.org/10.1016/j.lrp.2009.07.010

Christens, B. D., Winn, L. T., & Duke, A. M. (2016). Empowerment and Critical Consciousness: A Conceptual Cross-Fertilization. *Adolescent Research Review*, 1(1), 15–27. https://doi.org/10.1007/s40894-015-0019-3

Clarke, A. C. (1984). *Profiles of the Future: An Inquiry into the Limits of the Possible*. ISBN 978-0-03-069783-8. Henry Holt & Co

Cocchia, A. (2014). Smart and Digital City: A Systematic Literature Review. In R. P. Dameri & C. Rosenthal-Sabroux (Ed.), *Smart City: How to Create Public and Economic Value with High Technology in Urban Space* (pp. 13–43). Springer International Publishing.

Codeluppi, V. (2015). *Il gusto. Vecchie e nuove forme di consumo*. Vita e Pensiero.

Colucci-Gray, L., Trowsdale, J., Cooke, C. F., Davies, R., Burnard, P., & Gray, D. S. (2017). Reviewing the potential and challenges of developing STEAM education through creative pedagogies for 21st learning: How can school curricula be broadened towards a more responsive, dynamic, and inclusive form of education? *British Educational Research Association*. https://www.bera.ac.uk/promoting-educational-research/projects/reviewing-the-potential-and-challenges-of-developing-steam-education

Cooke, P., & Schwartz, D. (Ed.). (2012). *Creative Regions: Technology, Culture and Knowledge Entrepreneurship*. Routledge

Cooper, R. G. (1990). Stage-gate systems: A new tool for managing new products. *Business Horizons*, 33(3), 44–54. https://doi.org/10.1016/0007-6813(90)90040-I

Corbin, J. M., & Strauss, A. L. (2008). *Basics of Qualitative Research: Techniques and Procedures for Developing Grounded Theory* (3rd edition). Sage Pubns.

D'Aveni, R. (2015, maggio 1). *The 3-D Printing Revolution*. Harvard Business Review. https://hbr.org/2015/05/the-3-d-printing-revolution

Daclon, C. M. (2020). *Scenari di geopolitica per il millennio*. Aracne. Retrieved on October, 15th 2022 on http://www.aracneeditrice.it/aracneweb/index.php/pubblicazione.html?item=9788825531244

Dardot, P., & Laval, C. (2014). *Commun: Essai sur la révolution au XXIe siècle*.

Editions La Découverte.

Darlington, H. (2011). Good Practice in Science Teaching: What Research has to Say (2nd ed.). *International Journal of Science Education*, 33(2), 321–322. https://doi.org/10.1080/09500693.2010.533908

De Kerkove, D. (2011, settembre 27). *Nell'era di Facebook siamo tutti Pinocchio*. La Stampa. Retrieved on August 13th 2023 from https://www.lastampa.it/cultura/2011/09/27/news/de-kerckhove-nell-era-di-facebook-br-siamo-tutti-pinocchio-1.36932774/

de Lange, M., Synnes, K., & Leindecker, G. (2019). Smart Citizens in the Hackable City: On the Datafication, Playfulness, and Making of Urban Public Spaces Through Digital Art. In C. Smaniotto Costa, I. Šuklje Erjavec, T. Kenna, M. de Lange, K. Ioannidis, G. Maksymiuk, & M. de Waal (Ed.), *CyberParks – The Interface Between People, Places and Technology: New Approaches and Perspectives* (pp. 157–166). Springer International Publishing. https://doi.org/10.1007/978-3-030-13417-4_13

Deleuze, G., & Guattari, F. (1972). *L'anti-OEdipe: Capitalisme et schizophrénie* (1re édition). Les Editions de minuit.

DeLisle, J., & Grissom, T. (2013). An Empirical Study of the Efficacy of Mixed-Use Development: The Seattle Experience. *Journal of Real Estate Literature*, 21(1), 25–57. https://doi.org/10.1080/10835547.2013.12090352

Dembskl, F., Wössner, U., Letzgus, M., Ruddat, M., & Yamu, C. (2020). Urban Digital Twins for Smart Cities and Citizens: The Case Study of Herrenberg, Germany. *Sustainability*, 12(6), Art. 6. https://doi.org/10.3390/su12062307

Denaro, G. (2021). *Progettazione e produzione 4.0 nell'abbigliamento italiano. Una mappatura per la comprensione del contributo del Design nella Moda* [Doctoral Thesis, Sapienza University of Rome]. Iris Sapienza. https://iris.uniroma1.it/handle/11573/1653968

Denning, P. J., & Hayes-Roth, R. (2006). Decision making in very large networks. *Communications of the ACM*, 49(11), 19–23. https://doi.org/10.1145/1167838.1167852

Dewey, J. (2010). *Dewey, J: My Pedagogic Creed*. Nabu Press.

Diez Ladera, T., Ferro, C., Niaros, V., Parikh, M., & Jusic, I. (2022). The Fab City Full Stack: A Multiscalar Framework for Distributed Production Strategies in Cities and Regions. *Proceedings of the Fab 17 Research Papers Stream*, 5–11. https://doi.org/10.5281/ZENODO.7432027

Diez, T. (2018). Fab City: The Mass Distribution of (almost) Everything. Iaac. https://fab.city/assets/documents/FabCity_Book.pdf

Dinetti, F. (2012). *Trasformazioni del lavoro e forme di vita nel 20° secolo: I nuovi paradigmi del lavoro nel passaggio dal fordismo al postfordismo, fino al lavoro contemporaneo* [Doctoral Thesis, Università degli studi di Firenze : Dipartimento di scienze politiche e sociali]. https://opac.bncf.firenze.sbn.it/bncf-prod/resource?uri=BVE0609357&v=l&dcnr=4

dos Santos, A., Vezzoli, C., Garcia Parra, B., Molina Mata, S., Banerjee, S., Kohtala, C., Ceschin, F., Petrulaityte, A., Duarte, G. G., Dickie, I. B., Balasubramanian, R., & Xia, N. (2021). Distributed Economies. In C. Vezzoli, B. Garcia Parra, & C. Kohtala (Ed.), *Designing Sustainability for All: The Design of Sustainable Product-Service Systems Applied to Distributed Economies* (pp. 23–50). Springer International Publishing. https://doi.org/10.1007/978-3-030-66300-1_2

Drew, R. (2016). Technological Determinism. In A *Companion to Popular Culture* (Vol. 1, p. 67). John Wiley & Sons.

Driver, R., Guesne, E., & Tiberhien, A. (1985). Some features of children's ideas and their implications for teaching. In *Children's ideas in science* (pp. 193–201). Milton Keynes, Open University Press.

Duany, A., Plater-Zyberk, E., & Speck, J. (2010). *Suburban Nation: The Rise of Sprawl and the Decline of the American Dream* (Anniversary edition). North Point Pr.

Duarte, F., & Álvarez, R. (2021). U*rban Play: Make-Believe, Technology, and Space*. MIT Press.

Dunne, A., & Raby, F. (2013). *Speculative Everything: Design, Fiction, and Social Dreaming* (Illustrated edition). The MIT Press.

Eisenhardt, K. M. (1989). Building Theories from Case Study Research. *The Academy of Management Review*, 14(4), 532–550. https://doi.org/10.2307/258557

Elmquist, M., Fredberg, T., & Ollila, S. (2009). Exploring the field of open innovation. *European Journal of Innovation Management*, 12(3), 326–345. https://doi.org/10.1108/14601060910974219

Escobar, A. (2018). *Designs for the Pluriverse: Radical Interdependence, Autonomy, and the Making of Worlds*. Duke Univ Pr.

Ewing, R., & Cervero, R. (2010). Travel and the Built Environment. *Journal of the American Planning Association*, 76(3), 265–294. https://doi.org/10.1080/01944361003766766

Fasoli, A., & Tassinari, S. (2017). Engaged by Design: The Role of Emerging Collaborative Infrastructures for Social Development. Roma Makers as A Case Study. *The Design Journal*, 20(sup1), S3121–S3133. https://doi.org/10.1080/14606925.2017.1352819

Feenberg, A. (2009). *What is Philosophy of Technology?* (pp. 159–166). Brill. https://doi.org/10.1163/9789087908799_016

Ferrer, J.-R. (2017). Barcelona's Smart City vision: An opportunity for transformation. Field Actions Science Reports. *The Journal of Field Actions*, Special Issue 16, Art. Special Issue 16.

Findeli, A. (2010). *Searching for Design~Research Questions: Some Conceptual Clarifications* (pp. 278–293).

Fleischmann, K., Hielscher, S., & Merritt, T. (2016). Making things in Fab Labs: A case study on sustainability and co-creation. *Digital Creativity*, 27(2), 113–131. https://doi.org/10.1080/14626268.2015.1135809

Follesa, S. (2017). A tempo e a luogo. Conoscenze, pratiche, direzioni per un design identitario. In G. Lotti & F. Tosi (Ed.), *La ricerca di design nelle Doctoral Thesis dell'Università di Firenze*.

Frate, F. (2018). *Il lavoro tra fordismo, post fordismo e rivoluzione digitale. Quale futuro si prospetta?* | Salvis Juribus. http://www.salvisjuribus.it/il-lavoro-tra-fordismo-post-fordismo-e-rivoluzione-digitale-quale-futuro-si-prospetta/

Frateili, E. (1969). *Design e civiltà della macchina*. Editalia.

Frayling, C. (1993). Resarch inArt and Design. In *Royal College of Art Research Papers* (Vol. 1, p. 9).

Friedman, K. (2008). Research into, by and for design. *Journal of Visual Art Practice*, 7(2), 153–160. https://doi.org/10.1386/jvap.7.2.153_1

Fry, T. (2010). *Design as Politics*. Berg Publishers.

Fry, T., Dilnot, C., Stewart, S., Willis, A.-M., & Norton, L. (2015). *Design and the Question of History*. Bloomsbury Academic

Fuad-Luke, A. (2009). *Design Activism: Beautiful Strangeness for a Sustainable World*. Routledge

Fusco, R. D. (2009). *Storia del design*. Illustrated Edition (26th edition). Laterza.

Gagliardi, P. (2017). Teorie dell'innovazione. In viaggio per Itaca. *Antologia tra cultura e organizzazione*, 573–579. Retrieved on December 14th, 2019 from https://pasqualegagliardi.it/content/teorie-dell%E2%80%99innovazione

Gallino, L. (1987). *Della ingovernabilità: La società italiana tra premoderno e neo-industriale*. Comunità

Gandolfi, A. (2008). *Formicai, imperi, cervelli. Introduzione alla scienza della complessità*. Bollati Boringhieri.

Gasparotto, S. (2019). Open Source, Collaboration, and Access: A Critical Analysis of "Openness" *Design Field*. *Design Issues*, 35(2), 17–27. https://doi.org/10.1162/desi_a_00532

Gershenfeld, N. (2005). *FAB: The Coming Revolution on Your Desktop-From Personal Computers to Personal Fabrication*. Basic Books.

Gershenfeld, N. A., Gershenfeld, A., & Cutcher-Gershenfeld, J. (Ed.). (2017). *Designing reality: How to survive and thrive in the third digital revolution*. Basic Books.

Ghawana, T., & Zlatanova, S. (2013). 3D printing for urban planning A physical enhancement of spatial perspective. In *Urban and Regional Data Management, UDMS Annual 2013*—Proceedings of the Urban Data Management Society Symposium 2013.

Gibson-Graham, J. K. (2003). *An ethics of the local. Rethinking Marxism*, 15(1), 49–74. https://doi.org/10.1080/0893569032000063583

Gibson-Graham, J. K. (2006). *A Postcapitalist Politics* (NED-New edition). University of Minnesota Press. https://www.jstor.org/stable/10.5749/j.ctttt07

Gibson-Graham, J. K., & Roelvink, G. (2009). Social Innovation for Community Economies. In *Social Innovation and Territorial Development* 1st ed., pp. 41–54. Routledge. https://doi.org/10.4324/9781315609478-13

Giorello, G., & Donghi, P. (2019). *Errore*. Il Mulino.

Glaser, B. G., & Strauss, A. L. (1967). *The Discovery of Grounded Theory: Strategies for Qualitative Research*. Aldine Transaction.

Graser, K., Hunhevicz, J., Jähne, R., Walzer, A., Seiler, F., Wüst, R., & Hall, D. (2021). A Qualitative Technology Evaluation Scoreboard for Digital Fabrication in Construction. https://doi.org/10.22260/ISARC2021/0135

Greenfield, A. (2018). Radical Technologies: The Design of Everyday Life (p. 368). Verso Books.

Guallart, V. (2012). *La ciudad autosuficiente: Habitar en la sociedad de la información*. RBA Libros.

Guallart, V. (2014). *The Self-Sufficient City: Internet has changed our lives but it hasn't changed our cities, yet*. Actar.

Gulari, M., & Fremantle, C. (2015). Are design-led innovation approaches applicable to SMEs?. *DS 82: Proceedings of the 17th International Conference on Engineering and Product Design Education (E&PDE15), Great Expectations: Design Teaching, Research & Enterprise*, E&PDE, Learning Paradigm (556-561) Loughborough, UK, 03-04.09.2015. 978-1-904670-62-9

Guyotte, K. W., Sochacka, N. W., Costantino, T. E., Walther, J., & Kellam, N. N.

(2014). *Steam as Social Practice: Cultivating Creativity in Transdisciplinary Spaces. Art Education*, 67(6), 12–19. https://doi.org/10.1080/00043125.2014.11519293

Hardt, M., Negri, A., & Pandolfi, A. (2010). *Comune. Oltre il privato e il pubblico.* Rizzoli.

Harvey, D. (2019). *Rebel Cities: From the Right to the City to the Urban Revolution.* Verso Books.

He, B., & Bai, K.-J. (2021). Digital twin-based sustainable intelligent manufacturing: A review. Advances in Manufacturing, 9(1), 1–21. https://doi.org/10.1007/s40436-020-00302-

Henning, K., Wolf-Dieter, L., & Wolfgang, W. (2011). Industrie 4.0. Mit dem Internet der Dinge auf dem Weg zur 4. *Industriellen Revolution*. VDI-Nachrichten, 13(1), 2.

Henriksen, D., & Mishra, P. (2018). Creativity as Invention, Discovery, Innovation and Intuition: An Interview with Dr. Richard Buchanan. *TechTrends*, 62. https://doi.org/10.1007/s11528-018-0279-4

Hill, D. (2014). *Dark Matter and Trojan Horses: A Strategic Design Vocabulary.* Strelka Press.

Hirshberg, P., Dougherty, D., & Kadanoff, M. (2016). Maker City: A Practical Guide to Reinventing Our Cities. Maker Media Inc.

Holman, W. (2015). Makerspace: Towards a New Civic Infrastructure. *Places Journal*. https://doi.org/10.22269/151130

Honavar, V., Miller, L., & Wong, J. (1998). Distributed knowledge networks. *1998 IEEE Information Technology Conference, Information Environment for the Future* (Cat. No.98EX228), 87–90. https://doi.org/10.1109/IT.1998.713388

Honey, M. (Ed.). (2013). *Design, Make, Play: Growing the Next Generation of STEM Innovators* (1st edition). Routledge.

Houpert, C. (2019). The New Role of Libraries: Places for All. *European Journal of Creative Practices in Cities and Landscapes*, 2(2), Art. 2. https://doi.org/10.6092/issn.2612-0496/10429

Ihde, D. (2004). Philosophy of Technology. In P. Kemp (Ed.), *Philosophical Problems Today: World and Worldhood* (pp. 91–108). Springer Netherlands. https://doi.org/10.1007/1-4020-3027-4_3

Ito, J. (2016). Design and Science. *Journal of Design and Science*. https://doi.org/10.21428/f4c68887

Jacobs, J. (1961). *Death and Life of Great American Cities*. Random House.

Jaworski, B. J. (2018). Reflections on the Journey to be Customer-Oriented and Solutions-Led. *AMS Review*, 8(1), 75–79. https://doi.org/10.1007/s13162-018-0117-z

Jonas, W. (2007). Design Research and its Meaning to the Methodological Development of the Discipline. In R. Michel (Ed.), *Design Research Now: Essays and Selected Projects* (pp. 187–206). Birkhäuser. https://doi.org/10.1007/978-3-7643-8472-2_11

Jones, J. C. (1983). Continuous design and redesign. *Design Studies*, 4(1), 53–60. https://doi.org/10.1016/0142-694X(83)90008-X

Joshi, A., Kale, S., Chandel, S., & Pal, D. (2015). Likert Scale: Explored and Explained. *British Journal of Applied Science & Technology*, 7(4), 396–403. https://doi.org/10.9734/BJAST/2015/14975

Juliei, G. (2013). From Design Culture to Design Activism. *Design and Culture*, 5(2), 215–236. https://doi.org/10.2752/175470813X13638640370814

Kamel Boulos, M. N., Tsouros, A. D., & Holopainen, A. (2015). Social, innovative and smart cities are happy and resilient: Insights from the WHO EURO 2014 International Healthy Cities Conference. *International Journal of Health Geographics*, 14(1), 3. https://doi.org/10.1186/1476-072X-14-3

Keeley, L., Pikkel, R., Quinn, B., & Walters, H. (2013). *Ten Types of Innovation: The Discipline of Building Breakthroughs* (1. edition). John Wiley & Sons Inc.

Kelley, D. (1999). *The Deep Dive: One Company's Secret Weapon for Innovation* [Video]. ABC Nightline. http://films.com/title/9249

Kempf, H. (2014). *Fin de l'Occident, naissance du monde*. Points.

Khine, M. S., & Areepattamannil, S. (Ed.). (2019). *STEAM Education: Theory and Practice*. Springer International Publishing. https://doi.org/10.1007/978-3-030-04003-1

Klaus, P., & Nguyen, B. (2013). Exploring the role of the online customer experience in firms' multi-channel strategy: An empirical analysis of the retail banking services sector. *Journal of Strategic Marketing*, 21(5), 429–442. https://doi.org/10.1080/0965254X.2013.801610

Klein, N. (2015). *This Changes Everything: Capitalism vs. The Climate*. PEenguin books ltd.

Kohlbacher, F. (2006). The Use of Qualitative Content Analysis in Case Study Research. *Forum: Qualitative Social Research*, 7.

Kostakis, V., Niaros, V., Dafermos, G., & Bauwens, M. (2015). Design global, manufacture local: Exploring the contours of an emerging productive model. *Futures*, 73, 126–135. https://doi.org/10.1016/j.futures.2015.09.001

Kuckartz, U. (2019). Qualitative Text Analysis: A Systematic Approach. In G.

Kaiser & N. Presmeg (Ed.), *Compendium for Early Career Researchers in Mathematics Education* (pp. 181–197). Springer International Publishing. https://doi.org/10.1007/978-3-030-15636-7_8

Lange, B., Harding, S., & Cahill-Jones, T. (2019). Collaboration at New Places of Production: A European View on Procedural Policy Making for Maker Spaces. *European Journal of Creative Practices in Cities and Landscapes*, 2(2), Art. 2. https://doi.org/10.6092/issn.2612-0496/9556

Lanza, A. (March 3rd, 2017). *Parola di Andra Branzi. Abitare.* https://www.abitare.it/it/ricerca/recensioni/2017/03/03/andrea-branzi-design-intervista/

Laszlo, E. (1986). *Evoluzione.* Feltrinelli.

Latouche, S. (2006). *Le pari de la décroissance.* Fayard.

Latour, B. (2017). *Où atterrir? Comment s'orienter en politique.* La Découverte.

Laureti, M. (2020). *Scenari di ricerca nel design. Una proposta di mappatura internazionale della ricerca nel design, delle arti e nuovi media* [Doctoral Thesis, Sapienza University of Rome]. Iris Sapienza. https://iris.uniroma1.it/handle/11573/1533059

Lazzarato, M. (2004). From Capital-Labour to Capital-Life. Ephemera: theory & politics in organization. *Theory of multitude*, 4(3), 187–208.

Liao, C. (2016). From Interdisciplinary to Transdisciplinary: An Arts-Integrated Approach to STEAM Education. *Art Education*, 69(6), 44 49. https://doi.org/10.1080/00043125.2016.1224873

Lipson. (2012). *Fabricated: The New World of 3D Printing* (1. edition). John Wiley & Sons.

Long, F. (2009). Real or Imaginary: The effectiveness of using personas in product design. *Irish Ergonomics Review*, Frontend.

López, M. G. (2022). Temporary Autonomous Home: Free parties and migration on the margins of the urban night. *Crossings: Journal of Migration & Culture*, 13 (Night Stories: Urban Narratives of Migrant Lives in Europe), 27–42. https://doi.org/10.1386/cjmc_00053_1

Luckman, S. (2011). *What are they raving on about: Temporary Autonomous Zones and «Reclaim the Streets».*

Lupton, E. (2017). *Design Is Storytelling* (1st edition). Cooper-Hewitt Museum of.

Lyotard, J. F. (1979). *La condition postmoderne. Rapport sur le savoir.* Minuit

MacCallum, D. (2009). *Social Innovation and Territorial Development.* Ashgate Publishing, Ltd.

MacFarquhar, R., & Schoenhals, M. (2008). *Mao's Last Revolution* (Illustrated edition). Belknap Press: An Imprint of Harvard University Press.

MacKenzie, D. A., & Wajcman, J. (Ed.). (1999). *The social shaping of technology* (2ⁿᵈ ed). Open University Press.

Maffei, S., & Bianchini, M. (2014). City Making: Nuovi metabolismi urbani tra micro e autoproduzione. *DIID, Disegno Industriale Industrial Design*, 57(2), 58–64.

Maffei, S., Menichinelli, M., Bianchini, M., Carosi, A., Bombardi, F., & Carelli, A. (2015). *Makers' Inquiry*. ISBN: 9-788897-748069. Libraccio Editore

Maffesoli, M. (1998). *Le temps des tribus: Le déclin de l'individualisme dans les sociétés de masse*. LGF.

Magone, A., & Mazali, T. (2016). *Industria 4.0: Uomini e macchine nella fabbrica digitale* (1ˢᵗ edition). goWare & Guerini e Associati Edizioni.

Malakuczi, V. (2015). *Design computazionale e fabbricazione digitale: Un diverso approccio per il design. Definizione di un design tool per la comprensione e lo sviluppo di prodotti personalizzabili* [Doctoral Thesis, Sapienza University of Rome]. https://iris.uniroma1.it/handle/11573/1097364

Malakuczi, V., & D'Elia, L. (2020). Tracing Design's Value in Distributed Manufacturing. *Design Management Journal*, 15, 34–42. https://doi.org/10.1111/dmj.12058

Malakuczi, V., D'Elia, L., & Monaco, L. (2020). Makerspaces e amministrazioni locali: Un toolkit a sostegno degli spazi del fare collaborativo. *MD Journal* [10] 2020 Design for citizenship, MD Journal, 304.

Maldonado, T. (1977). Disegno industriale. In *Treccani*. https://www.treccani.it/enciclopedia/disegno-industriale_(Enciclopedia-del-Novecento)

Manzini, E. (2012). SLOC, The Emerging Scenario of Small, Local, Open and Connected. In *Grow Small Think Beautiful* (Stephan Harding). Floris Books.

Manzini, E. (2014, luglio 25). Design for social innovation vs. Social design. *DESIS Network*. https://www.desisnetwork.org/2014/07/25/design-for-social-innovation-vs-social-design/

Manzini, E. (2015). *Design, When Everybody Designs: An Introduction to Design for Social Innovation*. (R. Coad, Trad.). The MIT Press.

Manzini, E. (2018). Per un circolo virtuoso tra progettualità sociale e Politica. *Progettualità sociale e politiche*, 8.

Manzini, E. (2021). *Abitare la prossimità. Idee per la città dei 15 minuti*. EGEA.

Manzini, E., & M'Rithaa, M. K. (2016). Distributed Systems And Cosmopolitan Localism: An Emerging Design Scenario For Resilient Societies. *Sustainable Development*, 24(5), 275–280. https://doi.org/10.1002/sd.1628

Manzini, E., & Menichinelli, M. (2021). Platforms for re-localization. Communities and places in the post-pandemic hybrid spaces. *Strategic Design Research Journal*, 14(1), Art. 1. https://doi.org/10.4013/sdrj.2021.141.29

Mari, E. (2002). *Autoprogettazione?* (Bilingual edition). Corraini.

Marquet, O., & Miralles-Guasch, C. (2015). The Walkable city and the importance of the proximity environments for Barcelona's everyday mobility. *Cities*, 42, 258–266. https://doi.org/10.1016/j.cities.2014.10.012

Martilla, J. A., & James, J. C. (1977). Importance-performance analysis. *Journal of Marketing*, 41(January), 77–79. Scopus.

Martin, A. (2019). *Industria 4.0. Sfide e opportunità per il made in Italy. Tecnologie. Scenari. Casi di successo*. Editoriale Delfino.

Martín-Páez, T., Aguilera, D., Perales-Palacios, F. J., & Vílchez-González, J. M. (2019). What are we talking about when we talk about STEM education? A review of literature. *Science Education*, 103(4), 799–822. https://doi.org/10.1002/sce.21522

Mason, P. (2016). *PostCapitalism: A Guide to Our Future* (1st edition). Penguin.

Mayntz, R. (1998). Tecnica e tecnologia. *Enciclopedia delle scienze sociali - Treccani*. https://www.treccani.it/enciclopedia/tecnica-e-tecnologia_(Enciclopedia-delle-scienze-sociali)

Mayring, P. (2014). *Qualitative content analysis: Theoretical foundation, basic procedures and software solution.*

McGrath, R., & MacMillan, I. (July 1st, 1995). *Discovery-Driven Planning. Harvard Business* Review. https://hbr.org/1995/07/discovery-driven-planning

McLuhan, M. (1972). *Take today; the executive as dropout*. Harcourt Brace Jovanovich.

McNeil, I. (Ed.). (1996). *An Encyclopedia of the History of Technology* (1st edition). Routledge.

Menichinelli, M. (2016). Mapping the structure of the global maker laboratories community throughTwitter connections. In C. Levallois, M. Marchand, T. Mata, & A. Panisson (Eds.), *Twitter forResearch Handbook* 2015 – 2016 (pp. 47–62). Lyon: EMLYON Press. Retrieved fromhttp://dx.doi.org/10.5281/zenodo.44882

Menichinelli, M. (2020). *Open and collaborative design processes—Meta-Design, ontologies and platforms within the Maker Movement*. Aalto University. http://urn.fi/URN:ISBN:978-952-64-0091-4

Menichinelli, M. (2020a). Exploring the impact of Maker initiatives on cities and regions with a research through design approach. *Strategic Design Research Jour-*

nal, 13(1), Art. 1. https://doi.org/10.4013/sdrj.2020.131.07

Menichinelli, M., & Cangiano, S. (2021). Open Design as an approach for the commoning of design. The collaborative experience of openly defining Open Design with an open source process. In *Conference: Design as Common Good - Swiss Design Network Symposium* 2021 25-26 March 2021, held online

Menichinelli, M., & Schmidt, A. G. S. (2019). First Exploratory Geographical and Social Maps of the Maker Movement. *European Journal of Creative Practices in Cities and Landscapes*, 2(2), Art. 2. https://doi.org/10.6092/issn.2612-0496/9640

Menichinelli, M., Bianchini, M., & Maffei, S. (2020). Editorial: Open & Distributed + Design & Production: Design Strategies for Enabling Indie Designers and Makers. Strategic Design Research Journal, 13(1), 1–5. https://doi.org/10.4013/sdrj.2020.131.01

Micelli, S. (2011). *Futuro artigiano*. Marsilio Editori SPA.

Micelli, S. (2016). *Fare è innovare. Il nuovo lavoro artigiano*. Il Mulino.

Middendorp, J. (2000). Toolspace. In *LettError*. Charles Nypels. https://letterror.com/index.html

Mikheev, A. A., Krasnov, A., Griffith, R., & Draganov, M. (2021). The Interaction Model within Phygital Environment as an Implementation of the Open Innovation Concept. Journal of Open Innovation: Technology, Market, and Complexity, 7(2), 114. https://doi.org/10.3390/joitmc7020114

Ministero dello Sviluppo Economico. (2018). *Piano Nazionale Industria 4.0.* https://www.mise.gov.it/images/stories/documenti/guida_industria_40.pdf

Minstrell, J., & Zee, E. V. (2000, ottobre 1). *Inquiring into Inquiry Learning and Teaching in Science.*

Mirata, M., Nilsson, H., & Kuisma, J. (2005). Production systems aligned with distributed economies: Examples from energy and biomass sectors. *Journal of Cleaner Production*, 13(10), 981–991. https://doi.org/10.1016/j.jclepro.2004.12.018

Monaco, L., D'Elia, L., & Malakuczi, V. (2021). Making in Proximity: Design Policies for collaborative making cultures. *Design Culture(s). Cumulus Conference Proceedings Roma 2021*, Volume #2, 2920–2930.

Morace, F. (2016). *ConsumAutori. I nuovi nuclei generazionali*. EGEA.

Morace, F., & Lanzone, G. (2010). *Verità e bellezza. Una scommessa per il futuro dell'Italia*. Nomos Edizioni.

Morelli, N., & Sbordone, M. A. (2018). Il Territorio delle Relazioni, Il Design infrastructuring per i contesti locali. *MD Journal* [05], Design e Territori, 176–185.

Moreno, C., Allam, Z., Chabaud, D., Gall, C., & Pratlong, F. (2021). Introducing the "15-Minute City": Sustainability, Resilience and Place Identity in Future Post-Pandemic Cities. *Smart Cities*, 4(1), Art. 1. https://doi.org/10.3390/smartcities4010006

Moulaert, F. (2000). *Globalization and Integrated Area Development in European Cities*. OUP Oxford.

Moulaert, F., Martinelli, F., Swyngedouw, E., & Gonzalez, S. (2005). Towards Alternative Model(s) of Local Innovation. *Urban Studies*, 42(11), 1969–1990. https://doi.org/10.1080/00420980500279893

Mulgan, G. (2019). *Big mind. How Collective Intelligence Can Change Our World* Princeton Univ Pr.

Mulíček, O., Osman, R., & Seidenglanz, D. (2015). Urban rhythms: A chronotopic approach to urban timespace. *Time & Society*, 24(3), 304–325. https://doi.org/10.1177/0961463X14535905

Murzio, A., Spallino, C., & Cancellato, F. (2019). *La dittatura degli algoritmi. Il dominio della matematica nella vita quotidiana*. DIARKOS.

Nabil, N. A., & Eldayem, G. E. A. (2015). Influence of mixed land-use on realizing the social capital. *HBRC Journal*, 11(2), 285–298. https://doi.org/10.1016/j.hbrcj.2014.03.009

National Research Council. (2000). *How People Learn: Brain, Mind, Experience, and School*: Expanded Edition. National Academies Press. https://doi.org/10.17226/9853

Neuhaus, F. (2013). *Urban Rhythms: Habitus and emergent spatio-temporal dimensions of the city* [Doctoral, UCL (University College London)]. In Doctoral thesis, UCL (University College London). https://discovery.ucl.ac.uk/id/eprint/1396239/

Newman, S. (2011). Postanarchism and space: Revolutionary fantasies and autonomous zones. *Planning Theory*, 10(4), 344–365. https://doi.org/10.1177/1473095211413753

Niaros, V., Kostakis, V., & Drechsler, W. (2017). Making (in) the smart city: The emergence of makerspaces. *Telematics and Informatics*, 34(7), 1143–1152. https://doi.org/10.1016/j.tele.2017.05.004

Nielsen, S. L., Christensen, P. R., Heidemann Lassen, A., & Mikkelsen, M. (2017). Hunting the Opportunity: The Promising Nexus of Design and Entrepreneurship. *The Design Journal*, 20(5), 617–638. https://doi.org/10.1080/14606925.2017.1349983

Norman, D. A. (1998). *The Invisible Computer: Why Good Products Can Fail, the Personal Computer Is So Complex, and Information Appliances Are the Solution* (1st edition). The MIT Press.

Norman, D. A. (2005). *Emotional Design: Why We Love (or Hate) Everyday Things* (1st edition). Basic Books.

Norman, D. A. (2014). T*he Design of Everyday Things, revised and expanded edition* (2nd revised and expanded ed edition). MIT Press.

Ostanel, E. (2017). *Spazi fuori dal Comune. Rigenerare, includere, innovare* (1st edition). Franco Angeli.

Ostrom, E. (1990). *Governing the Commons: The Evolution of Institutions for Collective Action*. Cambridge University Press.

Paoletti, A., Di Lucchio, L., & Imbesi, L. (2018). Industria 4.0 e formazione dei futuri designer. La formazione che parte dal basso tra Fab Lab e Scuola Pubblica. *MD Journal* [4] - DESIGN & INDUSTRY 4.0 REVOLUTION, 4, 100–109.

Papanek, V. (1971). *Design for the Real World: Human Ecology and Social Change*. Pantheon Books.

Pearce, J. M. (2012). Building Research Equipment with Free, Open-Source Hardware. *Science*, 337(6100), 1303–1304. https://doi.org/10.1126/science.1228183

Perignat, E., & Katz-Buonincontro, J. (2019). STEAM in practice and research: An integrative literature review. *Thinking Skills and Creativity*, 31, 31–43. https://doi.org/10.1016/j.tsc.2018.10.002

Phillips, R., Dexter, M., Baurley, S., & Atkinson, P. (2016). Standard deviation: Standardization and quality control in the mash-up era. *Disegno: TheJournal of Design Culture*, 3(1–2), Art. 1–2. https://doi.org/10.21096/disegno_2016_1-2rp-md-sb-pa

Phillips, W. E., & Marothia, D. K. (1981). Integrated area development approach to rural development: A conceptual framework. *Agricultural Administration*, 8(5), 325–335. https://doi.org/10.1016/0309-586X(81)90011-X

Pickton, D. W., & Wright, S. (1998). What's swot in strategic analysis? *Strategic Change*, 7(2), 101–109. https://doi.org/10.1002/(SICI)1099-1697(199803/04)7:2<101::AID-JSC332>3.0.CO;2-6

Pinch, T. J., & Bijker, W. E. (1984). The Social Construction of Facts and Artefacts: Or How the Sociology of Science and the Sociology of Technology might Benefit Each Other. *Social Studies of Science*, 14(3), 399–441. https://doi.org/10.1177/030631284014003004

Platone, & Zanatta, F. (2013). *Simposio* (11st edition). Feltrinelli.

Porcari, G. (2016). Munari e la metodologia Lego. In Metodoaperto. Rompere per conoscere. *Metodo aperto: Il metodo progettuale del designer Bruno Munari, dal futurismo alla robotica, dal Bauhaus al tinkering* (pp. 83–88). Amazon Fulfillment.

Porcari, G., Rendina, S., Mannino, W., Fiorio, D., & Tanchis, A. (2016). *Metodo aperto: Il metodo progettuale del designer Bruno Munari, dal futurismo alla robotica, dal Bauhaus al tinkering.* Amazon Fulfillment.

Potter, N. (1969). *What Is a Designer: Things, Places, Messages.* Hyphen.

Pouri, M. J., & Hilty, L. M. (2021). The digital sharing economy: A confluence of technical and social sharing. *Environmental Innovation and Societal Transitions*, 38, 127–139. https://doi.org/10.1016/j.eist.2020.12.003

Powell, W. W., & Snellman, K. (2004). The Knowledge Economy. *Annual Review of Sociology*, 30(1), 199–220. https://doi.org/10.1146/annurev.soc.29.010202.100037

Radziwon, A., Bilberg, A., Bogers, M., & Madsen, E. S. (2014). The Smart Factory: Exploring Adaptive and Flexible Manufacturing Solutions. *Procedia Engineering*, 69, 1184–1190. https://doi.org/10.1016/j.proeng.2014.03.108

Ranjbari, M., Morales-Alonso, G., & Carrasco-Gallego, R. (2018). Conceptualizing the Sharing Economy through Presenting a Comprehensive Framework. *Sustainability*, 10(7), Art. 7. https://doi.org/10.3390/su10072336

Resnick, M. (2007). All I really need to know (about creative thinking) I learned (by studying how children learn) in kindergarten. *Creativity and Cognition 2007, CC2007 - Seeding Creativity: Tools, Media, and Environments*, 6. https://doi.org/10.1145/1254960.1254961

Ricciardi, A. (2018). I distretti industriali italiani: Recenti tendenze evolutive. *Sinergie Italian Journal of Management*, 91, 21–58. https://doi.org/10.7433/s91.2013.03

Rifkin, J. (2011). T*he Third Industrial Revolution: How Lateral Power Is Transforming Energy, the Economy, and the World.* Griffin.

Rifkin, J. (2015). *The Zero Marginal Cost Society: The Internet of Things, the Collaborative Commons, and the Eclipse of Capitalism* (Reprint edition). Griffin.

Ritz, J. M., & Fan, S.-C. (2015). STEM and technology education: International state-of-the-art. *International Journal of Technology and Design Education*, 25(4), 429–451. https://doi.org/10.1007/s10798-014-9290-z

Rosa, P., Guimarães Pereira, Â., & Ferretti, F. (2018). Futures of work. Perspectives from the Maker Movement (KJ-NA-29296-EN-N; p. 98). *European Commission, Joint Research Centre.* https://doi.org/10.2760/96812

Ruffolo, G. (2009). *Un paese troppo lungo. L'unita' nazionale in pericolo.* (IED edition). Einaudi.

Rullani, E. (2009). Lo sviluppo del territorio: L'evoluzione dei distretti industriali e il nuovo ruolo delle reti di città. *Economia Italiana*, 2, 427–472.

Sala, G., Aboutaleb, A., Aki-Sawyerr, Y., Cantrell, L., Capp, S., Durkan, J., Kam-sing, W., Medina, F., Plante, V., Calle, D. Q., & WonSoon, P. (2020). *C40 Mayors'agenda for a green and just recovery* (C40 Cities, p. 43).

Sandelowski, M. (2000). Whatever happened to qualitative description? Research. *Nursing & Health*, 23(4), 334–340. https://doi.org/10.1002/1098-240X(200008)23:4<334::AID-NUR9>3.0.CO;2-G

Santachiara, D. (2017). *Download design. Manutenzione straordinaria della cultura materiale*. 24 Ore Cultura.

Savoldi, P. (2007). *Giochi di partecipazione. Forme territoriali di azione collettiva* (1st edition). Franco Angeli.

Schuhmann, A. (2014). How to be political? Art activism, queer practices and temporary autonomous zones. Agenda, 28(4), 94–107. https://doi.org/10.1080/101309 50.2014.985469

Schulze, J. (2021). Design Nonfiction: Cultural Invenvtion (with Jack Schulze) [Interview]. *Design Nonfiction*. Retrieved from https://www.tellart.com/projects/designnonfiction

Schwab, K. (2017). *The Fourth Industrial Revolution*. Portfolio Penguin.

Schwab, K. (2022). *Governare la quarta rivoluzione industriale* (1st edition). Franco Angeli.

Scolari, C. A. (2013). Media Evolution: Emergence, Dominance, Survival and Extinction in the Media Ecology. *International Journal of Communication*, 7(0), Art. 0.

Scolari, C. A. (2021). *Las Leyes De La Interfaz*. GEDISA.

Scott, A. J. (Ed.). (2001). *Global City-Regions: Trends, Theory, Policy* (1st edition). Oxford University Press.

Sellars, S. (2010). Hakim Bey: Repopulating the Temporary Autonomous Zone. Journal for the Study of Radicalism, 4(2), 83–108. https://doi.org/10.1353/jsr.2010.0007

Selloni, D. (2018). La Politica a scuola di design: Coltivare le capacità progettuali dei policy-maker. *Progettualità sociale e politiche*.

Semi, G. (2015). *Gentrification. Tutte le città come Disneyland?* Il Mulino.

Sennett, R. (2008). *The Kraftman*. Yale University Press.

Sennett, R. (2019). *Building and Dwelling: Ethics for the City* (Reprint edition). Farrar Straus & Giroux.

Sinek, S. (2011). *Start with Why: How Great Leaders Inspire Everyone to Take Ac-

tion (Reprint edition). Portfolio.

Smiley, K. T., & Emerson, M. O. (2020). A spirit of urban capitalism: Market cities, people cities, and cultural justifications. *Urban Research & Practice*, 13(3), 330–347. https://doi.org/10.1080/17535069.2018.1559351

Smith, A., Fressoli, M., Abrol, D., Arond, E., & Ely, A. (2016). Grassroots Innovation Movements. In *Grassroots Innovation Movements*. https://doi.org/10.4324/9781315697888

Snyder, H. (2019). Literature review as a research methodology: An overview and guidelines. *Journal of Business Research*, 104, 333–339. https://doi.org/10.1016/j.jbusres.2019.07.039

Steinberg, M. (2010, settembre). Welcome to HDL Global 2010. *Welcome to HDL Global 2010* - Helsinki Design Lab. Retrieved from http://helsinkidesignlab.rip/blog/welcome-to-hdl-global-2010.html

Stiglitz, J., Sen, A., & Fitoussi, J. (2009). The Measurement of Economic Performance and Social Progress Revisited. *Commission on the Measurement of Economic Performance and Social Progress*, Paris.

Stroud, A., & Baines, L. (2019). Inquiry, Investigative Processes, Art, and Writing in STEAM. In M. S. Khine & S. Areepattamannil (Ed.), *STEAM Education: Theory and Practice* (pp. 1–18). Springer International Publishing. https://doi.org/10.1007/978-3-030-04003-1_1

Sundararajan, A. (2016). *The Sharing Economy: The End of Employment and the Rise of Crowd-based Capitalism*. Mit Pr.

Taleb, N. N. (2013). *Antifragile. Prosperare nel disordine*. Il Saggiatore.

Taylor, C. W. (1993). Alternative World Scenarios for a New Order of Nations. *Strategic Studies Institute*, US Army War College.

Taylor, N., Hurley, U., & Connolly, P. (2016). Making Community: The Wider Role of Makerspaces in Public Life. *Proceedings of the 2016 CHI Conference on Human Factors in Computing Systems*, 1415–1425. https://doi.org/10.1145/2858036.2858073

Taylor, P. C., & Taylor, E. (2019). Transformative STEAM education for sustainable development. *Empowering Science and Mathematics for Global Competitiveness*. CRC Press.

Thewihsen, F., Karvska, S., Czok, A., Pateman-Jones, C., & Krauss, D. (2016). *If 3D printing has changed the industries of tomorrow, how can your organization get ready today? The trends, sector use cases and steps to accelerate your 3D printing journey* (p. 24). EY GM Ltd.

Thorpe, A. (2012). *Architecture & Design versus Consumerism: How Design Activism Confronts Growth*. Routledge. https://doi.org/10.4324/9780203119518

Toffler, A. (1980). *The Third Wave*. Pan Books.

Toker, Z., & Pontikis, K. (2011). An inclusive and generative design process for sustainable urbanism: The case of Pacoima. *Journal of Urbanism: International Research on Placemaking and Urban Sustainability*, 4(1), 57–80. https://doi.org/10.1080/17549175.2011.559956

Tonkinwise, C. (2004). Is Design Finished? Dematerialisation and Changing Things. *Design Philosophy Papers*, 2(3), 177–195. https://doi.org/10.2752/144871304X13966215068191

Tosi, F., & Rinaldi, A. (2010). *Prodotti e complementi per l'arredo d'alta gamma. Un'esperienza progettuale per Giuliano Fujiwara*. Alinea.

Transit. (2017). *Manifesto for Transformative Social Innovation*. Retrieved from https://tsimanifesto.org/manifesto/tsimanifesto.org

Tullini, P. (2016). Economia digitale e lavoro non-standard. *Labour & Law Issues*, 2(2), Art. 2. https://doi.org/10.6092/issn.2421-2695/6489

Uitermark, J., Duyvendak, J., & Kleinhans, R. (2007). Gentrification As a Governmental Strategy: Social Control and Social Cohesion in Hoogvliet, Rotterdam. *Environment and Planning A: Economy and Space*, 39, 125–141. https://doi.org/10.1068/a39142

UN-Habitat (Ed.). (2020). *World Cities Report 2020. The value of sustainable urbanization*. United Nations Human Settlements Programme (UN-Habitat).

van den Dool, A., Marchington, E., Ripken, R., Hsieh, A., Petrasova, M., Bilic, D., Idrisova, A., Pena, A., Ashraf, V., Capelán, N., Vijitpan, T., Yao, C., Coll Besa, M., Eckert, J., Pilibaityté, V., Min, S., & Lu, L. (2009). *The future is distributed: A vision of sustainable economies*. IIIEE, Lund University.

Van Herpt, O. (2014). *Adaptive Manufacturing—Olivier van Herpt*. oliviervanherpt.com. Retrieved on October 13th, 2019 from https://oliviervanherpt.com/adaptive-manufacturing/

Vargas, S., & Yamnitsky, M. (2014). *3D Printing Drives Digitization Further Into Products, Processes, And Delivery Models*. Forrester.

Villari, B. (2012). *Design per il territorio. Un approccio community centred* (1A edition). Franco Angeli.

von Hippel, E. (2005). *Democratizing Innovation*. MIT Press.

Weng, M., Ding, N., Li, J., Jin, X., Xiao, H., He, Z., & Su, S. (2019). The 15-minute walkable neighborhoods: Measurement, social inequalities and implications for building healthy communities in urban China. *Journal of Transport & Health*, 13, 259–273. https://doi.org/10.1016/j.jth.2019.05.005

Wided, B. (2022). *Strategies for the Digital Customer Experience: Connecting Customers with Brands in the Phygital Age*. Edward Elgar Publishing.

World Bank & Decentralization Thematic Team. (2013). *Different Forms of Decentralization*. Retrieved from http://www.ciesin.org/decentralization/English/General/Different_forms.html

World Bank. (2013). *Inclusion Matters: The Foundation for Shared Prosperity. World Bank*. Retrieved from https://openknowledge.worldbank.org/handle/10986/16195

Zatsarinnaya, Y., Rep'ev, E., & Gainullin, R. (2021). Distributed generation as a trend in the transformation of the electric power industry in Russia. *2021 International Conference on Electrotechnical Complexes and System*s (ICOECS), 64–67. https://doi.org/10.1109/ICOECS52783.2021.9657417

Zheng, J., & Chan, R. (2013). A property-led approach to cluster development: «creative industry clusters» and creative industry networks in Shanghai. *The Town Planning Review*, 84(5), 605–632.

Zuboff, S. (2015). Big other: Surveillance Capitalism and the Prospects of an Information Civilization. *Journal of Information Technology*, 30(1), 75–89. https://doi.org/10.1057/jit.2015.5

Zuboff, S. (2019). *The Age of Surveillance Capitalism: The Fight for a Human Future at the New Frontier of Power* (1st edition). Public Affairs.

Zwick, D., & Denegri-Knott, J. (2009). Manufacturing Customers: The Database as New Means of Production. *Journal of Consumer Culture - J CONSUM CULT*, 9, 221–247. https://doi.org/10.1177/1469540509104375

INDEX

May this book, this part of a tree, come back to the earth and be a tree again.

May its file, set of bytes, find sustainable store or be discarded to be no more.